OBSERVING THE OBSERVER:
THE STATE OF ISLAMIC STUDIES IN AMERICAN UNIVERSITIES

OBSERVING THE OBSERVER:

THE STATE OF ISLAMIC STUDIES IN AMERICAN UNIVERSITIES

EDITED BY

MUMTAZ AHMAD,
ZAHID BUKHARI & SULAYMAN NYANG

THE INTERNATIONAL INSTITUTE OF ISLAMIC THOUGHT
LONDON • WASHINGTON

© The International Institute of Islamic Thought, 1433AH/2012CE

The International Institute of Islamic Thought
P.O. BOX 669, HERNDON, VA 20172, USA
www.iiit.org

LONDON OFFICE
P.O. BOX 126, RICHMOND, SURREY TW9 2UD, UK
www.iiituk.com

ISBN 978–1–56564–580–6 *limp*
ISBN 978–1–56564–581–3 *cased*

Typesetting and cover design by Sideek Ali
Printed in Malta by Gutenberg Press Ltd

CONTENTS

FOREWORD   VII

INTRODUCTION
Sulayman S. Nyang, Mumtaz Ahmad, Zahid H. Bukhari   IX

CONTRIBUTORS   XXVIII

1. Quixotic Quests: In Pursuit of Islam   I
   Anouar Majid

2. Origins and Development of Islamic Studies in the U.S.:   12
   A Historical Overview of Trends and Institutions
   Seyyed Hossein Nasr

3. Changing Western Approaches to Islamic Studies   28
   John O. Voll

4. The Territory of the Qur'an: "Citizens," "Foreigners,"   53
   and "Invaders"
   Farid Esack

5. Islam and Gender in Muslim Societies: Reflections of   70
   an Anthropologist
   Saba Mahmood

6. The Academic Studies of Sufism at American   88
   Universities
   Marcia Hermansen

7. Teaching Islam in American Theological Schools   112
   Jane I. Smith

8. The Constitutionality of Teaching Islam: 137
   The University of North Carolina Qur'an Controversy
   Christopher Buck

9. Islam 101: A Survey of "Introduction to Islam"   178
   Courses in American Colleges and Universities
   Faisal Islam and Zahid H. Bukhari

10. Islamic Studies in American Universities: 219
    Conversations, Discourses, and Dialogue with Scholars
    Mumtaz Ahmad

CONCLUSIONS   252

FOREWORD

THE STATE OF ISLAMIC STUDIES IN AMERICAN UNIVERSITIES
was a project undertaken by IIIT and the Center for Islam and
Public Policy (CIPP) between the years 2004 and 2007. The current state of relations between the U.S. and the Muslim world, as
well as debates about Islamic education and study programs in
American campuses, necessitated a thorough and rigorous study of
Islam in American universities. Through both qualitative and quantitative research, the project sought to develop an understanding of
the origins, history, and growth of the discipline, tracing the historical roots of Islamic studies in American universities, examining their
current state, presenting and analyzing the theoretical frameworks
and methodologies of approaching the study of Islam and Muslim
world affairs, and collecting and disseminating data on the major
academic programs for the study of Islam and Muslim world affairs
in American universities.

As part of the project research, a scholarly, edited volume was
compiled forming this work: *Observing the Observer: The State of
Islamic Studies in American Universities*, a collection of papers covering a wide variety of topics, including the historical development of
the field, Western approaches to Islamic studies, the study of Qur'an,
gender, and Sufism in Islamic studies programs, conversations with
scholars, and analysis of Islam 101 courses.

We hope that both general and specialist readers benefit from the
perspectives offered and the overall issues examined in the book.

Where dates are cited according to the Islamic calendar (hijrah)
they are labelled AH. Otherwise they follow the Gregorian calendar
and labelled CE where necessary. Arabic words are italicized except for
those which have entered common usage. Diacritical marks have been

added only to those Arabic names not considered modern. English translations taken from Arabic references are those of the author.

The IIIT, established in 1981, has served as a major center to facilitate serious scholarly efforts based on Islamic vision, values and principles. The Institute's programs of research, seminars and conferences during the last thirty years have resulted in the publication of more than four hundred titles in English and Arabic, many of which have been translated into other major languages.

We express our thanks and gratitude to the contributors for their cooperation throughout the various stages of production. We would also like to thank the editorial and production team at the IIIT London Office and all those who were directly or indirectly involved in the completion of this book including, Shiraz Khan, Dr. Maryam Mahmood, Tahira Hadi, and Salma Mirza. May God reward them for all their efforts.

IIIT LONDON OFFICE
March 2012

INTRODUCTION

THE field of Islamic studies in the U.S. developed due to the keen desire of Americans to probe the historical sources of Islam and document encounters between American society and the peoples of the Muslim world. Inspired by a series of historic events in U.S. history, the study of Islam and Islamic societies has been growing significantly in American institutions of higher learning and research. Such events include the founding of the Republic, diplomatic and economic relations of the U.S. with Muslim countries, migration of millions of Muslims into the country over the last century and a half, conversion of a large number of Americans to Islam, U.S. interests in the Arab oil resources, involvement of Muslims in the American public square; challenges of the Cold War, and the rise of militancy and international terrorism associated with some fringe groups in Muslim societies.

The events of 9/11 gave further impetus, even urgency, to the need to understand and analyze Islam, primarily to examine the possible links between the teachings of Islam on the one hand, and the incidence of violence and terrorism on the other. Although for the wrong reasons, the tragedy of 9/11 has engendered such an interest in Islam that some observers have noted the rise of an "Islam industry" in the U.S., run primarily by fly-by journalists, think tank pundits, and cut-and-paste "experts."

Some observers have pointed out to another aspect of understanding the history and development of Islamic studies in America and in the West: the loss of the Cold War as a unifying emotional and psychological connection between Muslims and Americans. Since both the West and most leaders of the Muslim World shared a common allergy to communism and its godless ideology, and because many Muslims feared the political ambitions of the Soviets in Muslim lands, they saw in the West, and particularly in the U.S., a bulwark against the penetration of Communist ideas and Soviet power into their territories.

Real or imagined, this state of affairs contributed immeasurably to the phenomenon of coincidence of interests between liberal democratic capitalists of the West on the one hand and the authoritarian Muslim royals, and military dictators of the Muslim World, on the other. The logic of the Cold War, and the strategic importance of winning the support of the Muslim countries against the Soviets, gave rise to area studies programs in American universities of which the study of Islam and Muslim societies formed an important part.

The volume begins with Professor Anour Majid's chapter which presents a critical analysis of the origins and development of Islamic studies in the U.S. Working on the assumption that Islamic studies in the United States cannot be understood without being linked to the U.S. and its history, Majid sees the link between Islam and the U.S. in dialectical terms. America, in his view, "was established as the antithesis of Islam, first the refuge of pure Christianity, the community of saints, then a beacon of freedom that stands in sharp contrast to Islamic despotism and the slavish conditions of Muslims in general."

Majid sees an interesting dialectic between the creation of America and the enslavement of persons of African origins in the U.S. He suggests that American Muslims today cannot understand the perception of their fellow Americans of Judeo-Christian backgrounds if they do not take into consideration the categories in which America placed the Muslims since its existence. First, Muslims came as slaves during the antebellum period; then they emerged as freed men along with the other captives from Africa; subsequently, they were Arab or other Muslim immigrants from distant lands in search of the American Dream and a toehold, if not a foothold, in the American society. Finally, they emerged as full citizens with rights to vote and be voted into Congress.

Majid draws our attention to the African–American experience with the middle passage and the implications thereof for Muslims, and reminds us about early American republican encounters with the North African groups that attacked Americans from across the Atlantic Ocean. Known to Americans as peoples of the Barbary Coast in the eighteenth and nineteenth centuries, their threat to the American trade interests became the first encounter with the Islamic world, thus prompting President Monroe and his successors to set the stage for the earliest articulations of American attitude toward Islam. Hence the paradox: though Morocco was the first country to recognize and establish diplomatic relations with America, the activities of the pirates from the Barbary Coast left a bitter taste in the mouths of American leaders and the people.

Majid sees the struggle between Islam and the West or the U.S. as unacademic and rooted in individual self-definition. He traces this source of conflict to his metaphor of the Islamic gene, which is critical and rebellious. For him, the Islamic message harbors both interfaith dialogue and critical analysis of other religions. Islamic perspectives about the world, the purpose of creation and the role of man in this world have always been in conflict with those of its Semitic cousins in the West. The emergence of America in 1776 and the many scientific and intellectual developments that took place since the eighteenth century have not altered the equation between Islam and the West.

Like the original equation of Islam as the final revelation, the present situation in the relationship between the U.S. and the Muslim world is affected by mutual self-definition. Majid's view finds echoes in other writings as well. Citing the works of Timothy Marr on *American Orientalism,* he approvingly quotes Marr's assertion that "America's 'national project' wouldn't have been the same without negative references to Islam." Majid also endorses the observation of Robert J. Allison in *The Crescent Observed* who provides some powerful data about the literary utility of Islamic history and experience to the American thinkers and writers looking for an American antidote to the Muslim experience. Majid reminds us that this "the literature conveyed a persistent picture of the Muslim world, an inverted image of the world the Americans were trying to create anew."

The Christian right and its dreams at home and abroad serve as another avenue of potential hostility or prospective healing between Americans and Muslims. Majid discusses the impact of history on American studies of Islam and Muslims by pondering how and why the activities of the U.S. against the Taliban and other targets in the

Middle East and beyond contribute to the study of Islam and Muslims. With a deep sense of appreciation of how history plays games with humans through irony and paradox, he shows how Islamic fundamentalists in Afghanistan assumed different and conflicting roles during the times of the Cold War and then during the times of war against international terrorism.

As Professor Seyyed Hossein Nasr argues in the third chapter of this volume, a concatenation of historical circumstances has made Islam a subject of international significance. Not only does Islam have a past that lingers in the western mind and imagination, but also inside western nations such as America, "several million Muslims constitute an element of American society which can no longer be ignored." Despite this proximity in terms of inter-civilizational and intercultural ties from the past, Nasr argues, the state of Islamic studies in America is far from satisfactory.

Professor Nasr identifies a number of reasons why Islamic studies has yet to emerge as a strong and formidable field of study when compared with European centers of learning. The first problem relates to the history of the development of the discipline in the U.S. The earlier role of Christian missionaries in the study of Islam gave it an antagonistic bias. Although some of these early American students of Islam were of Rabbinical backgrounds, their objectivity before the triumph of Zionism in the Middle East has almost disappeared.

According to Nasr, not only did the Christian missionaries and Jewish scholars interested in religious studies affect the direction of Islamic studies, but Christian Arabs living and working in the West also contributed a great deal. Nasr mentions the late Professor Phillip Hitti who wrote many books about the Arabs and Islam trained a large number of students at Princeton over half a century of his teaching and research. In addition, western writers best known as Middle East area studies experts produced a type of scholarship that owed a great deal to the Cold War and the U.S. attempt to win and influence peoples of the Third World.

He laments that Islam lacks due recognition and attention. Nasr believes that Muslims were to some extent the targets of false propaganda, and sees problems not only in the failure to develop and train competent scholars in the field, but also in the lack of proper attention to Islam and its major languages. He sees the study of African Islam as neglected territory. Yet while acknowledging this disparity, Nasr tells us that social sciences have, in recent years, tried to fill the gap in the field of Islamic studies.

Nasr's evaluation of the field of Islamic studies reminds American readers of the global nature of the Islamic presence and the urgency of dialogue and communication. He cites the incredible distortion of Islam as a major obstacle to greater communication and understanding, and hopes the development of Islamic studies "cannot but be the greatest benefit to both America and the Islamic World."

The fourth chapter of this study is a historical analysis by Professor John Voll of the Center for Muslim-Christian Understanding, Georgetown University. Professor Voll offers a number of remarkable observations about the historical and intellectual circumstances that contributed to the evolution and development Islamic studies in the United States with reference to the contribution of Professor Hossein Nasr. Through a careful and effective combination of personal memories of his early encounters with Professor Nasr and the subsequent follow-up with his writings, Professor Voll traces the intellectual traditions and methods that provided the basis for Nasr's thought. He reminds us that prior to the arrival of Professor Nasr at Harvard University in the 1950s, Islamic studies in the U.S. had undergone some changes that were linked to intellectual developments taking place in Europe. Drawing heavily on the writings of American and western scholars of Islam in the West, Voll notes the scholastic antecedents and how that tradition created new perspectives about Islam and Muslims. Caught in the web of Christian polemics and with the intent to offer their religion as the better one vis à vis Islam, early Christian writers wrote not to shed light about the realities and subtleties of Islam but to portray it as negatively as possible.

This polemical attitude faded away, and during the Renaissance and the Reformation new views entered the Christian mainstream, although the rivalry between Catholicism and Protestantism did not dissipate their mutual antagonism against Islam. Another point shown in the Voll's analysis of the transition in the western portrayal of Islam was the gradual breaking away from a strictly religious approach to Islam, and the beginning of enlightened understanding of Islam in the west. Beginning with the American and French Revolutions, the study of Islam began to undergo another transformation. The scholars who wrote from the late eighteenth to the later part of the nineteenth and early twentieth centuries laid the foundation of what came to be known later as orientalist tradition.

One unique characteristic of this intellectual caravan and its tribal chiefs of scholarly tradition was their total disregard of the lived Islam and the daily lives of Muslims they studied. Rather, they preferred to engage with classical texts, medieval manuscripts and ancient languages. Voll quotes Anne Marie Schimmel as saying that people like her who studied Arabic never saw an Arab and were not instructed in an Arab country. It appears that this closing the eyes to the existence of the people and the cultures of Islam largely resulted from the colonial mentality of emerging dominant European powers. Concerned with governing their colonial subjects but mindful of the role and place of power differentiation, many European students of Islam became the intellectual apologists of colonial domination by reading both Islam and Islamic history as deficient.

In tracing the history of Islamic studies in the West, Voll tells us that from 1917, when the British created their Department of African and Oriental Studies, to the last days of empire and the Cold War, Islamic studies underwent several transformations. During the last century, particularly before the Iranian Revolution, theorists of modernization, whether Marxist, liberal, or conservative, promoted the notion that religion was a dying breed of human thought. Peter Berger and Harvey Cox were widely cited as harbingers of radical change of human thought patterns due to the interconnected processes of industrialization and secularization.

Since modernizing societies were supposed to fit into this dominant western pattern of simultaneous industrialization and secularization; sociologists like Daniel Lerner, in his *The Passing of Traditional Societies* announced the end of the public role of Islam in the new pattern of behavior among the Middle Eastern Muslims and boldly predicted the eventual triumph of secularism in Muslim societies as a result of the expansion of education, communication technologies and industrial-ization. The Iranian Islamic revolution of 1979 and the increasing role of Islam in the public affairs of several Muslim societies since the 1970s, however, saw the emergence of a new generation of Islamic scholars who were not only more sensitive to the new "realities" of Islam but were also theoretically more sophisticated and discerning.

Farid Esack's chapter on "The Territory of the Qur'an: 'Citizens,' 'Foreigners,' and 'Invaders'" is a brilliant metaphorical tour de force to describe the approaches of scholars toward the study of the Qur'an by using the categories of citizens, foreigners and invaders. Professor Esack employs the theme of beauty to tie together different approaches to the Qur'an and Qur'anic scholarship and draws on an analogy of the personality and body of a beloved and how she is seen and approached. For Esack, the first level of interaction with the Qur'an is analogous to that between a lover and beloved in that the "presence of the beloved can transport the lover to another plane of being that enables him to experience sublime ecstasy ..." At this level of interaction with the Qur'an, the relationship is only "to be enjoyed rather than interrogated or agonized over." This is the type of relationship that one can identify with the position of ordinary Muslims towards the Qur'an – consoling his "aching heart."

The second level of interaction is that of a lover "who wants to explain to the world why his beloved is the most sublime ... that cries out for universal acclaim and acceptance." This is the position of "con-fessional Muslim scholarship" that wants to share its own experience of the awe-inspiring beauty and wisdom of its beloved with others.

The third level of interaction with the Qur'an, according to Esack, takes place at the intersection of both profound love and commitment for, and a critical and interrogative stance toward, the beloved. This is the path taken by critical Muslim scholarship of the Qur'an – a path that leads Muslim scholars to ask questions, not to deny the divinity of the beloved but to gain a deeper understanding and reaffirmation of one's love for her.

Continuing the analogy of the beloved, Farid Esack categorizes the "outsiders" who study the Qur'an as "participant observers," "disin-terested observers," and "polemicist observers." The participant observer does not claim to be a lover but shows "enormous sense of responsibility to the sensitivities of the lover ..." This is the Qur'anic scholar who, in the words of Fazlur Rahman, "may not be a full citizen of the world of the Qur'an, but is certainly no foreigner either – let alone an invader!" The disinterested observer, on the other hand, feels no such responsibility of showing empathy for the lover and claims that "he is merely pursuing the cold facts surrounding the body of the beloved regardless of what she may mean to her lover." Then we have this polemicist observer who is, in fact "besotted with another woman, the Bible or secularism." Terrified by "the prospect that his Muslim enemy's beloved may be attracting a growing number of devotees," he now resorts to telling the Muslim "how ugly his (i.e., the Muslim's) beloved is." It is this kind of "scholarship," informed by religious prejudices and political goals that blames the Qur'an for all kinds of violence and militancy in the contemporary world and wants the world to believe that there could be no peace in the world as long as Muslims adhere to the teachings of the Qur'an.

Professor Farid Esack concludes his chapter by examining the "beginnings of the emergence" of hermeneutics as a new discipline in Qur'anic studies and emphasizes the need for the Qur'an to be "decoded in the light of its historical, cultural and linguistic milieu."

In Professor Saba Mahmood's paper, "Islam and Gender in Muslim Societies: Reflections of an Anthropologist," one finds some interesting perspectives about Islam and the manner that scholars in the field of anthropology have come to address the issue. Mahmood brings a great deal to the table. Not only is she deeply immersed in the theories and perspectives in her own discipline, but she is also mindful of the impact of the debates and the challenges generated by these theories for the study of the gender issue in western academia. Reminding us of the timeline when gender became a cause of disagreement for anthropologists and others in the field of social science in the 1960s, Mahmood gives us a guided tour of the scholarship that has developed significantly in the field in general and within Islamic studies in particular.

Mahmood unpackages the theoretical perspectives and approaches that ruled over the discipline and the male bias that informed women studies and gender relations. She argues that the increase in the representation of women researchers in the field changed the way gender issues were identified and analyzed. In her view, the turning point in the development of a more gender-friendly approach was the 1970s. In her critical survey of the literature on gender and the question of the Muslim women Mahmood states, "It was not until the 1970s ... that gender as an analytical category emerged in the study of Muslim societies, substantially transforming the conceptual presuppositions of the literature produced on Islam."

Mahmood reminds us that during this transition to new paradigmatic views and approaches to the study of gender, anthropologists writing on Muslim world affairs soon found it useful to see gender not a biological divide between male and female but as a relational category "that marks the difference in power between men and women." In Mahmood's view, gender in this circumstance "is not synonymous with women, but elucidates the broader production of social inequality in a variety of social domains, including politics, economics, law, and religion."

What is most interesting in Mahmood's analysis is her elucidation of how some new approaches to gender relations are crucial to the operation of modern capitalism and the market economies, to the sustenance of ideological boundaries such as public/private and production/reproduction, to the valuation of religious and spiritual practices, and to the operation of law and politics.

Having established the robustness of gender theorizing in the field of anthropology, Mahmood goes on to introduce two critical currents that swept through the discipline in the 1980s. The first current concerned the debate about the colonial origins of the field and the impact of colonial rule on how colonized people were presented or represented by colonial anthropologists. Talal Asad's *Anthropology and the Colonial Encounter* (1973) was the work of a founding pioneer who was almost immediately followed by Edward Said's *Orientalism*. In Mahmood's view, these two texts, particularly Said's:

> exposed how scholarly tropes used to describe non-western societies were not only misrepresentations of the social reality they purportedly captured but were also premised on assumptions of western superiority that helped facilitate projects of imperial and colonial rule.

Mahmood amplifies this fact by saying:

> Talal Asad differently emphasized how the power of western forms of knowledge lies not only in their ability to re-present social reality but also to intervene and remake non-western traditions, practices, and institutions, thereby transforming what it means to live as a Muslim subject in the modern world.

Professor Mahmood notes that since the appearance of these texts, things have changed radically in the field and a vast amount of scholarly work has come to light that genuinely enhanced our understanding of the gender question within the Muslim world.

The second current that changed the theoretical landscape in the 1980s focused more specifically on the discipline's claim to "objective" knowledge, drawing attention to those aspects of fieldwork and ethnographic writings that entail ambiguity, approximation, subjective judgment, and inequality of relations between the observer and the observed. Mahmood reports that some of her colleagues in the field have coined a new genre of anthropological writings better known as "reflexive anthropology," in which the anthropologist "foregrounds her privileged position as a researcher, drawing attention to the problems of reductionism, reification, ventriloquism, and essentialism that are endemic to any anthropological enterprise."

After having explored these theoretical and conceptual transformations, Mahmood demonstrates that Islamic studies, particularly in areas focused on women, benefited from these path breaking works in that they allowed Muslims and others to dispose of the colonial charge that Islam – rather than a complex of social, cultural and historical factors – was the web that kept Muslim women subdued and dominated. Mahmood shows how subsequent scholarship on gender and Islam has helped displace the stereotype that Muslim women are passive victims of patriarchal oppression. She reminds us about the cultural pluralism that exists in Islamic societies. Paying attention to such diversities could prove helpful in our attempt to understand the complex nature of the Muslim world.

Writing on post-Orientalist scholarship, Mahmood tells us that the

search for greater understanding of gender and Islam is not straightforward; there are conceptual booby traps to be avoided, and problems
reflective of shifting historical realities also deserve considerations. She
raises the question about the persistence in the use of the term "Muslim
women" in the literature. She argues that the term "Christian
women" is hardly used when writing about women in non-Muslim
lands. In addition to this persistence of terminologies in the literature,
she also talks about the failure to tackle the problems of gender in relational terms. Arguing that even in predominantly Muslim-populated
countries there are sizable non-Muslim populations – which makes
theorizing about "Muslim women" difficult – Mahmood contends
that the coexistence of Muslims and others from different religious
backgrounds complicates the drawing of conclusions without taking
into account the influence of such cultural relationships.

Furthermore, she cites the case of Indian Muslims who live in a predominantly Hindu society but whose sizable numbers makes it
dangerous and unwise to describe their condition as inhabitants of a
Hindu culture. Due to these theoretical difficulties, she writes:

> It is crucial for scholars interested in these issues to ask how the rubric of
> 'Islamic cultures' articulates with the narrow discourse of nationalism that
> reduces heterogeneous forms of religion and ethnic belonging into the
> simplistic calculus of minority and majority culture.

Mahmood also addresses the question of economic transformation in
Muslim societies and how such a process affects women. She analyzes
the relationship between this phenomenon and the rise of the Islamic
revivalism. She sees a paradox in the embrace of Muslim women in
Islamist movements and the problematic complication of the gender
questions.

In the chapter written by Professor Marcia Hermansen, we come to
learn a great deal about "The Academic Study of Sufism at American
Universities." Hermansen's paper examines three interrelated issues:
the place of Sufism within the broader curriculum in Islamic studies, as
well as some themes and approaches to this subject taken by western
scholars; the academic context in which Sufi studies are located; and

the role of contemporary positions in Islamic and western thought in shaping the academic study of Sufism. Hermansen also addresses issues she believes would be of interest to Muslims who are likely to find this study helpful in discerning western opinions on and attitudes towards Islam in general and Sufism in particular.

Hermansen begins by looking at the institutional foundations for the study of Sufism. She raises a number of theoretical and practical points. With respect to the institutional basis for the study of Sufism as a phenomenon and an object of academic inquiry, she wants the readers to notice the difference between the western and the Muslim contexts. In Muslim lands, colleges and universities patterned after their western counterparts tend to harbor their academic programs in theology departments or halls of learning that parallel their Catholic or Protestant counterparts in the U.S.

Another institutional point is the difficulty in defining what is specifically American in terms of scholarship and scholars. Hermansen states that the period after World War II led to the hegemonic presence of European scholars such as Hamilton Gibb, Gustave von Grunebaum, and Franz Rosenthal. According to her, one aspect of this Orientalism "was the sense of 'Islam' as constituting a unifying essential and somewhat static factor unifying disparate cultural, intellectual and social realities in Muslim societies."

Echoing some of the points mentioned earlier about the interplay between area studies and Islamic studies (and by extension Sufi studies), Hermansen reviews the transformation in the academy with respect to the location of Islamic studies programs. By the 1970s, she maintains, within the academy, programs such as Near Eastern studies departments were becoming rare and their services were being channeled elsewhere. The growth in area studies as a companion partner to Islamic studies in certain universities led not only to the primacy of the social sciences in the degree-granting institutions, but also led in the 1960s and 1970s to the majority of M.A. and Ph.D. graduates in non-western traditions to come out of area studies programs.

Hermansen addresses how the establishment of religious studies as an important component in many universities created the opportunity for courses on Sufism to thrive among undergraduates.

Hermansen then traces the effects of the Cold War on the American development of centers of learning that focused on the languages of the Muslim world. Taking note of the circumstances that came together to make this possible, she argues that the rigorous qualifying requirements limited the number of potential recruits for Islamic studies or Sufism. Those who embarked upon such a task were expected to gain command of two European languages and two Muslim languages, particularly Arabic. Some of the students who wished to specialize in Islamic studies or Sufism had to develop proficiency in these languages and, at one point, were expected to service in the government. In this context, the role of Public Law 480, which gave the U.S. access to the academic resources of the developing countries, was critical in promoting American scholarship of foreign countries.

Identifying those who became students in such Islamic studies and Sufism studies programs, Hermansen tells us that in the 1970s they could be characterized as "a part of the 'generation of seekers' who pursued personal edification as well as intellectual depth in graduate programs." Building on this point, she argues, "unlike the European experience, the American academic encounter with Islam was more comparative and of varied interests in aspects of Islam and therefore in Sufism."

Explaining how Islamic studies and Sufism studies developed in the American academy, Hermansen tells us that the dominant approach to comparative religion during the 1960s and 1970s was the "Patternist school" inspired by the works of Mircea Eliade of the University of Chicago. This approach to the study of mythology and traditional metaphysics beyond the Abrahamic religions created room for the study of Sufism. Together with phenomenology, this patternist approach allowed Sufism to shine in the academy.

In addition to these two theoretical approaches within the study of comparative religion, another important development that took place related to the debates within the walls of social sciences and the humanities. In her view, this led "to the increased role of theory derived from anthropology and literary theory as well as new critical initiatives such as feminism, post-modernism, and post colonial theory that interrogated the very foundations of the production of authoritative knowledge." Hermansen sees Edward Said's seminal work on *Orientalism* "as a major force in the challenge to occidental hegemony that heretofore dominated the views of other outside of the West." Yet, while noting and appreciating this development, she argues that despite the paradigm shifts, the marginalization of Sufism has largely remained unchanged in the academies of Muslim countries as well as in Muslim organizations in the West.

Looking at the teaching of Sufism in the American academy, Hermansen talks about the pervasive hypothesis or trope on the decline of Islam in general and Sufism in particular. This idea was decline dominant in the years after the end of World War II. Since the 1960s, what Daniel Lerner called "the passing of traditional society" was also upheld proudly by many secular modernizers in the Muslim world. That idea has been discarded by the scholars now and religion is back with a vengeance. Due to this state of affairs, she argues, scholars writing on the subjects of Islam and Sufism are caught in the struggle between competing paradigms about Muslim life and culture. She argues that Sufism is increasingly perceived as a desirable intellectual and spiritual lifestyle that could serve as a bridge in the ideological contest between the radical and the moderate Muslims.

Besides this analysis of the theoretical changes in the study of Islam and its mystical dimension, Sufism, Hermansen explores the approaches to the study of the subject and the development of discipleship within the academic realm and beyond. She argues that scholars such as Naser, Schuon, and others have created networks of students and disciples and their writings are widely sought.

Jane Smith's contribution in this volume is unique in that the topic of the study of Islam in Christian theological seminaries has rarely been studied with such thoroughness and perception, and with a wealth of personal experience in teaching Islam in a Christian theological seminary. Professor Smith notes that students in these seminaries want to include Islam in their program of studies to know more about Islamic scriptures, traditions, theology and law, and to understand the similarities and differences between Christians and Muslims. More recent interests of students in Christian seminaries focus on the reasons of the rise and spread of Islam in America and Europe; Islam and violence;

Islamic theology of jihad; the status and welfare of Christians in Muslim majority societies; the place of Islam and Muslims in the religious pluralism of Western societies; and potential for Christian-Muslim understanding and cooperation in projects from welfare work in local communities to global peacemaking.

Of course, as Professor Jane Smith notes, some faculty members in these seminaries teach Islam primarily "with a hope of advancing the cause of the Christian mission" but there is also an interest in the academic study of Islam and the motivation to engage Muslims in interfaith dialogue. Interestingly, a few seminary institutions now have full-time faculty positions in Islamic studies that are filled by Muslims and "more Muslim students are finding their way into seminary classrooms."

Christopher Buck's chapter on "The Constitutionality of Teaching Islam: The University of North Carolina Qur'an Controversy" is a brilliant case study of the "perils" of studying Islam – even in an academic environment – in a political context charged with both fear of, and hostility toward, Islam in the post-9/11 era. The controversy generated by the University of North Carolina (UNC) at Chapel Hill faculty requirement that its 2002 incoming freshman class, as part of its Summer Reading Program, read and discuss Michael Sell's *Approaching the Qur'an: The Early Revelations* raised a number of important constitutional and pedagogical issues. Michael Sell's translation of the Qur'an was included in the reading list to promote a better understanding of Islam through the study of its founding text. Although the reading list was compiled by the faculty on purely academic grounds, a conservative Christian activist group, the Family Policy Network (FPN), filed a suit in the U.S. District Court in July 2002 seeking a preliminary injunction to prevent UNC from conducting its summer program. The FPN alleged that UNC violated the Establishment clause of the First Amendment and abridged students' right to the free exercise of religion by requiring them to study Islam against their will.

The FPN lost the case in the District Court and again at the 4th Circuit Court of Appeals but what made the national headlines was, in the words of Michael Sells, "suing the Koran on behalf of the Bible." It was also a case testing the limits of both religious pluralism and possibilities and limits of academic freedom in American universities. To see and interpret the inclusion of the Qur'an in the summer reading program for freshman students as an attempt by the UNC to convert the students to Islam – a violation of both the Establishment clause and the Free Exercise clause of the First Amendment – is to ignore the very nature and purpose of the study of religion in a secular academic setting. As Professor Buck argues in his chapter, "To acknowledge the beauty and depth of the Qur'an is not to convert to Islam, but to converse with it and with Muslims who are enlivened by it." To know the Qur'an, therefore, is "to better prepare oneself for inevitable encounters with Muslims both in America and abroad – not as the exotic "other" somewhere in the distant Orient, but as the religion and way of life of our fellow compatriots at home – friends, neighbors, and, through increasing religious intermarriage, that of our immediate and extended families."

Professor Buck's paper, in order to gain a proper perspective on the rationale behind teaching the Qur'an in the university, begins with a brief introduction to the Qur'an, its world-historical significance, a history of its revelation, collection and editing, and a succinct discussion of its major themes. These discussions are then followed by an examination of Sells' *Approaching the Qur'an* and then a detailed discussion and analysis of the legal case brought against the University of North Carolina at Chapel Hill and how the courts resolved the issue in favor of UNC taking into account the constitutional norms and with reference to a broad spectrum of cases that form the body of educational law related to the teaching of religion in public schools and in higher education institutions. Professor Buck's paper in this volume is the first comprehensive study of the religious, political, legal-constitutional, and pedagogical aspects of the "teaching the Qur'an" controversy that engaged the media, courts, religious groups, and educational institutions for more than two years and brought the issue of Islam and its study into sharp focus in the post-9/11 America.

In this volume, we also address the question of Islamic studies in terms of the contents of courses that introduce American students to the history, tradition, and culture of Islam. Working on the assumption that the collective efforts of scholars teaching and writing about Islam have over the years converged on a number of points, we set out to explore their course outlines. Our study shows that teaching Islam at introductory level involves a variety of approaches. Some scholars focus primarily on Islamic beliefs and practices and the life and teachings of the Prophet (ṢAAS).* The focus on the biography of the Prophet is central to all the narratives in any Introduction to Islam course. Some other scholars rely heavily on the reading of religious texts – selected portions of the Qur'an, a selection of Prophetic Hadith, and some juristic texts. Those instructors who come from comparative religion background emphasize on Islamic theology and belief patterns as well as on major intellectual currents in Islam. Shariʿah and law constitute another popular focus in some cases. Another approach is to emphasize the role of Islam in history, both as a decisive political force in its formative phase and as a world civilization in later years. In recent years, instructors have shown increasing interest in contemporary Islamic developments, allocating considerable time for discussion of topics such as Islam and politics, Islamic resurgence and modern Islamic movements, Islam and the west, Islam and democracy, Islam and human rights, Islam in the west, and Islam and violence. Instructors of introductory courses on Islam often bring their own research interests to the classroom, sometime spending inordinate time on specialized topics such as Sufism and the issues related to gender in Islam. An interesting insight emerges when one looks at the intellectual preferences of male and female instructors: Male instructors tend to be more focused on Islamic history, Islam in the modern world, and Islamic institutions. Female teachers, on the other hand, tend to focus on gender, human rights, and law and Shariʿah.

Our study shows that the universe of instructors of men and women who teach these 101 courses includes persons specializing in eight different disciplines. 48 percent are in Religious Studies (excluding Islam), 15 percent are in Near Eastern/Middle Eastern Languages and Civilizations, 12.6 percent are in History, and 12.6 are in Islamic Studies. Overall, the statistical evidence suggests instructors are not

---

*(ṢAAS) – *Ṣallā Allāhu ʿalayhi wa sallam*: May the peace and blessings of God be upon him. Said whenever the name of the Prophet Muhammed is mentioned.

Islamic studies specialists and the pool of available talents is truly multi-disciplinary in training and research.

This finding reinforces what Brannon Wheeler and his colleagues reported earlier: the instructors of Islam 101 courses are invariably drawn from outside the field of mainstream Islamic studies. Some enter the domain of Islamic studies because of their earlier interest in Biblical, Jewish, or Indian religion studies. What is remarkable about our findings is that most American colleges and universities have not yet found it necessary to recruit persons of high quality and training to teach introductory courses on Islam. While several scholars have lamented this fact, the situation remains largely unchanged despite considerable interest in all things Islamic in recent years in the west.

Also noteworthy are the scholars' responses to the "publish or perish syndrome." Almost 78 percent of the scholars had published at least one book related to their area of expertise. Almost 39 percent had published two to five books and 16 percent of the instructors had published more than five books. Twenty-two percent of all the scholars in our sample have published articles and book chapters. It is important to note, however, that not all – or even majority – of these publications of in the mainstream of Islamic studies as such.

Another interesting finding in our study is the list of the most widely used textbooks for introductory courses on Islam. Our survey gives us the following breakdown of authors whose texts are most widely used in these courses: Frederick Mathewson Denny's *Introduction to Islam* is number one; 27 percent of instructors required this text for their classes. Professor Denny's book is followed by John Esposito's *Islam: The Straight Path* and Michael Sells's *Approaching the Qur'an: The Early Revelations*. Besides these three texts, there is N.J. Dawood's translation of the Qur'an is also widely used by the instructors.

In addition to scholarly papers, the volume also includes a report of two focus group discussions among a group of leading Islamic studies professional that were held at Georgetown University, Washington, DC and Temple University, Philadelphia. The idea was to elicit insights of the scholars based on their personal experiences and observations on the problems associated with the study of Islam in American universities. These conversations were supplemented by written responses to our questionnaire by scholars who could not personally attend the focus group meetings at Georgetown and Temple. Professor Carl Ernst's observations in this chapter are drawn from his notes published elsewhere. These informal conversations that were conducted without any structured questionnaire eventually formed their own structure as they gained momentum and enthusiasm. A rare exercise in the field, these conversations contain an enormous wealth of insights into the state of Islamic studies in American universities – the origin and the development of the discipline; its theoretical approaches and methodological orientations; the training of scholars and the institutional structures that evolved to impart this training; the development and consolidation of sub-fields; government and private funding sources and their impact on the direction of research and teaching; the growth and the role of area studies centers; orientalist and post-orientalist approaches to the study of Islam and Islamic societies; and the impact of 9/11 on how Islam and Muslims are seen and studied.

This volume is intended to inform and educate the general reader and to invite our colleagues in the field to join the dialogue about the nature, history, and the current state of Islamic studies in the U.S. and to critically examine the factors as to why Islamic studies as a discipline has lagged behind the study of other Semitic religions in the American academy. The essays included in this volume provide much-needed data and analysis that could be useful in enhancing the quality of teaching Islam in colleges and universities and in opening new avenues of research in the field. Additionally, there are data and analyses that will be immensely valuable for educational planners and administrators who are interested in strengthening programs of Islamic studies in institutions of higher learning.

SULAYMAN S. NYANG, MUMTAZ AHMAD AND
ZAHID H. BUKHARI

CONTRIBUTORS

AHMAD, MUMTAZ

Dr. Mumtaz Ahmad is Professor of Political Science at Hampton University, Hampton, VA, and Executive Director, Iqbal International Institute for Research & Dialogue, International Islamic University, Islamabad. He has a Ph.D. in Political Science from the University of Chicago. Before joining Hampton University in 1990, he was a Research Fellow at the Brookings Institution, Washington DC. Ahmad is President of the South Asian Muslim Studies Association, and member of the editorial advisory boards of several professional journals. Dr. Ahmad was a member of the "Islam and Social Change" project of the University of Chicago, a member of "Fundamentalism Project" of the American Academy of Arts and Sciences, and a Senior Consultant on "Muslims in American Public Square" project of Georgetown University. He was a Senior Fulbright Fellow in India, Pakistan and Bangladesh; the United States Institute of Peace (USIP) Fellow in Sudan, Malaysia and Pakistan; and Senior Fellow of the American Institute of Pakistan Studies and the American Institute of Bangladesh Studies. He has published extensively on Islamic political movements and radical groups, *madrasah* education in South Asia, and the politics of Islamic resurgence in the Middle East and South Asia. Dr. Ahmad is the author of nine books and numerous journal articles, book chapters, and encyclopedia entries on Islam and politics.

BUCK, CHRISTOPHER

Dr. Christopher Buck, PhD is a Pennsylvania attorney and independent scholar, who taught at Michigan State University (2000-2004), Quincy University (1999-2000), Millikin University (1997-1999), and Carleton University (1994-1996). His publications include: Religious Myths and Visions of America: How Minority Faiths Redefined America's World Role (2009); Alain Locke: Faith and Philosophy (2005); Generation Y Speaks Out: A Policy Guide (2002); and Paradise and Paradigm: Key Symbols in Persian Christianity and the Baha'i Faith (1999), as well as a number of book chapters, encyclopedia articles, and scholarly journal articles. Many of Buck's publications may be downloaded for free at Christopher Buck's academic website at www.christopherbuck.com.

BUKHARI, ZAHID

Dr. Zahid Bukhari serves as Executive Director of the Center for Islam and Public Policy (CIPP). He served as Director, American Muslim Studies Program (AMSP) at the Prince Alwaleed Center for Muslim-Christian Understanding, Georgetown University, Washington, DC. From 1999-2004, he also worked as Director, Project MAPS: Muslims in American Public Square at Georgetown University. Dr. Bukhari was elected national president of the Islamic Circle of North America (ICNA) for 2009-10. He has been serving as a member of Governor of Maryland Commission on Middle Eastern American Affairs for 2008–2011. Dr. Bukhari's research interests focused on religion and politics in the United States and South Asia. He has a vast experience in all aspects of survey research. From 1978-1983, he worked as executive director of the Pakistan Institute of Public Opinion (PIPO), Islamabad, a member of Gallup International. He has published and presented papers on Islam in the West, Muslim public opinion in the US, Interfaith Relations in the USA, and other related topics in national and international forums. He is also editor of a research volume, *Muslims' Place in the American Public Square: Fears, Hopes and Aspirations* (2004).

ESACK, FARID

Dr. Farid Esack is the chair of the Islamic Studies at the University of Johannesburg. A native of South Africa, Dr. Esack was trained in both traditional *madrasahs* in Pakistan and Western universities. Dr. Esack played an integral role in the United Democratic Front struggle against apartheid. He served as Commissioner for Gender Equality in the South African government during the Presidency of Nelson Mandela, and has taught in several international universities, including Harvard, West Cape, St. Xavier, Amsterdam, Hamburg and Union Theological Seminary, New York. He was Chair of Ethics, Religion, and Society Program at Xavier University. Dr. Esack is the author of *Qur'an,*

Liberation and Pluralism (1997), *The Qur'an: A User's Guide* (2005), *The Qur'an: A Beginner's Guide* (2009) and *On Being A Muslim: Religious Path in Today's World* (2009). Dr. Farid Esack has lectured in universities and community centers all over the world and has actively participated in inter-religious solidarity work for justice.

HERMANSEN, MARCIA
Dr. Marcia Hermansen is Director of the Islamic World Studies Program and Professor in the Theology Department at Loyola University, Chicago where she teaches courses in Islamic Studies and the academic study of religion. She received her Ph. D. from the University of Chicago in Arabic and Islamic Studies. In the course of her research and language training she lived for extended periods in Egypt, Jordan, India, Iran, Turkey and Pakistan and she conducts research in Arabic, Persian, Turkish and Urdu as well as the major European languages. Her book, *The Conclusive Argument from God*, a study and translation (from Arabic) of Shah Wali Allah of Delhi's, *Ḥujjat Allāh al-Bālighah* was published in 1996. Dr. Hermansen has also contributed numerous academic articles in the fields of Islamic Thought, Sufism, Islam and Muslims in South Asia, Muslims in America, and Women in Islam.

ISLAM, FAISAL
Faisal Islam is a doctoral candidate in the field of educational research and evaluation at McGill University, Montreal, Canada. He has a Master degree in Sustainable International Development from Brandeis University, Massachusetts, USA.

MAHMOOD, SABA
Dr. Saba Mahmood is Associate Professor of sociocultural anthropology at University of California, Berkeley. Her research interests include exploring historically specific articulation of secular modernity in post-colonial societies, particular emphasis on issues of subject formation, religiosity, embodiment and gender. Dr. Mahmood's book, *Politics of Piety; the Islamic Revival and the Feminist Subject* (Princeton University, 2005) has been acclaimed as a seminal work on ethnography of Muslim women's piety movement in Egypt. Dr. Saba Mahmood has been a fellow of Center for Advanced Study of Behavioral Science, Stanford

University; American Council of Learned Society; and Carnegie Foundation.

MAJID, ANOUAR

Dr. Anouar Majid is Director of the Center for Global Humanities and Associate Professor for Global Initiatives at the University of New England. His research work deals with the place of Islam in the age of globalization and Muslim-Western relations since 1492. He is the author of such highly acclaimed works as *Unveiling Traditions: Post-Colonialism Islam in a Polycentric World* (Duke University Press, 2000); *Freedom and Orthodoxy: Islam and Difference in the Post-Andalusian Age* (Stanford University Press, 2004); *A Call for Heresy: Why Dissent is Vital to Islam and America* (University of Minnesota Press, 2007); and *We are all Moors: Ending Centuries of Crusades Against Muslims and Other Minorities* (University of Minnesota Press, 2009). Professor Majid has lectured and given keynote addresses in major universities in the United States and around the World.

NASR, SEYYED HOSSEIN

Dr. Seyyed Nasr is a University Professor of Islamic Studies at George Washington University, and a prominent Islamic philosopher and scholar of comparative religion. Dr. Nasr has lectured and published extensively on Sufism, philosophy of Science, metaphysics, spirituality, art and architecture, and civilizational dialogue. Professor Seyyed Hossein Nasr is the author of more than three dozen scholarly books including, *Ideals and Realities of Islam, An Introduction of Islamic Cosmological Doctrine, Sadr al-Din Sherazi and His Transcendental Theosophy, Three Muslim Sages, Science and Civilization in Islam* and *History of Islamic Philosophy*. Dr. Nasr has helped with the planning and expansion of the Islamic and the Iranian Studies in several Universities in the United States and has been honored by the Universities and Cultural Institutions around the World for his scholarly work.

NYANG, SULAYMAN

Professor Sulayman Nyang serves as President of the Center for Islam and Public Policy (CIPP). He teaches at Howard University in Washington, D.C. where he serves as Professor of African Studies. From. 1975 to

1978 he served as Deputy Ambassador and Head of Chancery of the Gambia Embassy in Jeddah, Saudi Arabia. He also served as co-director of Project MAPS: Muslims in the American Public Square, a research project housed at Georgetown University, Washington, DC and funded by The Pew Charitable Trusts. Professor Nyang has served as consultant to several national and international agencies. He has served on the boards of the African Studies Association, the American Council for the Study of Islamic Societies and the Association of Muslim Social Scientists. He is listed on the editorial boards of several national and international scholarly journals. He has lectured on college campuses in Africa, Asia, Europe and the Americas. Professor Nyang has written and published extensively on Islam in Africa and Islam in America.

SMITH, JANE

Dr. Jane Smith is Professor of Islamic Studies and Co-Director of Duncan Black Macdonald Center for the Study of Islam and Christian–Muslim Relations at Hartford Seminary, Hartford, CT. Professor Smith has done extensive work on Muslim communities in America, Christian theology in relation to Islam, historical relations between Christians and Muslims, Islamic conceptions of death and afterlife, and the role and status of women in Islam. Currently, Dr. Smith is co-editor of *The Muslim World*, a journal dedicated to the study of Islam and Christian–Muslim relations. She is editor of the Islam section of the new *Encyclopedia of Women in World Religions*, convener of the North American Regional Research Team for the Pew Program on "Christian Theological Education in Muslim Contexts," a member of the Commission on Interfaith Relations of the National Council of Churches and serves on the Executive Committee and Globalization Task Force for the Association of Theological Schools. Among Dr. Smith's recent publications are *Islam in America* (Columbia Press, 1999); "Islam and Christendom" in *The Oxford History of Islam* (Oxford University Press, 1999); *Muslim Communities in America* (State University of New York Press, 1994); and *Mission to America: Five Islamic Communities in the United States* (University Presses of Florida, 1993).

Contributors

VOLL, JOHN O.

Dr. John Voll is Professor of Islamic history and Associate Director of the Prince Al-Waleed bin Talal Center for Muslim-Christian Understanding at Georgetown University. He taught Middle Eastern, Islamic, and world history at the University of New Hampshire for thirty years before moving to Georgetown in 1995. Prof. Voll received his Ph.D. degree from Harvard University. He has lived in Cairo, Beirut, and Sudan and has traveled widely in the Muslim world. The second edition of his book *Islam: Continuity and Change in the Modern World* appeared in 1994. He is co-author, with John L. Esposito, of *Islam and Democracy* and *Makers of Contemporary Islam* and is editor, author, or co-author of six other books. He is a past President of the Middle East Studies Association (MESA) and also of the New England Historical Association. He has published numerous articles and book chapters on modern Islamic and Sudanese history.

Quixotic Quests: In Pursuit of Islam

ANOUAR MAJID

TO discuss the state of Islamic studies in the U.S. is ultimately to talk about America, if one chooses the narrow scope of geographies involved, or of the West, if one expands the scope of analysis beyond the territorial limits of the U.S. The layers of analysis keep unfolding ad infinitum, as the nucleus of our long quest for meaning keeps eluding us and shifting toward new sets of theoretical challenges. Islam may well be an impossible subject of study – it is too broad a category, one that comes awfully close to mimicking life itself. Just as college students cannot sign up for a course on life (despite what many may think), no one can seriously major in Islam. We know that Islam is *dīn wa dunyā*, a philosophy that covers the spiritual and the temporal life on this earth and in the hereafter. Islam, in short, claims to cover the whole human experience, a cradle-to-grave road map that leaves nothing to improvisation. No detail falls outside the all-seeing eye of the faith; everything, with the help of the ever-ready *'ulamā'*, the religious scholars, must bend to its dictates. Islam, for Muslims, is nothing short of life itself.

How then does one approach the study of Islam in American colleges and universities? Naturally, the description of basics is essential: contexts and actors in the saga of the religion's appearance; the nature and pillars of the faith; the study of the large and complex corpus of canon law and jurisprudence; the main schools, or *madhāhib*; and the historic split and differences between the Sunnis and the Shia, a division that has acquired significant meaning in the post-Saddam Hussein

Middle East. To describe such matters would require a good deal of time and attention, for, as with other subject areas, these are complex matters with voluminous literatures. One could therefore spend a good number of years studying the nooks and crannies of the faith, wrestling, for instance, with what constitutes legitimacy and authority in Islam. If the study of Islam were confined to such matters, the study of Islam would resemble the study of other Oriental religions that are significant to interested scholars, American Muslims, and, perhaps, people interested in the study of world cultures.

However, Islam is not a mere religion; it is, perhaps, more *dunyā* than *dīn*. Islam is often compared and contrasted to the West, a secular entity, as it used to be with Christianity in the past. Not only that, but the meaning of Islam in the U.S. cannot be read outside of the process of America's self-definition, for, like Europe and the West in general, the U.S. was established as the antithesis of Islam: first the refuge of pure Christianity, then as a beacon of freedom in sharp contrast to Islamic despotism and the slavish condition of Muslims in general.

To study Islam in the U.S. one must study America itself, or, at least, the aspects of American history that shed light on the experience of Islam in this continent. The 2006 election of Keith Ellison from Minnesota to the U.S. Congress was the first time in American history a Muslim was so honored, and reached back to the legacy of Muslim slaves in antebellum America. The line between, say, the West African Job ben Solomon and Keith Ellison turns and twists the longer we depart from the eighteenth and early nineteenth centuries, but the legacy of the stoic African pioneers is certainly not erased. The spirit of resistance and the quest for justice continues to animate U.S. Muslim minorities, whether native-born or immigrant, not least because the plight of Muslims in America cannot be read outside the historic clash of Islam and Christendom, beginning with the emergence of Islam itself in the lands of Arabia.

For if America is a progeny (however idiosyncratic) of European culture, the transatlantic extension of a long history of struggle with an upstart Arabian religion borrowing from, and claiming to surpass, the Church in matters of divine legitimacy, then such a history, which found expression in the statements of the first Protestant, Martin

Luther, was bound to emigrate to the U.S., as had Iberian prejudices to the lands south of the border. The Christian dispute with Islam, we need to recall, has never been a purely academic matter; the rivalry of the faiths was about self-definition. Europe would not be Europe without Islam, and Islam would not be Islam without Christianity or Judaism. The spirit of defiance was born with Islam itself, intensifying the Christian march toward orthodoxy. Despite all exhortations in the Qur'an to respect other monotheistic faiths, the clash of religions, and, therefore, of civilizations, was born with the advent of Islam. Things have not changed much since then, and are unlikely to change in the future, as long as faiths, with their universalist outlooks, make blanket claims on our lives.

Islam, then, was marked by its critical, rebellious gene, but Europe, too, emerged as the antithesis of *dar al-Islām*, the stronghold of the Christian faith. Just as Europe cannot be imagined without Islam, just as the U.S., not to mention the entire American continent, is inconceivable without the long war to defeat the dangerous imposture of Muhammad. It is not an accident that the 1492 defeat of the Nasirid kingdom in Granada, the last bastion of Islam on Iberian soil was also the beginning of a new world order, the discovery of a continent of natives whose fate was subjection to the sword, enslavement, or policies of annihilation. The New World was imagined as the long-sought-after utopia, a world without Muslims (although the natives quickly acquired quite a few Muslim traits), but such fantasies were soon tempered by the realities of globalization, for one cannot do much in this world without coming across Muslims. Thus Islam, despite restrictive immigration policies, found its way to America, shaping theologies and philosophies of liberation, even as the preachers of freedom enslaved Muslims and non-Muslims alike.

To what extent is the study of Islam in the U.S. such an undertaking different from the first medieval Latin translations of the Qur'an or from George Sale's English version in 1734? Christian leaders, like their secular descendants today, wanted better knowledge of this mysterious faith, but the driving impulse was not knowledge for its own sake, but an understanding that culminates in the evisceration of Islam – knowledge, in other words, for domination and control. Edward

Said famously lamented and condemned such an approach. Governments act out of interest, to increase, or perpetuate, the power of the nation they represent; to expect them to act out of mere curiosity is unrealistic. Muslims also conquered without seeking to know the cultures they conquered. The only piece of information needed was that the conquered were not Muslim. Even today, despite centuries of defeat and struggle, the study of Christianity, Judaism, and non-monotheistic religions remains laughably peripheral. The Muslim superiority complex is etched in graying rock.

Study of Islam in the U.S. exposes the vexed and troubling histories of Islam and the West. Timothy Marr's recent book on American Islamicism, a particular form of American Orientalism, leaves no doubt that Islam "has provided a powerful reservoir of global rhetoric and imagery that Americans have regularly appropriated to authorize and to criticize cultural constructions of national mission, religious faith, moral behaviors, ethnic identity, and gender performance." America's "national project" would have been different without negative references to Islam.[1] As Robert J. Allison argued in his classic, *The Crescent Obscured*:

> a flood of books on the Muslim world poured from the American presses in the 1790s: captivity narratives; histories, including two biographies of Muhammad; novels and poems; and the first American edition of the *Arabian Nights*. This literature conveyed a persistent picture of the Muslim world, an inverted image of the world the Americans were trying to create anew.[2]

The belief that Islam fostered tyranny was deeply ingrained in the revolutionary mindset, and no sooner had the U.S. got its independence (first officially recognized by the Muslim nation of Morocco) that it found itself fighting the Muslim Barbary states and ransoming American hostages from Muslim rulers. Sounding like suicide bombers today, Americans, in plays and action, prided themselves in their willingness to die in the fight against such a mighty foe. In a five-act play called *The Young Carolinians, or, Americans in Algiers*, published in 1818, a young gambler is redeemed by taking up the cause of rescuing captive sailors, stating "our sailors shall make the crescent bend to our fixed stars."3 The Islamic threat justified the construction of a naval force and fanned the nation's nascent sentiments of patriotism. By trumpeting the exploits of Stephen Decatur and William Eaton, "the Navy was no longer a threat to Americans but had itself been transformed into an emblematic instrument of national honor."4 Even the U.S. national anthem, celebrating the victory of 1814, echoes an older version commemorating the defeat of Muslims in the Mediterranean:

> *And pale beam'd the Crescent, its splendor obscur'd*
> *By the light of the star-spangled flag of our nation*
> *Where each flaming star gleam'd a meteor of war*
> *And the turban'd head bowed to the terrible glare*
> *Then mixt with the olive and the laurel shall wave*
> *And form a bright wreath for the brow of the brave.*5

By 1831, the U.S. Navy could reduce the town of Kuala Batu in Sumatra to ashes because the Malays, a "band of lawless pirates," in President Andrew Jackson's formulation, had captured an American vessel following a trade dispute. That same year, the Naval Monument, honoring the lives of Americans who had fought Libyans in the Mediterranean, was placed near the Capitol in Washington.6 It was only after the Ottoman power ebbed in the 1830s that repulsion gradually gave way to pure exoticism, and even a more realistic portrait of Turks, for instance.

The essence of Islam, however, would remain unchanged, or, more accurately, caught between the extremes of existential threat and benign exoticism. The new nation kept Britain's imperial outlook, as Malini Johar Schueller argued, deploying the same language of liberty to launch missions against Arabs and Muslims. While military victories opened the way to the long-term scramble for hegemony in the region. Islamicism, with its Orientalist tropes, started guiding, as Douglas Little showed in *American Orientalism*, national foreign policy toward Arabs and Muslims in general. America's "imperialism of virtue"7 would henceforth be the strategy of choice for such an intractable people.

We are accustomed today to the incendiary discourse of the evangelical right, with its dedicated support to the state of Israel and long-term goal of converting Jews in anticipation of the second advent of Christ. Perhaps we think this is the outcome of a new fundamentalism, no older than the twentieth century itself. Not so. The recapture of the Holy Land, through the removal of Ottoman/Muslim obstacle, and the return of the Jews to their Promised Land in anticipation of the Second Coming was a driving goal of the American Board of Commission for Foreign Missions (ABCFM), founded in 1810. When Levi Parsons, a pioneering missionary in Palestine and western Asia died, less than five years after the Middle East mission was launched in 1819, a requiem celebrated him with such lines: "Thy spirit, Parsons, lur'd by seraph's song/...who like him [shall] destroy Mohammed's sway?"8

The defeat of Islam in its native lands was a longstanding policy of the U.S. Although Americans cheered the breakdown of the Ottoman Empire and the schisms within the Islamic community, Islam proved to be resilient, a fact that not only led to disappointment, but also induced some grudging admiration on the part of a few missionaries. The failure to convert Muslims, however, channeled missionary energies into public works, which, over time, "had a lasting impact in the region and help[ed] to foster the rise of Arab nationalism."9

Through islamicist consciousness, anything that seemed out of the bounds of Protestant morality or republican values was orientalized and dismissed as some sort of Islamic outpost within the expanding territory of the U.S. Thus, no sooner had the small community of Yerba Buena been baptized by Anglo-Saxon occupiers as San Francisco, and soon attracted all the vices of the sea to its waterfront district, that the latter was named the "Barbary Coast." Orientalizing "western spaces" helped contain the Mormon movement, during its westbound exodus to the Rockies, around the same time San Francisco was established in 1846.

The initial reaction to Mormonism, its leader and prophets, was nothing less than a call to arms to resist the Muslim infiltration of America. Mormons were seen as what one what might today call "sleeper cells," fifth columnists for the Muslim powers in some distant, nebulous East. The Mormon migration was dubbed a hijrah, and Utah, the Holy Land, and Salt Lake City, a new Makkah. Joseph Smith Jr. was "the Yankee Mahomet," or "the American Mahomet," and his Book of Mormons, a new Qur'an. Brigham Young, who took over after Smith's death, was also called "the New World Mohammed" and "the Mahomet of Salt Lake." And so it went, with the issue of polygamy giving further ammunition to the new religion's detractors. Novels, plays, and poems depicted a world of harems and seraglios. In her 1882 book, *The Women of Mormonism*, Frances Willard, the President of the Woman's Christian Temperance Union, saw Utah as nothing less than Turkey in America: "Turkey is in our midst. Modern Mohammedanism has its Mecca at Salt Lake, where Prophet Heber C. Kimball speaks of his wives as "cows." Clearly the Koran was Joseph Smith's model, so closely followed as to exclude even the poor pretension of originality in his foul "revelation.""[10]

In the end, such animus, as during the Barbary wars and now after 9/11, turned out to be the proverbial negative advertisement, leading many to inquire about this new (and perhaps exotic) faith at home. And so, like Islam, it kept growing. Moreover, the dwindling power of the Ottoman Empire, and, therefore, of Islam, and the rising commercial and military might of the U.S. attenuated the anxiety associated with Islam and replaced it with a continuous romantic exoticism that influenced American customs and costumes. American "howadjis" undertook "cultural pilgrimages" to the Levant in search of fabled Circassian and eastern female beauties. "The Eastern Beauty is another glory than the pale sweetness of your Blonde," wrote well-known traveler George William Curtis in 1852.[11] Yet no heavenly bodies were to be found in the East, only regular, heavily-clad women, leading to quite a few disappointed tourists. The only nudity found was in Hiram Power's sculpture, *The Greek Slave*, depicting an angelic woman in Turkish captivity. So popular was this sculpture that it toured the country between 1847 and 1850, giving average Americans their first exposure to nudity in art (conveniently displaced onto the Orient).

Islam influenced women's fashion, too, allowing women to use models of Turkish and Islamic dress to resist their sartorial degradation that weighed them down with layers of clothing and restricted their movement and agility. Thus, Amelia Jenks Bloomer introduced her pair of Turkish-style trousers, allowing American to appropriate islamicist notions of eastern beauty and reclaim the harem as a site of freedom. However, the press pilloried the women's dress reform movement. American women were depicted as allies of Muslim infidels, waging holy war on Christians. In 1852, a critic wrote for the *Knickerbocker*, asking incredulously, "Shall the harems of the East set the fashion for the boudoirs of the West?...Have we quit Paris, dear delightful Paris! for the Sublime Porte and her mantua-makers for the Blue Beards of Constantinople?"[12] Under relentless pressure and persecution, the reform movement eventually died, only to be reborn "during the bicycle craze of the 1890s."[13] By that time, American elite crack troops had taken to wearing Algerian costumes. These were the Zouave soldiers, named after their French namesakes, who adopted the dress after conquering Algiers in 1830. As the nineteenth century wore on, freemasons established Arabic orders and orientalized the habit of smoking, turning Islam into a symbol of liberty as much as it had been one of despotism, only a few decades earlier.

Islamicism, then, cuts both ways. It exoticizes Islam by embellishing it with lavish displays of Orientalia and, at the same time, denounces it as a mortal threat to the republic and its way of life. One could see this cultural habit playing itself out in the Maghreb – Morocco, Algeria, and Tunisia – in the post-World War II period, when American troops landed in Casablanca, Oran, and Algiers during Operation Torch to chase the Germans out of North Africa. General George S. Patton, who led the U.S. contingent in Morocco, saw in Morocco a mixture of Old Testament and the Arabian Nights, while not failing to note, as other writers did, "the similarity between the Arab and the Mexican."[14]

Even as Morocco was being exoticized in films like *Casablanca* (released soon after Operation Torch was launched), army publications were describing the local Arabs as lazy and good-for-nothing natives. The Algiers edition of *Stars and Stripes* could write matter-of-factly in 1943, "if the Arab was often a pest and pretty generally a nuisance, he nevertheless was indispensable. He shined our shoes, sold us oranges, delivered eggs to our front lines right through enemy fire, and continually reminded us what blessings we had in the form of chewing gum, chocolate, and cigarettes." No longer a warrior, the North African Arab has thus been reduced to a neutral, small–time peddler.[15]

Images of Morocco as an undisturbed biblical landscape (the same topography one finds in Barbary captivity narratives in the late eighteenth and early nineteenth centuries) and a land of Oriental mystery were part of the lore that attracted Americans. Brian Edwards detailed other images in his *Morocco Bound*. Tangier, the safe house for all sorts of western malcontents, was equally admired and condemned for its excess and licentiousness, a free republic, as one writer put it, beholden to no state or nation, surviving on the wits of its residents and refugees, the whole representing almost every race and creed in the known world.

The remarkably constant image of Islam in America's changing ideological make–up legitimizes American patriotism and contributes to the country's strong sense of exceptionalism. "Since the beginnings of the settlement of what is today the U.S.," Marr wrote,

> The Islamic world has formed an extrahemispheric horizon that Americans have engaged to define the cultural contours of their changing sense of worldliness. The cultural discourse of islamicism dislocated Islam from its diverse everyday practices and recalibrated it into an imaginary resource for articulating local, regional, and national situations within a broader planetary perspective. Because early Americans were largely unable or unwilling to understand the religious ethos held by Muslims themselves, they imported islamicist images instead and then applied and elaborated them in attempts to generate a more global relevance for their varied domestic productions. Islamicist expression therefore is ultimately an invented appropriation of the difference of Islam used to mark American boundaries rather than an intercultural means of measuring Muslim meanings.[16]

In other words, Americans have consistently failed to meet Islam in its own terms. How then does one begin to teach about Islam in a cultural and political environment impregnated with deeply–rooted prejudice, whether such prejudice has some basis in fact or not? Not all

American criticisms of Islam were necessarily cut from the same Orientalist cloth. It would be too simplistic to overlook the world-historic event of the American Revolution and the zealotry for universal freedom (echoes of which are still being heard today) that it unleashed. Islam, like Catholicism and monarchical regimes, seemed relics of a dysfunctional past.

The emotions, views, and philosophies that emerge from such an event are certainly qualitatively different from the anti-Islamic attitudes of the earlier colonial period or of European ones (although in Europe, too, attitudes changed after the French Revolution, launched on the heels of the American one). The U.S. has never had a problem accepting private Islamic practices, but the country, which tied its future to remaking the world in its own image, has always found Muslim nations wanting in matters of economic and political freedom. Islam has not done well politically in its control of worldly matters.

This is a rather simplistic sketch of the tensions that traverse American-Muslim relations, one that nevertheless helps us to conceptualize, perhaps a little bit more concretely, the points of what may be unbridgeable differences and contention. Whenever the subject of Islam is raised in America (including in the classroom or in scholarship), it never appears as a neutral category, cleansed from polemics. The response to Islam may vary in intensity, as the ghosts of non-Muslim enemies occupy center stage every now and then, but Islam always returns as the reliable phantom to haunt the American imagination. The Taliban were supported during the last days of the Communist threat, but, today, they are America's mortal foe. Islam is the enemy that never fails to acquit itself of its historic function as archenemy most of the time and strategic ally on occasion. As the African-American Democratic presidential hopeful, Barack Obama survived a first round of slanderous attacks linking him to Islam, via his middle name (Hussein) or to a *madrasah* (since all *madrasahs*, or religious schools, are imagined as breeding grounds for Muslim terrorists). The deployment of Islam to disqualify an African-American from the U.S. presidency, or, as had happened a few months earlier in the case of the Muslim Keith Ellison, from the U.S. Congress, prove that Islam has lost none of its spectral powers.

NOTES

1   Timothy Marr, *The Cultural Roots of American Islamicism* (New York: Cambridge University Press, 2006), p.9.

2   Robert J. Allison, *The Crescent Obscured: The U.S. and the Muslim World 1776-1815* (New York: Oxford University Press, 1995), p.xvii.

3   Marr, *The Cultural Roots of American Islamicism*, p.65.

4   Ibid., p.69.

5   Robert J. Allison wrote: "The parallels between this song and the one [Key] wrote after watching the British bombard Fort McHenry in September 1814 are striking. The tune is the same, as is the rhyme scheme of the chorus. In the more famous later version, the fate of the 'star-spangled flag of our nation' is in doubt throughout the perilous fight. In this song, however, it obscures the Muslim crescent, whose hollow splendor is cast in shadow by the true glory of the American flag and the republic it symbolizes." Allison, *The Crescent Obscured*, pp.205-6.

6   Marr, *The Cultural Roots of American Islamicism*, pp.78-79, 81.

7   Ibid., p.35; Douglas Little, *American Orientalism: The U.S. and the Middle East Since 1945* (Chapel Hill: University of North Carolina Press, 2002).

8   Ibid., p.85.

9   Ibid., p.131.

10   Ibid., p.207.

11   Ibid., pp.271-272.

12   Ibid., p.286.

13   Ibid., p.287.

14   Brian T. Edwards, *Morocco Bound: Disorienting America's Maghreb, from Casablanca to the Marrakech Express* (Durham, NC: Duke University Press, 2005), pp.29-32.

15   Ibid., pp.56-57.

16   Ibid., pp.296-97.

ESSAY II

Origins and Development of Islamic Studies in the U.S.: A Historical Overview of Trends and Institutions

SEYYED HOSSEIN NASR

THE name of Islam appears in the news nearly daily and several million Muslims constitute an element of American society that can no longer be ignored. The thought of Islamic philosophers and the contribution of Islamic scientists is embedded in one way or another in the background of the philosophy and science being cultivated in the western world including America; and words of Arabic and Persian origin are used in American English more than are Japanese, Chinese, or Hindi words. The adobe architecture of the American Southwest reflects clearly its Islamic influence through both its forms and its building techniques as well as in the word adobe itself; and the poetry of the Islamic peoples is read and the music heard to an ever-greater degree in this land. Yet, despite all these and many other similar facts, the state of Islamic studies in America is far from satisfactory.

In this essay, which is confined to Islamic studies in American colleges and universities, we wish to consider some of the factors that prevent Islamic studies from occupying a position one would expect for a field that embraces the culture and history of a billion people stretching across the Afro-Asian land mass with important extensions into Europe and now to an ever greater degree in the Americas. One should ask why whole areas of the Islamic world, such as Southeast Asia, fail even to be considered in most centers of Islamic studies, and why, despite so many universities where Islamic studies is taught, America has produced so few outstanding scholars in this field who can be compared to such European Islamicists as Louis Massignon, Sir Hamilton Gibb, or Henry Corbin. In addition, much of the fruit of scholarship in Islamic studies in America is so strongly opposed by Muslims despite the attempt by a number of American scholars to cultivate a more sympathetic view of Islam than what was developed by classical European orientalism.

The existing state of affairs can in part be explained by the history of the development of Islamic studies as a discipline here. The early American scholars of Islam were mostly missionaries with an often open and vocal opposition to Islam. A number of early scholars, however, came from the background of Rabbinical studies, and since they belonged to the era preceding the partition of Palestine in 1948, they did not feel compelled to produce the polarized and "motivated" scholarship associated with Zionism that has affected Islamic studies so greatly since the 1950s.

Among them were some outstanding figures who contributed greatly to Islamic studies: such scholars as Harry A. Wolfson, who although primarily a scholar of Jewish thought, made notable contributions to the history of Islamic theology *(kalām)* and philosophy. Among the pioneers of Islamic studies were also a number of Maronites like Phillip Hitti, who while being outstanding scholars of Arabic, were not Muslims, although they were seen by many in America as authentic voices of Islamic scholarship since most people almost naturally equated Islam with Arabs. Many of these early scholars, however, had little love for the specifically Islamic dimension of the subject they were studying, although they helped to advance the cause of Arabic studies.

Despite the appearance of a number of scholars of distinction, there was from the beginning a trait in Islamic studies in America that distinguished it from Chinese, Japanese, or Indian studies, for example. This trait was an opposition to or even disdain for Islam and its culture among many scholars in this field. Usually, when an American went into the field of Far Eastern studies, with the exception of a few missionaries, he was attracted by some aspect of that civilization or religion that he loved and defended, as seen by the attitude of Langdon Warner of Harvard University, who played such an important role in saving

Kyoto from being bombed during World War II. This attitude of love and empathy has manifested itself much less frequently in Islamic studies.

After World War II, when America actively entered the international scene, a new phase opened in the history of Islamic studies, which caused the field to expand but at the expense of depth and concern for the historical and religious dimension. Centers of regional studies began to develop in many universities throughout the country, from Harvard to UCLA, usually under the name of Middle Eastern but also occasionally Near Eastern studies. Oriented mostly toward the present day and based in social sciences rather than theology, religion, or the humanities, these centers taught many subjects concerning the Islamic world but minimal reference to Islam itself.

A whole generation of scholars was trained, some of whom became decision-makers in America, and affected the history of the Islamic world itself, usually in an adverse manner, while the majority became experts and scholars of the central regions of the Islamic world. With a number of notable exceptions, however, few of these scholars made any outstanding contributions to Islamic studies or could predict any of the major transformations in the region of their specialization: transformations such as the revival of Islam in various forms in the 1970s. Only the events of the past ten years in the Islamic world have forced many of these centers to pay more attention to Islam in the Middle East.

Even to this day, however, in many of the major centers of Middle Eastern studies, everything is taught seriously except Islam itself. One sees often in such centers numerous courses on history, anthropology, languages, sociology, political science, and similar subjects pertaining to the Islamic world, but little in-depth study of Islam as the religion that forms the heart and arteries of the body of the society and civilization being considered.

In America, there is in fact only a handful of institutions of higher learning like the University of Chicago and Temple University where Islam is studied seriously in religion departments as a religion and not as something else. Moreover, despite the rapid expansion of religious studies on this continent during the past four decades to include "non-western" religions, and the establishment of centers for the study of religion on a worldwide scale such as those at Harvard, Colgate, and Claremont, Islam has not fared as well as Hinduism, Buddhism, or the Chinese religions. The discipline of comparative religion in fact has produced very few Islamicists of note. Besides the historical opposition to Islam in the Christian West, going back to the Crusades and the Reconquest in Spain, which affects almost unconsciously the attitude of many modern Westerners including those who do not even consider themselves Christian, there is the question of how religious studies have evolved.

During the nineteenth century, there developed in the field of "the science of religions" (*Religionwissenschaft*) the idea of the evolution of religion from so-called "primitive" to higher forms, reaching its peak with Christianity. Such a conception of religious history, which continued into this century, obviously had great difficulty coming to terms with such a major postscript as Islam. In reaction to this historicism, there developed the school of phenomenology, whose most influential representative in America was M. Eliade, who made major contributions to nearly every field of religious studies except Islam. With its emphasis upon myths and symbols, this school was much more attracted to such traditions as Hinduism, whose truths are for the most part expressed in mythological language, than to Islam, whose metaphysical and theological teachings are couched mostly in an "abstract" language and whose teachings include a sacred law that is central to the understanding of the religion.

To these factors were added the age-old distortions of Islam as the "religion of the sword" or the "dry" religion of the desert, whose blindingly clear spirituality was supposedly somehow borrowed from foreign sources and grafted upon the body of Islam. As a result, the teaching of Hinduism used such sublime texts as the *Baghavad-Gita*, not laws of inheritance in various castes and sub-castes, and Hindu art rather than social and commercial conflicts. In the case of Islam, only the most external aspects of the religion came to be taught along with a distorted history of a religion seen in constant conflict and war.

As a result, Islamic studies has not fared well as religious studies even when compared to Hindu, Buddhist, or Chinese religious studies, despite or perhaps because Islam is theologically much closer to Judaism and Christianity and Islam has shared so much more common history with the Christian West than the Indian and Far Eastern religions. The incredible synthesis that developed in Muslim Spain and in the culture under Muslim rule, where Muslims, Jews, and Christians lived at peace for several centuries, contributing to a glittering civilization in which they all played a role, is passed over more or less in silence. Almost no one refers to the Judeo/Christian/Islamic tradition. Instead, in forgetfulness of the reality of Abrahamic monotheism and to abet the cause of passing political goals, most scholars juxtapose the Judeo-Christian heritage to the Islamic.

Islamic studies has fared poorly by and large in the field of religion, and has been more or less neglected in the field of the humanities. Whether in philosophy or history, literature or the arts, Islamic studies in America has not succeeded in flowering in any notable manner in comparison with, for example, Japanese studies. In medieval European universities, the Islamic humanities played a greater role than they do today in America. Even during the Romantic movement in England and Germany, there was greater interest in at least the literature of the Islamic peoples than one finds today.

Only in the field of the social sciences have subjects related to the Islamic world been treated fairly extensively in America. Here, however, there stands the major question of whether western models apply to the Islamic world. Is it possible to study Islamic society based on theories of Durkheim, or to carry out an anthropological study of a part of the Islamic world based on the theories of Levi-Strauss? These major questions are now being debated, and one hopes that as a result more serious contributions will be made to Islamic studies in those fields that in the West are called the social sciences. Until then, even in this domain where so much effort is being spent, the results will usually not have much to do with the social and religious reality of the Islamic world.

As for law, which plays such an important role in Islam, only during the past decade have certain American law schools begun to teach Islamic law, and mostly for practical reasons. The teaching of the Divine Law, or Shariʿah, however, has not become part and parcel of

Islamic studies and few American scholars have made notable contributions to this field.

At the heart of Islamic studies stands not only the religion of Islam, but also the languages involved with the study of that religion and the civilization Islam created. Arabic is the most important of Islamic languages and has been taught in America since the eighteenth century. In recent decades, however, despite the appearance of several eminent Arabists who either themselves or their families migrated from the Islamic world, such as George Makdisi and Irfan Shahid, and a number of fine American Arabists such as James Bellamy, William Brenner, Victor Danner, Richard Frank, and Nicholas Heer, the teaching of Arabic has still suffered regarding Islamic studies.

The main reason has been the emphasis upon "modern" Arabic at the expense of the classical language. Until recently in most centers of Arabic studies, Qur'anic Arabic was made subservient to the prose of *al-Ahram* and little attention was paid to the fact that among many literate Arabs, the Qu'ran is read and understood first, and only later is modern literary Arabic mastered. During the past decade, some changes have been made in the direction of classical Arabic, and more students are now being trained who can read classical texts. Still, the training is far from complete because too few students even with advanced degrees are actually able to read classical Arabic texts with full in-depth comprehension of their meaning.

The situation of the second major Islamic language, Persian, is much more deplorable. First, even the name of the language is now used incorrectly, frequently called "Farsi" as if in English one called French *français* or German *Deutsch*. Second, it is usually forgotten that not only is Persian (by whatever name it is called) still the spoken and written language of Iran, Afghanistan, and Tajikistan as well as that of many people in Iraq, the Persian Gulf, and Pakistan, but that for a thousand years it was the *lingua franca* of Asia. Qur'anic commentaries in China were written in Persian, while even after World War II just before Albania became Communist, Persian books continued to be printed in this western outpost of the Islamic world.

Without knowledge of Persian, the Muslim culture of India and most of its medieval history, both Hindu and Muslim, is a closed book, and later Islamic thought as it developed in the eastern lands of Islam is a forbidden territory. The remarkable indifference to the teaching of Persian in many American universities has done much to weaken Islamic studies and to prevent well-rounded students from being trained. Persian is essential not only for the study of eastern history, literature, and the arts, but also for Islamic studies, where some of the most important figures such as Ghazāly wrote in both Arabic and Persian.

The other major Islamic languages such as Turkish, Urdu, Bengali, and Malay are taught here and there but rarely as integral parts of Islamic studies. This is partly due to an unfortunate classification of religions that is detrimental to Islamic studies – the division between eastern and western religions. In many universities, Islam is taught as a western religion despite being "non-western." This is correct to the extent that Islam is an integral part of Abrahamic monotheism, of which Judaism and Christianity are the other two branches. Yet whereas these branches grew primarily in the West, Islam was destined to spread as much in the East as in the West. There are more Muslims in Southeast Asia today than in the whole of the Arab world. The religious life and culture of several hundred million Muslims in South Asia, Bangladesh, Indonesia, Malaysia, and China is hardly ever mentioned in general courses on Islam and not even known to any appreciable degree by advanced students in the field.

Likewise, African Islam is rarely treated as part of Islamic studies. General courses on Islam and its history deal only accidentally and tangentially with Africa south of the Sahara, and courses on Africa rarely relate the advent and history of Islam in Africa to the rest of the Islamic world. One can attain the highest degree in Islamic studies and know nothing about either the great Islamic empires of Mali or the millions of Muslims living in Xinjiang (Sinkiang). A work such as the *Venture of Islam* by Marshall Hodgson, one of the most gifted American scholars of Islam, covers the whole of the Islamic world in time as well as geographically in an exceptional manner, far from the usual treatment that is given to the subject.

The criticism made of Islamic studies in America is not intended to detract from the achievements in this domain by a number of

American scholars in so many fields such as Islamic history, anthropology, sociology, the history of art and archaeology, music, literature, philosophy, the history of science, and several aspects of the religion of Islam itself. Yet considering the importance of the subject, the distortions and high price in terms of practical matters that the Islamic world and America have paid and continue to pay as a result of the misunderstanding of Islam and the Islamic world in America, it is necessary to investigate how to improve the situation.

It must, therefore, be asked what can be done to improve the condition of Islamic studies while benefiting from the achievements of the past few decades and learning from its mistakes. This question must, moreover, be asked in light of the fact that Islamic studies in America involves to an even greater degree the Islamic world due to a large number of Muslim students in America, as well as a number of Muslim scholars and teachers whose works have extensive influence not only upon these students but also within Islamic countries.

The first and most important step that must be taken in Islamic studies is to study this field within the framework of religion rather than as a discipline, which no matter how significant, is not concerned with religion as such. As already mentioned, in the vast majority of institutions of learning in America, Islam is studied as history, language, culture, a political system, and the like, but not as religion. The heart of Islamic studies must be moved from all these other disciplines or regional centers and placed in religion departments where the central religious significance of all things Islamic can be developed. In the Islamic world, not only theology and ethics, but also law, economics, politics, arts, and sciences possess much greater religious significance than their counterparts in post-medieval European civilization. There is no greater source of distortion than applying the secularist perspective of the past few centuries in the West to a religion and civilization where it does not apply. The activity in the bazaar of a Muslim city is economic activity but also possesses a religious dimension that is crucial to its understanding and without which any study of it will be superficial, to say the least.

Stating that Islamic studies should be placed in religion departments, however, is not meant to imply that contemporary western religious categories should be applied blindly to Islam. For example, in Christianity, theology is much more central than law, whereas in Islam, law is more central. In Christianity, mysticism was never organized into orders independent of the authority of the Church, whereas in Islam, Sufi orders have always been independent of the exoteric 'ulamā'. In fact, the whole question of religious authority is posed differently in the two traditions. There is need to make use of a theology and metaphysics of comparative religion that can deal with Islam in a manner that does justice to the nature of that tradition and yet is comprehensible to the western worldview.

The prejudices that have marred the study of Islam in the West since the time of Peter the Venerable, when the Qur'an was first rendered into Latin and even beforehand, must finally be overcome if in-depth understanding is to be achieved. Unfortunately, despite so many claims to objectivity, much of western scholarship concerning Islam remains distorted due to many old prejudices, to which new ones have been added, resulting from the Arab-Israeli conflict and the rise of so-called fundamentalism.

Islam must first and foremost be studied as a religion and not simply a social force or historical event. This task is made easier by the appearance of a number of works in European languages during the past few decades that speak with sympathy and authority about Islam. Most have been written by westerners who understand the Islamic tradition or speak from within that tradition. Also, a number of books in this category of writings have been written by Muslims in European languages, primarily English and French. Although some of these works do not address the western mind and the questions usually posed by a westerner in quest of understanding Islam, others do succeed in creating a bridge between the Islamic world and the West. In any case, the thorough and sympathetic yet objective study of the Islamic religion and the placing of this study at the heart of Islamic studies is a necessary task already facilitated by the research, study, and writings of those western and Muslim scholars who speak with such authority that they are accepted by Muslims and at the same time are comprehensible to the western audience.

There is under present circumstances no excuse for the large number of Middle Eastern, Near Eastern, or Islamic studies programs in which Islam is relegated to a single introductory course, and everything else Islamic, whether it be history, art, sociology, or economics, is taught almost completely detached from the Islamic tradition, which in reality is the lifeblood of all those other domains. Nor is there any excuse for the remarkably weak representation of Islam in so many comparative religious studies programs throughout the country where there are often several professors in Hindu, Buddhist, and Far Eastern religious studies but hardly any in Islam. Of all the major world religions, Islam fares worst in most religious studies programs in America. Until that weakness is solved, there is little hope for a serious improvement in the situation of Islamic studies.

Once Islamic studies is reconstituted to centralize the religion and its study, it will be necessary to relate this central concern to a number of fields such as sociology, economics, international relations, political science, and humanities for those students who wish for interdisciplinary education. This is particularly true of Muslim students coming to America for advanced education. To an ever-greater degree, such students are interested in studying economics, sociology, anthropology, history of art, and history of science. They are primarily interested in Islam in relation to those fields. In light of the present-day interest within the Islamic world in the process that has become known as "the Islamization of knowledge," this type of interdisciplinary approach could become one of the most fruitful developments in Islamic studies in America with far-reaching consequences for the Islamic world. Yet the condition of success in this program remains a carefully prepared core Islamic studies program grounded in religious studies.

The second important consideration in improving Islamic studies is the proper teaching of the Islamic languages. Fortunately, much attention is paid to Arabic but still not enough to classical Arabic. As already stated, emphasis should be placed upon classical Arabic to serve as the basis for modern Arabic, not vice-versa. Also, greater attention should be paid to the reading and interpretation of classical texts according to the traditional methods of hermeneutics. Earlier orientalism, despite its numerous prejudices, rendered much service to Islamic studies by critically editing many important texts. Even this art, however, is being lost, especially in America where so many young scholars prefer to write about texts without being able to read them carefully, not to speak of editing them. The fault in this matter lies most of all in the manner that Arabic is taught.

As for Persian, the whole philosophy of teaching it must be changed. Persian must first of all be recognized for what it is, namely as already mentioned the *lingua franca* of what Toynbee called the Iranic zone of Islamic civilization stretching from Iraq to China. After Arabic, Persian is the most important Islamic language and the only language other than Arabic that became global within Islamic civilization. No program of Islamic studies can be serious without the teaching of Persian. Semitic philology is an independent field of study, as is Islamic studies. Arabic is of course very important for Semitic linguistic studies, where it is studied along with Hebrew, Aramaic, Syriac, and other Semitic languages. However, this relationship has little to do with the relationship of Arabic to Persian and through Persian to other major Islamic languages such as Turkish and Urdu. Islamic studies, in contrast to Semitic studies, must emphasize this latter relationship and teach both Arabic and Persian to serious students of Islamic studies, especially as far as Islamic thought is concerned.

As for the other Islamic languages, they must also be offered in major centers while a number of centers will naturally specialize in a particular region of the Islamic world such as North Africa, South Asia, or Southeast Asia, in which case, Berber, the Indian language, or Malay must be taught. Yet such languages and even such a major language as Turkish are vernacular languages, while Arabic and Persian constitute the classical and universal languages of the Islamic world. These languages, because of their immense richness and long history, must be mastered in-depth and based on a program that would enable at least a small number of students to gain full mastery of them.

American institutions of learning have not until now been as successful in this endeavor as the amount of effort spent would lead one to expect. There has, however, been more success in the field of Arabic than Persian, where there are very few American scholars who possess complete mastery over the classical literature. The flowering of Islamic studies requires a deepening of language teaching so that at least a number of young scholars are trained every year who can read and translate with precision the texts with which Islamic studies is concerned.

As for different aspects of Islamic studies, the situation varies from one field to another. A number of gifted young scholars have been trained in history, but there is a shortage of competent scholars in the field to the extent that many of the works written around the turn of the century continue to be reprinted and taught despite many important new discoveries that have been made since they were written. It is necessary to encourage a greater number of students with a real flair for history to turn to the subject of Islamic history by emphasizing not only the significance of the field itself, but also its relation to other major fields of history such as medieval European history, Indian history, and the like.

In the field of philosophy, Islamic studies in America suffers particularly from the fact that the prevalent philosophical trend in America since World War II has been particularly opposed to the religious and metaphysical concerns of Islamic philosophy. This, added to the lack of attention paid to the study of philosophy in secondary schools, has prevented Islamic philosophy from attracting as many gifted students as one finds in Europe. There are very few centers in America, even major ones, where Islamic philosophy is taught seriously, and where it is, rarely is it related to the Islamic tradition to which it is inalienably linked.

The situation of Islamic science is not much better. There is a small number of fine scholars in the field teaching in several centers, but in most cases the study of Islamic science is cut off from the rest of Islamic studies and taught more as a chapter in the history of western science. Rarely are the Islamic sciences seen as the fruit of the tree of Islamic civilization, nurtured and developed within a worldview that has its roots in the Islamic tradition.

The field of Islamic art, however, has come into its own during the past decade and there is a greater degree of interest in both Islamic art and architecture than even before. The Aga Khan program in Islamic art and architecture at Harvard and M.I.T. has been a catalyst in this domain and has caused a number of young Muslim architects, urban designers, and the like to come to America to pursue their studies in Islamic art and architecture. This very active domain of Islamic studies can be further developed by strengthening its link with the study of Islam itself and by not losing sight of the nexus between Islamic art and the religion that made the creation of this art possible.

The non-plastic arts, however, have not fared as well. The literature of the Islamic peoples has attracted a number of scholars, and a few like Herbert Mason have created literary works based on Islamic themes. Still, the situation is very far from that of Persian literature in Victorian and Edwardian England. There is need for studying anew the great masterpieces of Islamic literature, particularly Sufi poetry. Classical Persian Sufi poetry remains to this day a subject that attracts many who are drawn to mystical and spiritual subjects. More work is needed along the line of works by A.M. Schimmel, William Chittick, Omar Pound, and others to make this poetry as well as the literary masterpieces of Arabic, Turkish, Urdu, and other Islamic languages known and made part and parcel of Islamic studies.

As for the social sciences in relation to Islam, the works of American scholars are numerous and American centers remain very active in various social sciences such as sociology, anthropology, political science, and more recently economics. In some fields such as anthropology, American scholars like Clifford Geertz have produced works of great influence. By and large, these fields suffer from the imposition of alien models upon the Islamic world with often catastrophic results, as witnessed by the predictions made by so many American political scientists concerning the Islamic world during the past few decades.

These disciplines need to sink their roots more into the Islamic religion, its theology and philosophy, its Sacred Law, the politico-social and economic teachings that issue from it, and the history and culture of the Islamic peoples. Today in most American centers of Islamic studies, western social, economic, or political models are used for the study of the Islamic world, and there is little interaction between the social sciences and Islamic studies. The walls drawn around each discipline are so high and thick that it is difficult to either mount them or pierce through them. If Islamic studies is to be strengthened in this domain, there is no choice but to remove some of these obstacles;

otherwise studies whose results are usually contradicted by events will remain the order of the day.

In order for Islamic studies to flourish in America to the benefit of both America and the Islamic world, it should also be taught as part and parcel of the general education and liberal arts programs in American universities. The experience of Muslim Spain where Christians and Jews lived in harmony with Muslims and where communities interacted and collaborated to create one of the most glorious episodes of human history should be recalled and studied carefully, rather than purposefully forgotten because of current political or ideological interests. The western humanities should be taught as related both historically and morphologically to those of Islam. Simple mention of the "Arab philosophers" in an intermediate chapter linking late antiquity to the scholastics in the history of philosophy is not sufficient.

The Muslim philosophers must be taught fully not only as one of the pillars of the foundation of medieval western thought, but also as philosophers who while sharing the same Greco–Hellenistic intellectual heritage and Abrahamic religious background as western philosophers, developed their thought in a different direction from the post–medieval West. Islamic philosophy must be seen as not only a chapter in the history of western thought, but also as an independent school of philosophy, close to, yet different from western philosophy, and having its own history that continues to the present day. Islamic philosophy, moreover, should be taught in philosophy departments and not only in Middle East departments where neither the teachers nor the students are necessarily trained to understand philosophical discourse.

The same could be said for other disciplines. Islamic literature should be taught to students specializing in Islamic studies, and also to all students of world literature who should see Arabic literature in relation to Provençal poetry, to the *Divine Comedy* of Dante, to the treatises of Raymond Lull, to the introduction of rhyme into European poetry, or to the *Fables* of La Fontaine. They should read Persian poetry along with their study of Goethe and Ruckert, or English romantic poetry, or the American Transcendentalists, and come to understand the significance of the influence of the literature of

(1) ؏ạ4+/F
(2) ﺟﻌﺪ d ﺍ h
(3) m ﺍd/N4

25

these languages upon the European literary tradition. They should also study the literature of the Islamic peoples as literature.

In music, the origin of many European instruments should be made clear, as should the interaction between Spanish and Arabic music. Introduction of the Turkish military bands, as well as works of Mozart and Haydn with purported Turkish themes should be combined with familiarity with some Turkish music. Even in modern times, the study of Bartók and Kodály should be accompanied by some acquaintance with Arabic and other forms of music of the Muslim peoples in which they were so interested.

As for art, rarely is the history of western art taught with reference to the significance of the Cordoba mosque for medieval Gothic arching, or Arabic illuminations for the art of illumination, or for that matter the Persian miniature for certain aspects of the art of Matisse. Without denying the very different nature of European art from Islamic art, various forms of Islamic art, which over the centuries have fecundated or influenced European or American art, can be taught as a part of those subjects in the same way that Greek or Roman influences, which were of course influential on a much wider scale, are studied. Although Islam was not simply the foundation of western civilization as was Rome once Christianized, it was one of the elements that played a great role in the formative period of western civilization. Islamic studies should therefore be taught in the light of that role as well as independent of western studies.

Finally, every intellectual endeavor flowers and develops through the quality of the thought of those who lead, and not through the quantity of those who happen to study in the particular field in question. Islamic studies is no exception. In American centers until now there has not been enough emphasis upon a hierarchical concept of a program that would begin with many students and end with very few who would, however, be highly qualified. There is a tendency to offer too many courses that move in a parallel and horizontal direction rather than vertically. Too much emphasis is placed upon the quantity of teachers and students, as if the greatest Islamicists the West has produced were not products of universities where one or two outstanding scholars trained a very small number of gifted students over the years in a manner which did not simply widen their horizon but also deepened their scholarship and enabled them to penetrate more profoundly into the subject. No excellence in Islamic studies, or for that matter practically any other field of intellectual endeavor, is possible without emphasis upon quality and hierarchy in the sense of building an ever-higher intellectual edifice on a firm and broad foundation, and not only expanding the foundation horizontally.

The future of Islamic studies in America is not only a matter of theoretical or academic concern. The future of both the Islamic world and America depends on the knowledge or ignorance of the Islamic world in America. The incredible distortions of the image of Islam in the American mass media complements the lack of understanding of many facets of Islam by the "experts" upon whose views depend the decisions that affect the lives of millions of human beings. The Islamic world is too large and Islam too strong a force to be relegated to the status it possesses in the West and especially America today.

The development of Islamic studies upon a more solid foundation, with greater depth and based on more vigorous scholarship and intellectual honesty, can be of great benefit to both America and the Islamic world. The destinies of the Islamic world and the West are intertwined as such that ignorance of one world by the other is calamitous for both worlds. It is hoped that the bitter fruits of the past decade will help usher in a period in which Islamic studies can both provide a greater understanding of that world and enrich to the extent possible the religious, cultural, artistic, and educational life of America itself.

Changing Western Approaches to Islamic Studies

JOHN O. VOLL

THE study of Islam in the West has a long history in western intellectual tradition. Over the centuries, scholars and thinkers worked to gain some understanding of Islam and Muslims. These efforts were always shaped by the worldviews and perspectives of the westerners engaged in the study, as well as the historical and religious realities of Islam and actual Muslim experience. The methods and approaches used in the study reflected the scholarly disciplines and intellectual discourses of the time and place of study.

At the beginning of the twenty-first century, the study of Islam is entering a new era. In many ways, the old canons of western scholarship are being changed and challenged in the context of intellectual globalization. In the past, it was possible to identify separate worlds of scholarship in the study of Islam: western Europe (and in the past century, North America); and the Muslim world. While there was some contact between scholars from the two different worlds, especially in special situations like the medieval Iberian Peninsula in the era of Muslim control, the methods and perspectives represented two different intellectual worldviews and there were limited direct personal contacts. However, in the nineteenth century, important lines of communication and interaction developed among scholars from the two worlds who were studying Islam. The specific conditions of time and place shaped the nature of these contacts, since they developed in the context of western imperialist expansion and exploitation. Despite the limitations and distortions created by this situation, a new world of significantly interacting scholarship was beginning to develop.

During the twentieth century, many worlds of scholarship began to merge as students and scholars became more mobile. In this process, important Muslim scholars gradually became a significant part of the scholarly and academic institutions in the West. This was one of a number of factors that began the transformation in the West of the study of religion in general and the study of Islam in particular. These Muslim scholars made critical contributions to the transitions from Orientalism to area studies, and from theological studies to religious studies. At the beginning of the twenty-first century, they are now key contributors in developing ways of understanding and living in a single but religiously pluralistic world. Seyyed Hossein Nasr is an important figure in this process. An examination of his contributions, especially in the scholarship of religious experience and the understanding of Sufism, can provide a helpful key to understanding the intellectual and scholarly transformations involved in the study of Islam during the second half of the twentieth century.

Foundations for the Western Study of Islam

The transformations of scholarship in the second half of the twentieth century represent a reshaping of older traditions and the necessary creation of new conceptualizations. Older and more recent conceptualizations had to be reconstructed in the new contexts of the emerging pluralist, globalized world. The older western intellectual constructs and images of Islam needed (and need) to be reshaped, and more recent grand theories like modernization theory and theories of secularization needed to be either rejected or reconceived.

The old, established western conceptualizations of Islam have very deep historical roots. In the European medieval era, perspectives of theological scholasticism shaped the study of Islam, while in the Renaissance and Reformation eras, new modes of scholarship were used. Similarly, the atmosphere of the European Enlightenment in the eighteenth century set new conceptual frameworks for European understandings of Islam. At the same time, many of the specific descriptions and conceptualizations were passed on from generation to generation. During these centuries, a relatively coherent, established canon of western interpretation of Islam developed and maintained a remarkably high degree of continuity. This interpretation even survived Christendom's doctrinal unity and the growth of atheism and agnosticism. By the eighteenth century, some scholars made progress in creating a less religiously-committed body of information.[1]

One significant dimension of the scholarship involved in the development of the "western canon" is the absence of direct participation by Muslim scholars. Although European travelers went to Muslim lands and occasionally wrote travel accounts, western scholars who wrote about Islam tended to base their work primarily on written texts and had little direct contact with Muslim scholars. In the intellectual contexts of the pre-modern world, this is not surprising, since both Muslim and European scholars tended to see those rare times of meeting as being occasions for polemical debate rather than exchange of knowledge.[2]

One truly remarkable exception is the experience of al-Ḥasan ibn Muḥammad al-Wazzān (c.1489), a scholar born in Granada and educated in North Africa. He traveled widely in northern Africa and then was captured by pirates and given as a slave to Medici Pope Leo X. In Rome, he took the name of Leo Africanus, he wrote, under the patronage of the Pope, many works, including his "Description of Africa." Originally written in Italian and translated into a number of languages, it became an important source in Europe for information about Islam.[3]

By the eighteenth century, a tradition of academic study was developing that provided a growing body of translations of Islamic works. The sources tended to be historical and philosophical and the approach philological. The weakness of all this literature, and especially of the long series of translations is that, apart from the Qur'an, it ignored the major sources for knowledge of Islam. Moreover it tended, even when most just, to ignore the living spirituality of Islam.[4] This was an important part of the conceptual foundations of Orientalism as it developed by the late nineteenth century as the intellectual and scholarly mode for the study of Islam in the West.

The text-based analysis utilizing the tools of critical textual analysis that were providing the basis for scholarship in Biblical criticism was a major move beyond uncritical tales of travelers and the canon of anti-Islamic theological polemics. The Orientalists of the late nineteenth and early twentieth century may have been motivated by the missionary desire to know the nature of the competition or by the imperialist need to understand the worldview of subject peoples. However, their scholarship was shaped and judged within the framework of the emerging scholarly disciplines and subject to a type of modern scholarly critique not previously exercised. This scholarship could impress and influence Muslim intellectuals like Sir Sayyid Ahmad Khan in India, who tried to articulate a modern understanding of Islam. The dialogue between western Orientalists and some Muslim scholars had growing importance in the study of Islam in the West by the early twentieth century.

The Orientalist approach to the study of Islam became the dominant perspective in western scholarship during the first half of the twentieth century. It primarily involved text-based study and identified Islam with the "great tradition" of urban literate civilization in the Muslim world. It paid little attention to what were viewed as the superstitions and perversions of so-called "popular Islam." In the West, the establishment of professorial chairs, journals, and institutions like the School of Oriental and African Studies in London in 1917 reflected the dominance of the Orientalist approach to the study of Islam in the West until the middle of the twentieth century.

Following World War II, scholars in the West began a major reconceptualization of the disciplines and methods to be used for the study of non-western societies. The product of these efforts was the displacement of Orientalism by area studies as the dominant conceptual framework for the study of what had been conceived of as "the Orient." Initially, this effort was primarily an activity by western scholars. Annemarie Schimmel noted this isolation as she described her studies in the immediate postwar period: "For the modern student of Oriental languages, it seems unbelievable that we never saw an Arab, let alone studied in an Arab country."[5]

Although Schimmel described the situation specifically in

Germany, this was more generally the case, with early area studies scholarship being shaped by people who had contacts with the Muslim world due to family missionary activities or intelligence or policy work during World War II, and older Orientalists. However, by the 1950s, there was an important but small group of Muslim scholars that began to find places within the emerging area studies centers in the American academic world. In this context, Seyyed Hossein Nasr came onto the scene and began his long career of shaping how both Muslims and non-Muslims understood Islam in the complex, globalizing world of the second half of the twentieth century.

Islam and Area Studies

Area studies developed as a methodological approach for the study of human societies. The approach emphasized the need to view societies as whole entities, and to give attention to the actual operation of societies, not just to the literature of the literate urban educated elite. Its advocates called for a multi-disciplinary methodology and, in practice, the core disciplines were the social sciences, including history understood as a social science. This framework had implications for the study of religion in general and the study of Islam in particular.

Within the framework of area studies, Islam was identified with a particular area: the Middle East. Although scholars recognized there were Muslims in other regions, coverage of Islam, when it was covered, was primarily included in programs of "Middle Eastern" studies. Consequently, when Islam was discussed in the study of other areas, it tended to be viewed as an outside element. In this way, in discussions of Islam in sub-Saharan African studies and South and Southeast Asian studies, for example, attention would be given to "the spread of Islam" in the region and the interaction of Islam, as an intrusive element, with "indigenous" culture. Distinctive local expressions of Islamic faith and practice were viewed as departures from a "pure" Islam that tended to be defined in terms of Arab- Middle Eastern practice and traditions. Because the Middle East was identified as a distinctive region, "Middle Eastern" Islam was viewed as distinctive and definitive.

One widely-read area studies analysis at the time defined the Middle East as a "culture continent" and noted the importance of Islam in distinguishing the cultural configuration of the Middle East.[6] "However," the author added:

> the distribution of Islam is considerably wider than that of the Middle Eastern culture. There is, moreover, a marked difference between the cultures of the Middle Eastern Muslim peoples and those of the large Muslim ethnic aggregates residing beyond the boundaries of the Middle East.[7]

In this context, the definitive version of Islam was a culturally Middle Eastern one. Through analyses like these, Middle Eastern area studies became the scholarly location for the study of Islam within the new approach.

This approach reinforced the social science bias of area studies by viewing Islam as a social and cultural phenomenon rather than as a human faith experience. Scholars regularly noted that Islam "is more than a religion in the sense in which this concept is known to us from the western world...[and is] a total way of life."[8] However, treatment of Islam tended to be relegated to a separate chapter in the broader books describing the Middle East.[9] Islam was treated as a derivative element related to sociopolitical and economic forces.

In general terms, this social science approach in area studies was defined within the framework of the major theories of contemporary social change at the time, i.e., the various modernization theories. Whether the approach was Marxist, western liberal, or Cold Warrior conservative, there appeared a general consensus in support of the theory that the more "modern" a society, the less important the public role of religion. In this way, secularization was accepted as an inherent part of the modernization process. As a result, the study of Islam was seen as the study of a residual force within society that represented "conservative" resistance to the processes of modernization.

However, some intellectuals and scholars resisted this marginalization of religion and, in the long run, helped to correct gaps in area studies. Since the 1950s, there have been a number of phases in the evolution of area studies and in the development of scholarly studies of Islam. The era of consensual dominance of the conceptualizations of secularization theory continued until the late 1970s. Then, the dramatic events of the Islamic revolution in Iran in 1978-1979 highlighted societal changes around the world that strengthened the sense of need for a reassessment of the place of religion in modern and contemporary societies. Especially in the study of Islam, much of the scholarship of this next era concentrated on movements of militant revival that some called "fundamentalist." By the 1990s, however, a significant number of western scholars recognized that the continuing dynamism of Muslim experience was not monolithically "fundamentalist," and in fact, there was a more broadly-based reaffirmation of the vitality of Islam in the contexts of modern and contemporary societies around the world.

The works of Seyyed Hossein Nasr provide an important window into the debates and conceptualizations in these long-term changes. He was frequently a critic of the main developments in scholarship but always engaged rather than avoided the intellectual debates of the times. In each era, Nasr's writings and lectures represented timely critiques, adding needed dimensions to contemporary scholarship, and signals for significant changes that would be taking place.

Nasr and the Study of Islam

Seyyed Hossein Nasr entered the world of western scholarship on Islam in the late 1950s when the definition of area studies as an approach was becoming clear. As area studies evolved, the focus of Seyyed Hossein's critique shifted, but basic themes remained constant. There is a continuing assertion that religious faith is a primary, not a derivative, factor in human life. In addition, in terms of scholarship, there is also a continuing affirmation that individual religious faith and commitment are not contradictory to effective research and scholarship. In other words, one can be both a religious believer and a credible scholar. In many ways, these positions represent an affirmation of the legitimacy of the mainstream of Islamic faith and experience, which was and is a middle ground between perceived extremes of

"establishment Islam" and "folk Islam," and between agnostic secularism and "fundamentalism."

During the 1960s, Nasr engaged in the debates of the time that
concerned the most effective ways to understand Islam and religion.
His arguments ranged from direct to indirect, with his positions
reflected in his activities. In some of these efforts, Nasr joined new area
studies advocates in condemning aspects of the Orientalist tradition.
The shadows of the old medieval polemical canon still shaped some
discussions, and Nasr worked actively to defend Islam against attacks
from Orientalists. In this movement away from Orientalism, Nasr
reflected some of the emerging area studies perspectives.

Contrary to the developing scholarly mode, however, Nasr did not
present his analyses in the increasingly popular style of the social scientists. He conducted research in a field of great interest at the time – the
history and philosophy of science – but his interest in cosmology and
philosophy was expressed in religious terms. One of Nasr's areas of
greatest interest and commitment was Sufism, or what he called "the
inner dimension of Islam."

Nasr's approach to Sufism provides an important example of his
direct and indirect critique of current scholarly trends in the study of
Islam. In 1962, as a visiting lecturer at Harvard University, he taught
"An Introduction to Sufism," which was regularly attended by many
graduate students in the new area studies programs. At a time when the
area studies/social science mentality looked with great suspicion upon
anyone who admitted to being a religious believer, Nasr began his
course with a strong affirmation that he was going to discuss Sufism as a
living tradition, and as one who believes in it. He argued this was necessary since he wanted to present Sufism as it is.[10]

The presentation of Sufism in an academic context was in itself an
important critique of the emerging area studies/social science consensus. Many of the major Orientalists translated some of the classics of
Sufi literature and poetry because of their beauty and the appeal of generalized mysticism. Older Orientalists like Reynold Nicholson and
A.J. Arberry appreciated the great literature of the Sufis and presented
their writings in the Orientalist manner as part of a literary canon of an
urban educated elite. Classic Orientalist Nicholson affirmed,

"Mysticism is such a vital element in Islam that without some under-standing of its ideas and of the forms which they assume we should seek in vain to penetrate below the surface of Muhammadan religious life."[11]

However, like other Orientalists, Nasr covered major medieval texts with virtually no mention of Islamic mystical experience in the modern era. A. J. Arberry expressed the general Orientalist consensus that the "age of Ibn al-Farid, Ibn 'Arabi and Rumi [twelfth and thir-teenth centuries AC] represents the climax of Sufi achievement, both theoretically and artistically. Thereafter...the signs of decay appear more and more clearly."[12]

Speaking of the modern era, the Orientalist concluded, "Sufism, in its original as in its derived forms, may now be said to have come to an end as a movement dominating the minds and hearts of learned and earnest men."[13] In the 1960s, there was one area of agreement between emerging area studies scholarship and older Orientalism: Sufism was a part of "traditional" society that encouraged, among other things, a fatalistic passivity among peasants.[14] Young researchers at the time were frequently told by Muslim intellectuals and officials, as well as western social scientists, that "any talk of Sufism, and certainly of the turuq, seemed positively anachronistic."[15] Sufism, like "reli-gion" in general, was viewed as a residual element remaining from "traditional" society that would cease to be a major force in human life as the modernization processes went forward.

In this context, Nasr's presentation of Sufism as an intellectually credible and religiously authentic experience for humans in the mod-ern age was an important corrective to the non-religious and sometimes anti-religious tone of area studies scholarship. In his course, Nasr provided an introduction to writings by contemporary Sufis and sympathetic scholars of Sufism which, along with his own personal analysis and presentation, portrayed Sufism as a dynamic modern worldview that builds on a great tradition. Titus Burckhardt's writings provided a general foundation for this portrait.[16]

In the early 1960s, Martin Lings presented a portrait of a "Sufi saint in the twentieth century" that was an effective synthesis of academic scholarly analysis and religious commitment.[17] Nasr viewed this study as "indispensable,"[18] and helped to place Sufism in particular and religious faith in general at the center of what is needed in modern life. It becomes even a basis for a contemporary critique of western thought since, in Nasr's view, the

> tragedy of modern western philosophy lies, from the Muslim point of view, in confusing intellect and reason. The intellect to which the Sufi doctrine appeals and through which it is understood is that instrument of knowledge which perceives directly. It is not reason which is, at best, its mental image.[19]

This presentation of Sufism in the 1960s is an important example of how Nasr constructs a living mainstream that flows between extremes. Sufism in this articulation is neither an artifact of history nor a dying contemporary folk religion. Instead, as presented by Nasr, Sufism is a vibrant and dynamic dimension of contemporary Islamic experience, as capable of providing inspiration to people living in the modern era as it was for the medieval faithful. As such, Sufism is important to mainstream Muslim spiritual life in the modern world.

Islamic Studies and Religious Resurgence

The early 1970s saw signs of a new religious revival, despite dire predictions made in the 1960s by scholars like Peter Berger. Berger argued that all established religions were rapidly secularizing: "[I]n a surprise-free world, I see no reversal of the process of secularization produced by industrialization. The impact is the same everywhere, regardless of culture and the local religion. The traditional religions are likely to survive in small enclaves and pockets."[20]

However, as Vietnam war protests grew and alternative life styles developed among people living in the U.S. and western Europe, there was a major shift in orientation, especially among the younger generation. This led to a new interest in "eastern" religion, astrology, witchcraft, drugs, spiritualism, and other phenomena that were presumably incompatible with modern scientific knowledge. The result was that society underwent a profound mystical and religious revival, almost entirely outside the religious institutions.[21]

In this turn to "eastern" religions, Sufism was regularly identified as one of the "religions" of the counter culture. Anthologies of Sufi tales and other volumes of mystic teaching were compiled by people who became the articulators of an "Age of Aquarius"- style Sufism, whose books were sold along with the other "New Age" literature of the time. "Sufi dancing" was a popular form of the new "eastern" religious expression.[22] In this context, Nasr resisted becoming yet another exotic guru among visible but marginal religious groups. Instead, he strongly criticized what, in his view, became an entrepreneurial charlatanism that provided an oversimplified and often inaccurate image of Sufism.

The "new religious movements" of the late 1960s and early 1970s heralded the future renewal of religion among mainstream believers in the major traditions, but they themselves remained small and inhabited the exotic fringes of religious life. Their existence did attract the attention of serious scholars of religion. The academic study of religion in general, and gradually of Islam, began a transition from debating how the "inevitable" modern religion-less or fully secular society would look, to a new concern with trying to understand the continuing strength of religion. At first, this produced a concentration by sociologists of religion on the "new religious movements," which were now no longer counter-cultural "leftist" radicals but increasingly more traditional, but fundamentalist, evangelistic positions.

The new context for the study of religious movements and the study of Islam was transformed by the Islamic revolution in Iran in 1978-1979. Before this development, scholars of Islam increasingly recognized an "Islamic resurgence." In a now-famous article first published in 1976, Bernard Lewis spoke of "the return of Islam," and provided an account of the modern history of the Muslim Middle East, showing the continuing power and influence of Islam throughout that history.[23] This article has often been described as a prescient identification of the coming resurgence, but it was primarily a reiteration of ideas expressed in the 1960s,[24] within the conceptual framework of area studies and modernization theory.

In earlier discussions of Muslim responses to modernity, some attention was given to movements like the Salafiyyah. In its original form as articulated by the Egyptian thinker Muhammad Abduh (1849-1905), the Salafiyyah offered "something more substantial than empty hatred of the infidel or the mirage of a return to a largely mythical past...instead, it was willing to take account of modern thought as well as knowledge in a reformulation of Islamic modernism."[25]

The movements that attracted attention in the 1970s, culminating with the Islamic revolution in Iran, were more "fundamentalist" and frequently violent in their advocacy. They preempted "Islamic modernist" alternatives in the analyses of the new resurgence.[26] In the discussions of emerging "fundamentalist" movements, there was a return to the conceptualization of the Islamic resurgence as an anti-western, anti-modern movement. Islamic studies in the West tended to portray the world of Islam as polarized between relatively modern secularists and more rigidly traditional fundamentalists.

In terms of Islamic expression itself, a "dichotomy between official Islam and popular Islam" was presented in the scholarship.[27] Official Islam was seen as the position of governments and the educated intellectual elite (presumed to be primarily secularist in orientation), while popular Islam was defined in terms of movements that "seek to achieve renewal of society by ending the rule of infidels and domestic apostates, and returning to what they see as a pure and authentic Islamic order."[28] In this emerging polarized image of the Muslim world, it became possible for analysts to ask the question: Are there any Muslim moderates?[29]

Most Muslims in the 1970s and 1980s were neither members of radical fundamentalist organizations nor identifiable as supporters of the positions of the small secular intellectual class. The views of the majority spread across a wide spectrum of views between the two extremes. The general observation by Lewis in 1976 was that "Islam is still the most effective form of consensus in Muslim countries." This remains true at the beginning of the twenty-first century. However, Islam as the basis for societal consensus does not mean inevitable support for fundamentalist positions, or that the only alternative is a western-style secularism.[30] As Abdullahi An-Naim argued, "If presented with European secularism as the only alternative to the so-called Islamic state and application of Shari'ah, Islamic societies will clearly prefer the latter, however serious its conceptual faults and practical difficulties."[31] The two extremes were not the only options.

Seyyed Hossein Nasr worked to provide an articulation of an alternative Islamic perspective that reflected the main lines of the majority consensus within the framework of the historic traditions of Islam. In the early 1970s, Nasr criticized the "apologetic, modernized type of approach" that sought to cope with modernity "by bending backwards in a servile attitude to show in one way or another that this or that element of Islam is just what is fashionable in the West today."[32] At the same time, he recognized that the ʿulamāʾ, who are "the custodians of the Islamic tradition," had little understanding of the modern world with which they were trying to cope. Nasr argued that to meet the challenge of western modernity "a true intelligentsia at once traditional and fully conversant with the modern world" was needed,[33] and that such a group, though still small in the early 1970s, was emerging within the Muslim world. While Nasr's work did not create this emerging grouping, he clearly reflects its views and soon became one of its highly visible spokespersons.

In the many discussions of the dynamic visibility of Islamic movements following the Iranian revolution, the emphasis on "fundamentalists" intensified. While many scholars repeated that Islam is not "monolithic," there was a tendency to ignore the broader views of the majority and concentrate on the extreme alternatives. By the early 1980s, Nasr began to clarify this more mainstream position. He spoke of four types of movements within the Muslim world. One was the highly visible emerging "fundamentalism" and another was the "Mahdist," or apocalyptic visions aroused by the turmoil of the times. The third was the "modernist" approach which took different forms like "Islamic nationalism" or "Islamic Marxism," and which, in Nasr's view, threatened the authentic faith of many Muslims.

A fourth force within the Islamic world was one Nasr's viewed as greatly important but that had received little attention. "This force is the revival of the Islamic tradition from within by those who have encountered the modern world fully and who with full awareness of the nature of the modern world... have returned to the heart of the Islamic tradition." This "traditional" Islam involved the inner renewal (*tajdīd*) of Islamic society rather than the modern style of reform that dealt with externals and undermined traditional religious faith. In the early 1980s, Nasr affirmed that "Islam is still very much alive in the Islamic world today," but in many ways it was a "traditional" Islam that was the source of strength.34

In this framework, it was "essential to remember that in many parts of the Islamic world the majority of Muslims continue their lives in the traditional manner and are not involved in any of the theological, religious, or political reactions to the modern world." This "traditional" perspective neither blindly rejected modernity nor unquestioningly accepted it, that is, it was neither fundamentalist nor modernist. As the foundation for the faith of the majority of Muslims, it was the source of the continuing dynamism of the Islamic resurgence.

Scholars who tied their analysis to the older area studies conceptualization of the resurgence viewed the resurgence as a manifestation of anti-modern, anti-western fundamentalism, as an essentially conservative force working to maintain or restore some outmoded vision of the past. In this perspective, the resurgence could be interpreted as a Luddite-style attempt to maintain the old in a futile battle against modernity. This approach missed the dynamism of the resurgence that Nasr described as a movement of renewal that could operate effectively within modern conditions.

In missing this dynamism and in seeing the resurgence in the framework of secularization theory as a manifestation of religion doomed to failure as modernity progresses, scholars in the old area studies framework regularly and inaccurately predicted the end of the resurgence. In this way, Bernard Lewis speaking in 1980, at the same time that Nasr was defining the dynamism of "traditional Islam," could assert that "the Islamic resurgence has reached it peak, and that from now [1980] onwards it will probably decline rather than ascend," and cited as an example of this the weakness of the Islamic response to the Soviet invasion of Afghanistan. Similarly, almost a decade later, just weeks before the Muslim world was aroused by Ayatullah Khomeini's fatwa against Salmon Rushdi, Fouad Ajami write, "The political phenomenon we here identified as 'Islamic fundamentalism' is a spent force now. The power of the Iranian state remains, but the appeal of the revolution to classes and men beyond Iran's boundaries has been blunted."[35]

Nasr and other scholars in Islamic studies recognized that the Islamic resurgence represented an empirical refutation of secularization theory. His work defining "traditional Islam" as a vital religious dynamic in modern history reflected broader developments in scholarship that understood religion as something more than a derivative factor in the processes of historical change.[36] It was already clear by the mid-1980s to many scholars in the social sciences that the secularization model needed serious revision,[37] and there were by the 1990s, major scholars calling for its abandonment.[38] In the era of the concentration on Islamic fundamentalism in the social science studies of Islam, Nasr and scholars like him represented a realistic understanding of the mainstreams of Muslim life.

Islamic Studies and Globalization

By the 1990s, the context and content of the study of Islam in the West had been significantly changed by major world historical developments like globalization and post-Cold War understandings of modernity and post-modernity. The profound interaction of the major world societies raised critical questions about the nature of those societies and their relationships. Put in terms most commonly debated among scholars of Islam, one of the major issues was the degree to which the great global interactions, in religious terms, involved a "clash of civilizations" and the viability of effective civilizational dialogue.

The old area studies perspective had identified Islam with a particular regional and socio-cultural complex. Although still tied in many ways to concepts of "the Middle East," area studies scholarship began to see Islam and the Muslim world in broader terms. Rather than being tied to a region, in analytical terms, Islam was frequently identified as a "civilization," with some scholars, like Bernard Lewis, recognizing its significant trans-regional dimensions. In this view, Islam "created a world civilization, polyethnic, multiracial, international, one might even say intercontinental."[39] Defined within this framework, according to Samuel Huntington, "a civilization is a cultural entity... Civilizations are differentiated from each other by history, language, culture, tradition, and, most important, religion."[40] This emphasis on religion as the primary identifying feature of a "cultural entity" represents a continuation of the old area studies conceptualizations of religion as a derived cultural construct rather than as a primary element in human experience.

In this style of analysis, "the West" is the designation for "the larger civilization of which Europe is the source and America the leader."[41] Islam is viewed as another competing civilization, and "the interaction between Islam and the West is seen as a clash of civilizations."[42] Conflict among these major conceptualized units – "civilizations" – was predicted, by Samuel Huntington and scholars like Lewis, to be "the latest phase in the evolution of conflict in the modern era."[43] In earlier modern history, the major wars had been fought by nation-states and ideologies within western civilization, but, "with the end of the Cold War," from this perspective, "international politics moves out of its western phase and its centerpiece becomes the interaction between the West and non- western civilizations."[44]

Dealing specifically with Islam, some scholars like Lewis view the interactions of Islam and the West in a perspective that sees a struggle "lasting for some fourteen centuries. It began with the advent of Islam, in the seventh century, and has continued virtually to the present day. It has consisted of a long series of attacks and counterattacks, jihads and crusades, conquests and reconquests."[45] In the context of the modern era, this primordial conflict assumes a new form with the struggle between western modernity and Muslim efforts to maintain their traditions. Lewis argued:

> we are facing a mood and a movement far transcending the level of issues and policies and the governments that pursue them. This is no less than a clash of civilizations – the perhaps irrational but surely historic reaction of an ancient rival against our Judeo-Christian heritage, our secular present, and the worldwide expansion of both. [46]

While scholars adopting the "clash" perspective sometimes note that not all Muslims are militants or "fundamentalists," the real core is the broad and "ancient" rivalry between the two cultural entities. As Huntington describes the heart of the conflict:

> The underlying problem for the West is not Islamic fundamentalism. It is Islam, a different civilization whose people are convinced of the superiority of their culture and are obsessed with the inferiority of their power. The problem for Islam is not the CIA or the U.S. Department of Defense. It is the West, a different civilization whose people are convinced of the universality of their culture.[47]

Although this vision of a world of self-contained and competing civilizations was one possible line of analysis within the conceptual framework of area studies, the evolution of scholarship in international affairs and religious studies in general and Islamic studies in particular opened the way for important and different visions. In general terms, many scholars argue that neither the Muslim world nor the West are monolithic and that defining Islam and the Muslim world monolithically becomes more difficult as clear boundaries between Islam and the West evaporate in the increasingly global society.[48]

There has sometimes been a strong critique of using the concept of "civilization" itself. Andre Gunder Frank argues:

> There are no and have never been distinct pristine civilizations, societies, cultures, nor even peoples. The very ideas are nothing but ideology...All of those pundits and their misleading civilizational theses of civilizational clash between 'us' and 'them' are ideologically suspect and socio-politically.[49]

Some analysts suggest, somewhat less combatively, that it was important to go beyond the conceptual domination of the "civilizational narrative" in understanding the dynamics of contemporary global history.[50]

Scholars like worked within the context of these heated debates to understand the significance of religion in general and Islam in particular in the modern and contemporary world. In terms of the study of Islam, some scholars such as Nasr and Marshall G.S. Hodgson distinguished between the Islamic faith traditions and the various cultural expressions of that faith. Looking at the crises faced by Muslims in the contemporary world, Nasr used the concept of "civilization" to discuss the tradition and heritage of the Muslim world. However, he distinguished between the faith and the civilization. In the context of the contemporary world, Nasr argues that the "religion of Islam is still alive and strong but the civilization which Islam created has withered away to a great extent, having been attacked from many directions for several centuries."[51] In this conceptual framework, the "clash of civilizations" has no relevance to the significance of Islam in the contemporary world. In fact, in Nasr's view, the "fundamentalist" opposition to the West, which is the heart of the "clash of civilizations" ideology, represents "the transformation of Islam from a religion and total way of life into an ideology,"[52] and, in that sense, represents a paradoxical westernization of Islam.

This alternative approach identifies the basic Muslim mainstream, what Nasr calls "traditional Islam," as being neither fundamentalist nor westernizing. Nasr examined its implications for life in the contemporary world for many different areas but especially in his specialization of the history and philosophy of science. He notes that, in contrast to both fundamentalists and modernists, the traditional school "has tried to rethink, on the basis of the Islamic worldview, the foundations of western science and technology and to confront the challenges of modern thought, science and technology in depth rather than simply through emotional response."[53] The result is the activity of "trying to bring back to life the principles of Islam as they can be applied to the condition of contemporary humanity."[54] In this effort, there is little concern for preserving "Islamic civilization" as such and, in this framework, the analysis of the scholars of the "clash" school misses the crucial issues.

Nasr and scholars like him see the lines of conflict differently. "Religion" as an inclusive worldview is the key concept, rather than "civilization." In Nasr's view, the Qur'an "reasserts over and over the universality of religion and the fact that religion has been sent to all of humanity."[55] Within this framework, traditional Christianity and Judaism in the West "can become allies with Islam against the forces of materialism and secularism that are seeking to destroy or at best privatize all religions and banish them from the public realm." This reverses in important ways Lewis's concept of the "ancient rivalry" between Islam and the Judeo-Christian tradition. In this way, the real "clash" is not between Islam and the West, nor even between Islam and modernity. The fundamental clash in Nasr's perspective is between religion and various philosophies and ideologies that have emanated from the modern world. In this clash, Muslims need to recognize what they share with "the religious and sacred perspectives of other monotheistic religions which are, in fact, sisters of Islam and also members of the Abrahamic family of religions."[56]

Nasr argues that Muslims need to "distinguish between the authentic Islamic teachings... and local customs and habits which also surround their life," and recognize the diversity that results from the "different social and cultural contexts within which the teachings of Islam have manifested themselves." This view sharply contrasts with the views of those scholars who identify Islam with particular cultural constructs that can be identified in historic contexts as "Islamic civilization." Arguing from within the faith tradition, Nasr affirms that the Qur'an and Hadith "provide all the guidance of which Muslims young and old are in need, now or in the future, to the end of time."[57] This reflects both a position of faith and the mode of scholarly analysis of religions in general that recognizes that the major world religions are not tied to a particular civilization or region.

In a faith tradition that affirms "there is no human condition, no world, to which the teachings of Islam do not apply,"[58] it is possible to speak of "modern Islam," just as some scholars have spoken about other culturally identified manifestations of Islam like "Islamic civilization." This again reflects a broader line of scholarly analysis in the West that argues "modernity and westernization are not identical; the western pattern or patterns of modernity are not the only 'authentic' modernities, even if they were historically prior."[59] S.N. Eisenstadt speaks of "multiple modernities," noting that these modernities are not static and that "it is within the framework of such transformations that the upsurge and reconstruction of the religious dimension in the contemporary era is best understood."[60] Global interactions in this world of "multiple modernities," whether "clashes" or "dialogues," are misunderstood if conceptualized as interactions among static civilizations. The conceptual separation of religious principles from cultural manifestations becomes, as in Nasr's thought, a key to understanding the dynamics of the new world of globalization.

Conclusion

Since the development of area studies in the post-World War II era, the study of Islam in the West has undergone a number of important changes. The following half-century saw dominant modes of analysis and critiques of those modes. The scholarship of Seyyed Hossein Nasr since the early 1960s reflects the changes and provides, as it did in the various phases of scholarship, both critiques of the dominant modes and contributions to their development.

Since World War II, three general eras can be identified in terms of modes of studying Islam in the West. In the first, the social science orientation of area studies shaped the study of Islam, with emphasis on the interpretations involved in modernization and secularization theory. This approach viewed Islam, like all religions, as a cultural derivative and, under the expectations of secularization theory, doomed to a declining role in modernizing societies. In the 1960s, Nasr's scholarship presciently emphasized the importance of religion as a primary element in human experience. Scholarship like his helped pave the way for the revision of the social sciences' understanding of religion in society that was necessitated by the rise of the new religious movements and a worldwide religious resurgence that began to be visible in the 1970s.

The dominant mode of this revision gave special emphasis to the extreme styles of resurgence. At first, the focus was on the exotic religious movements such as the "Age of Aquarius" in the U.S., but attention soon shifted to what came to be identified as a "fundamentalist" resurgence. This was especially true when studying movements of resurgence in the Muslim world, and became a prominent analytical mode following the success of the Islamic revolution in Iran in 1979. However, again, some scholars viewed the resurgence as reflecting more mainstream concerns. In these discussions, where area studies scholars tended to speak in terms of a polarity in the Muslim world between the "modernists" and the "fundamentalists," Nasr identified and worked to define a mainstream "traditional" Islamic position in the context of the resurgence. Again, this type of conceptualization prepared the way for understanding the significantly more popular and populist movements of Islamic resurgence of the 1980s.

By the final decade of the twentieth century, the intensification of the processes of globalization and the end of the Cold War set new issues for scholarly analysis in the study of Islam in the West. One of the most prominent interpretations of the role of Islam in the world involved a conceptualization of global relations in terms of the "clash of civilizations." This involved a set of assumptions about the nature of "civilizations" as relatively static cultural entities predominantly identified by religion. Scholars in the "clash school" defined relations between Islamic civilization and western civilization as inherently conflictual, by the very nature of the "civilizations" involved. Other scholars like Nasr developed a variety of analytical structures for interpreting global interactions that argued that the concept of "clashing civilizations" was at best irrelevant and possibly counterproductive. Nasr distinguished between the historic "Islamic civilization" and the continuing religion of Islam. In this perspective, the conflicts are not between Islam and the West or Islam and modernity. In an area of multiple modernities, the clashes are to determine the nature of the modern human experience.

Nasr represents an important element in the transformation of the study of Islam in the West. He provides an example of the contributions that Muslims can make as scholars in the West. In the increasingly interactive world of the twenty-first century, such scholars are an important resource in shaping the relations among religious traditions, societies, and "civilizations." The evolution of Islamic studies in the West in the second half of the twentieth century reflects the importance of those scholars who could provide a corrective to the dominant modes of interpretation, helping to identify the weaknesses of analyses based on secularization theory, an emphasis on fundamentalism, and a vision of world relations as being a dangerous clash of civilizations.

NOTES

1   Norman Daniel, *Islam and the West: The Making of an Image* (Oxford: Oneworld, 1997), p.302.

2   See, for example, the account of the eighteenth century encounter described in Muradi between Muhammad al Tafilati and some monks in Malta. Muhammad Khalil al-Muradi, *Silk al-Durar fi aʿyān al-qarn al-thānī ʿashar* (Baghdad: Maktabah al-Muthannā, n.d.), vol.4, pp.102-108.

3   Al-Ḥasan ibn Muḥammad al-Wazzān (Leo Africanus), *Encyclopedia of Islam*, new edn. (Leiden: Brill, 1983), vol.5, pp.723-724. For a scholarly fictionalized account of his life, see Amin Maalouf, *Leo Africanus*, trans. Peter Sluglett (Lanham, MD: New Amsterdam, 1988).

4   Daniel, *Islam and the West*, pp.319-320.

5   Annemarie Schimmel, "The Charles Homer Haskins Lectures of the American Council of Learned Societies," *The Life of Learning*, eds. Douglas Greenberg and Stanley N. Katz (New York: Oxford University Press, 1994), p.166.

6   Raphael Patai, *Society, Culture, and Change in the Middle East*, 3rd edn. (Philadelphia: University of Pennsylvania Press, 1969), pp.46-47. The first edition of this book was published in 1962 and during the 1960s this was a widely read, widely-cited study.

7   Patai, *Society, Culture, and Change in the Middle East*, p.47.

8   Ibid.

9   Ibid.

10 He has said this on many occasions. One time was in the initial course handout in the course that he taught as a visiting lecturer at Harvard University, Spring Semester, 1962: "History of Religion 134: An Introduction to Sufism." Subsequent references to this course will be cited as "Nasr, HR 134" with an appropriate date. This is drawn from class notes taken by the author, who audited the course in 1962.

11 Reynold Alleyne Nicholson, *Studies in Islamic Mysticism* (Cambridge: Cambridge University Press, 1921), p.vi; A.J. Arberry, *Sufism: An Account of the Mystics of Islam* (London: George Allen & Unwin, 1950), p.119.

12 Arberry, *Sufism*, p.133.

13 Manfred Halpern, *The Politics of Social Change in the Middle East and North Africa* (Princeton: Princeton University Press, 1963), p.91.

14 Michael Gilsenan, *Recognizing Islam: Religion and Society in the Modern Arab World* (New York: Pantheon, 1982), p.229. This was the experience of Gilsenan doing research on the *Ḥamīdiyyah-Shādhiliyyah* in Egypt and also of the author when doing research at that time on the *Khatmiyyah* in Sudan.

15   See, especially, Titus Burckhardt, *Introduction to Sufism*, trans. D.M. Matheson (San Francisco: Thorsons/HarperCollins, 1995). This was first published as *An Introduction to Sufi Doctrine* (Lahore: Sh. Muhammad Ashraf, 1959).

16   Seyyed Hossein Nasr, *Ideals and Realities of Islam* (London: George Allen & Unwin, 1966), p.145.

17   Martin Lings, *A Sufi Saint of the Twentieth Century, Shaikh Ahmad al-Alawi*, 2nd edn. (Berkeley: University of California Press, 1971). This was originally published in 1961 as *A Moslem Saint of the Twentieth Century*.

18   Nasr, *Ideals and Realities of Islam*, p.136.

19   Luncheon talk at the New School for Social Research, as quoted in *The New York Times* (February 25, 1968).

20   Edward B. Fiske, "Religion in the Age of Aquarius," *The New York Times* (December 25, 1969).

21   See, for example, the discussion in Jacob Needleman, "Winds from the East: Youth & Counter Culture," *Mystery, Magic, and Miracle: Religion in a Post-Aquarian Age*, ed. Edward F. Heenan (Englewood Cliffs: Prentice Hall, 1973), p.78.

22   Bernard Lewis, "The Return of Islam," *Commentary* (January, 1976), vol.61, no.1, pp.39-49; reprinted in *Religion and Politics in the Middle East,* ed. Michael Curtis (Boulder: Westview Press, 1981), pp.9-29. Lewis is one of the foremost scholars in Islamic studies, and because he has been so prolific in his scholarship and is so widely read, his works will be the most frequently cited examples in this essay to illustrate what might be considered the standard scholarship of the times.

23   See, for example, the very similar analysis by Lewis presented in 1964 in Bernard Lewis, "The Revolt of Islam," *The Middle East and the West* (Bloomington: Indiana University Press, 1964), chapter V, pp.95-114.

24   Lewis, "The Return of Islam," p.41,44.

25   For example, while Bernard Lewis paid considerable attention to Muhammad Abduh and Islamic modernists in his 1964 analysis (Lewis, "The Revolt of Islam," pp.103-105), 'Abduh is not mentioned at all his 1976 discussion. (Lewis, "The Return of Islam")

26   Bernard Lewis, "Islamic Political Movements," *Middle East Review* (Summer, 1985), vol.17, no.4, p.27.

27   Lewis, "Islamic Political Movements," p.27.

28   An interesting later debate on the general subject was identified in the two interviews published in *Middle East Quarterly*: "Not Every Fundamentalist Is a Terrorist" Robert H. Pelletreau, Jr., and "There Is No Such Thing as a Moderate Fundamentalist" Mohammad Mohaddessin, *Middle East Quarterly* (September, 1995), vol.2, no.3.

29   Lewis, "The Return of Islam," p.48.

30 Abdullahi A. An-Naim, "Political Islam in National Politics and International Relations," *The Desecularization of the World: Resurgent Religion and World Politics*, ed. Peter L. Berger (Washington: Ethics and Public Policy Center, 1999), p.119.

31 Seyyed Hossein Nasr, "The Western World and its Challenges to Islam," *Islam: Its Meaning and Message*, ed. Khurshid Ahmad (London: Islamic Council of Europe, 1976), p.121.

32 Nasr, "The Western World," p.220.

33 Seyyed Hossein Nasr, "Islam in the Islamic World Today: An Overview," *Islam in the Contemporary World*, ed. Cyriac K. Pullapilly (Notre Dame: Cross Roads Books, 1980), p.16.

34 Nasr, "Islam in the Islamic World," p.18.

35 Fouad Ajami, "Bush's Middle East Memo," *U.S. News & World Report* (December 26, 1988/January 2, 1989), p.75.

36 This analysis was most fully presented in Seyyed Hossein Nasr, *Traditional Islam in the Modern World* (London: Kegan Paul, 1987; reprint edition 1995).

37 See, for example, the papers in Phillip E. Hammond, *The Sacred in a Secular Age* (Berkeley: University of California Press, 1985).

38 See, for example, Rodney Stark, "Secularization, R.I.P.," *Sociology of Religion* (Fall, 1999), vol.60, no.3, pp.249-273.

39 Bernard Lewis, *What Went Wrong? Western Impact and Middle Eastern Response* (New York: Oxford University Press, 2002), p.6.

40 Samuel Huntington, "The Clash of Civilizations?" *Foreign Affairs* (Summer, 1993), vol.72, no.3, pp.23,25.

41 Bernard Lewis, "Eurocentrism Revisited," *Commentary* (December, 1994), vol.98, no.6, p.50.

42 Huntington, "The Clash of Civilizations," p.32.

43 Ibid., p.22.

44 Ibid., p.23.

45 Bernard Lewis, "The Roots of Muslim Rage," *The Atlantic Monthly* (September, 1990), vol.266, no.3, p.49.

46 Ibid.

47 Huntington, Samuel P., "The Clash of Civilizations," *Foreign Affairs*, Summer 1993.

48 John L. Esposito, *Unholy War: Terror in the Name of Islam* (New York: Oxford University Press, 2002), p.128,141.

49 Andre Gunder Frank, "Toward Humano- and Eco-Centrism: Unity in Diversity, not Clash of Civilizations," paper presented at the United Nations University Conference on Dialogue of Civilizations, Tokyo and Kyoto (July 31-August 3, 2001).

50   See, for example, John O. Voll, "The End of Civilization is Not So Bad," *Middle East Studies Association Bulletin* (July, 1994), vol.28, no.1.

51   Seyyed Hossein Nasr, *A Young Muslim's Guide to the Modern World*, 2nd edn. (Chicago: Kazi, 1994), p.117.

52   Ibid.

53   Ibid., p.128.

54   Ibid.

55   Ibid., p.242.

56   Ibid., p.243.

57   Ibid., p.252.

58   Ibid.

59   S.N. Eisenstadt, "The Reconstruction of Religious Arenas in the Framework of 'Multiple Modernities,'" *Millennium* (2000), vol.29, no.3, p.593.

60   Ibid.

The Territory of the Qur'an: "Citizens," "Foreigners," and "Invaders"

FARID ESACK

MUSLIMS have often expressed their experience of the Qur'an in an array of metaphors. The Qur'an has, for example, been compared to a brocade: 'The patterned beauty of its true design bears an underside which the unwary may mistake, seeing what is there but not its real fullness. Or, the Book is like a veiled bride whose hidden face is only known in the intimacy of truth's consummation. It is like the pearl for which the diver must plunge to break the shell which both ensures and conceals treasure.'

Fazlur Rahman has also used the analogy of a country, using the categories of 'citizens,' 'foreigners,' and 'invaders' to describe approaches of scholars towards the Qur'an. The theme of beauty ties together an overview of approaches to the Qur'an and Qur'anic scholarship. In reflecting on the diverse scholarly approaches to the Qur'an, one can draw an analogy with the personality and body of a beloved and the ways she is approached. The body that comes to mind immediately is a female one and this itself is remarkable for what it reveals as much as what it conceals. The female body is usually presented and viewed as passive, and more often objectified as 'something' to be approached even when it is alive, and 'ornamentalized' as a substitute for enabling it to exercise real power in a patriarchal world.

Yet this body or person also does something to the one that approaches it. The fact that it is approached essentially by men also reflects the world of Qur'anic scholarship, one wherein males are, by and large, the only significant players. When the female body is approached by other women then it is a matter to be passed over in silence. Like the world of religion in general, where women are so vital in sustaining it and yet, when it comes to authority and public representation, they are on the periphery, Qur'anic scholarship is really the domain of men and the contribution of women, when it does occur, is usually ignored.

This analogy fits into many patriarchal stereotypes. Questions such as: 'Why does the Qur'an not lend itself to being made analogous with a male body?' 'What if a gender sensitive scholar insists on doing this, and how would my analogy then pan out?' 'What about multiple partners in a post-modernist age where one finds Buddhist Catholics or Christian Pagans?' etc, are interesting ones which shall be left unexplored and, like all analogies, this can also be taken too far and can be misleading in more than one respect.

The first level of interaction[1] with the Qur'an can be compared to that between a lover and his beloved. The presence of the beloved can transport the lover to another plane of being that enables him to experience sublime ecstasy, to forget his woes, or to respond to them. It can console his aching heart and can represent stability and certainty in a rather stormy world; she is everything. The lover is often astounded at a question that others may ask: 'What do I see in her?' 'What do you mean? I see everything in her; she is the answer to all my needs. Is she not 'a clarification of all things' (16:89), 'a cure for all [the aches] that may be in the hearts' (10:57)? To be with her is to be in the presence of the Divine.' For most lovers it is perfectly adequate to enjoy the relationship without asking any questions about it.

When coming from the outside, questions about the nature of the beloved's body, whether she really comes from a distinguished lineage, begotten beyond the world of flesh and blood and born in the 'Mother of Cities' (42:7) as common wisdom has it, or whether her jewelery is genuine, will in all likelihood be viewed as churlishness or jealousy. For the unsophisticated yet ardent lover such questions are at best seen as a distraction from getting on with a relationship that is to be enjoyed rather than interrogated or agonized over. At worst, they are viewed as a reflection of willful perversity and intransigence. This lover reflects the position of the ordinary Muslim towards the Qur'an.

The second level of interaction is that of a lover who wants to explain to the world why his beloved is the most sublime, a true gift from God that cries out for universal acclaim and acceptance. He goes into considerable detail about the virtues of his beloved, her unblemished origins, and her delectable nature. This pious yet scholarly lover literally weeps at the inability of others to recognize the utter beyondness of his beloved's beauty, the coherence of her form and the awe-inspiring nature of her wisdom. 'She is unique in her perfection, surely it is sheer blindness, jealousy and (or) ignorance that prevents others from recognizing this!'

This is the path of confessional Muslim scholarship based on prior faith that the Qur'an is the absolute word of God. Some of the major contemporary works[2] that have emerged from these scholars include the exegeses of Abul A'la Mawdudi (d.1977),[3] Amin Ahsan Islahi (d.1997),[4] Husayn Tabatabai (d.1981),[5] Muhammad Asad (d.1992),[6] Aishah Abd al-Rahman (Bint al-Shati),[7] and the work on Qur'anic studies by Muhammad Husayn al-Dhahabi,[8] Muhammad Abd al-Azim al-Zarqani,[9] (both contemporary Egyptian scholars), and Abul Qasim al-Khui (d.1992).[10] Others have written about specific aspects of the beloved's beauty, the finery of her speech, or the depth of her wisdom.

In addition to the world of books, the other relatively new domain of some of the lovers in this category is the internet, where a large number of Muslim researchers engage in vigorous combat with all those who challenge the divine nature of the Qur'an.[11] (In depicting the positions of the scholars in this category, this study, in the main, utilizes the works of earlier Cairene scholars such as Badr al-Dīn Zarkashī (d.794/1391) and Jalāl al-Dīn al-Suyūṭī (d.911/1505), and among the contemporary ones, Zarqani and Al-Khui.

The third kind of lover may also be enamored with his beloved but will view questions about her nature and origins, her language, if her hair has been dyed or nails varnished, etc, as reflecting a deeper love and more profound commitment, a love and commitment that will not only withstand all these questions and the uncomfortable answers that rigorous enquiry may yield, but that will actually be deepened by them. Alternately, this relationship may be the product of an arranged marriage, where he may simply never have known any other beloved besides this one and his scholarly interest moves him to ask these questions. As for the Qur'an being the word of God, his response would probably be 'Yes, but it depends on what one means by 'the word of God.' 'She may be divine, but the only way in which I can relate to her is as a human being. She has become flesh and I cannot interrogate her divine origins; I can therefore only approach her as if she is a worldly creature.'

"The study of the text," said Nasr Hamid Abu Zayd, "must proceed from reality and culture as empirical givens. From these givens we arrive at a scientific understanding of the phenomenon of the text." This is the path of critical Muslim scholarship, a category that may be in conversation with the preceding two categories – as well as the subsequent two categories - but that does not usually sit too well with them. What cannot be disputed is the devotion of this lover to his beloved. The anger with the objectification of the beloved by the first two categories, in fact, stems from an outrage that the 'real' worth of the beloved is unrecognized. Abu Zayd asked, "How much is not concealed by confining the Qur'an to prayers and laws?...We transform the Qur'an into a text which evokes erotic desire or intimidates. With root and branch do I want to remove the Qur'an from this prison so that it can once again be productive for the essence of culture and the arts in our society." Some of the major works by these scholars include the exegetical work of Fazlur Rahman (d.1988),[12] the linguistic-philosophical studies by Mohammed Arkoun,[13] the literary enquiry into the Qur'an and critique of religious discourse by Abu Zayd,[14] and the related literary studies done by Fuat Sezgin.[15]

The line between the last of the categories above, the critical lover, and the first below, the participant observer, is often a thin one. In the same way that one is sometimes moved to wonder about couples: 'Are they still in love or are they just sticking to each other for old time's sake?', one can also ask about one's intimate friends who display an unusual amount of affection to one's own beloved. In other words, is the critical lover really still a lover and is the ardent friend of both the lover and the beloved not perhaps also a lover? Similar questions have been raised about the extent to which the participant observer has internalized Muslim sensitivities and written about the Qur'an in a manner that sometimes make one wonder if they are not also actually in love with the Muslim's beloved. Thus, what these two categories have in common is that those at the other ends of the continuum really accuse them of being closet non-Muslim or closet Muslims.

The participant observer, the first in the category of those who do not claim to be lovers or who deny it, feels an enormous sense of responsibility to the sensitivities of the lover, who is often also a close friend of lover and beloved. 'Beauty is in the eye of the beholder,' he reasons, and if this is what the Qur'an means for Muslims and if they have received it as the word of God, then so be it.' 'We don't know if Gabriel really communicated to Muhammad and we will never know. What we do know is that the Qur'an has been and continues to be received by the Muslims as such. Can we keep open the question of 'whatever else it may be' and study it as received scripture which is also an historical phenomenon?'

Wilfred Cantwell Smith, who places more emphasis on the spiritual dimensions to this reception, in contrast to Montgomery Watt who emphasizes its sociological dimensions, is arguably the most prominent scholar who adopts this position.[16] "Given that it was first transmitted in an oral form," asked William Graham further, "can we focus on the Qur'an as an oral scripture rather than written text?"[17] Others in this category may have their own objects of adoration and love but acknowledge the beauty of the Muslim's beloved. They can possibly also love her although in a different sense but would be hesitant to declare this love for fear of being misunderstood. Said Watt, "I have always taken the view that Muhammad genuinely believed that the messages he received, which constitute the Qur'an, came from God. I hesitated for a time to speak of Muhammad as a Prophet because this would have been misunderstood by Muslims…"[18]

Another inspiring scholar in the genre is Kenneth Cragg, the Oxford-based Anglican clergyman whom Rahman has described as "a man who may not be a full citizen of the world of the Qur'an, but is certainly no foreigner either – let alone an invader!"[19] This irenic approach to the study of the Qur'an seemingly seeks to compensate for past 'scholarly injuries' inflicted upon Muslims and is often aimed at a 'greater appreciation of Islamic religiousness and the fostering of a new attitude towards it.' This category of scholar accepts the broad outlines of Muslim historiography and of claims about the development of the Qur'an. While the first two categories, the 'ordinary Muslim' and confessional scholar, the latter increasingly aware of their presence, find them annoying or even reprehensible, they are often in vigorous and mutually enriching conversation with the third category, the critical Muslim scholar.

The second observer in this category feels no such responsibility and claims he is merely pursuing the cold facts surrounding the body of the beloved, regardless of what she may mean to her lover or anyone else. He claims, in fact, to be a "disinterested" observer. Willing to challenge all the parameters of the received 'wisdom,' he may even suggest that the idea of a homogenous community called 'Muslims' that emerged over a period of 23 years in Arabia is a dubious one.

The beloved, according to him, has no unblemished Arab pedigree, less still 'begotten-not-created'; "Instead, she is either the illegitimate offspring of Jewish parents." ("The core of the Prophet's message...appears as Judaic messianism" or "almost exclusively of elements adapted from the Judeo-Christian tradition.") These scholars view the whole body of Muslim literature on Islamic history as part of its "Salvation History," which "is not an historical account of saving events open to the study of the historian; Salvation History did not happen; it is a literary form which has its own historical context...and must be approached by means appropriate to such; literary analysis."

Based on this kind of analysis, the work of John Wansbrough,[20] Andrew Rippin (who has done a good bit to make Wansbrough's terse, technical, and even obtuse writing accessible), and the more recent work by Christoph Luxenborg[21] seek to prove that the early period of Islam shows "a great deal of flexibility in Muslim attitudes towards the text and a slow evolution towards uniformity...which did not reach its climax until the fourth Islamic century."[22] While some of these scholars, often referred to as 'revisionists,' have insisted on a literary approach to the Qur'an, their views are closely connected to the ideas of Muslim history as essentially as a product of Judeo-Christian milieu argued by Patricia Crone and Michael Cook, two other scholars whose contribution to revisionist thinking is immeasurable.[23] The basic premise of this group of scholars is the indispensability of a source-critical approach to both the Qur'an and Muslim accounts of its beginning, the need to compare these accounts with others external to Muslim sources, and utilizing contemporary material evidence including those deriving from epigraphy, archaeology, and numismatics.

Needless to say, this approach, a kind of voyeurism, and its putative disinterestedness, has not been welcomed by those who openly acknowledge a relationship between themselves and the lover and/or the beloved. Like the voyeur who may delude himself into thinking that he is a mere observer without any baggage, these 'objective' scholars claim to have no confessional or ulterior motive in approaching the Qur'an other than that of examining the body in the interest of scholarship. Alas, there is no innocent scholarship.

Attached to this last category is a polemicist who really has little in common with the methodology of his sustainers, the revisionists, although the uncritical lover, and occasionally the critical lover as well, perhaps unfairly, lumps them all together.[24] This man is, in fact, besotted with another woman, the Bible, or secularism. Having seen his own beloved exposed as purely human, although with a divine spirit in the case of the former; i.e., the Bible as beloved, and terrified of the prospect that his Muslim enemy's beloved may be attracting a growing number of devotees, he is desperate to argue that 'Your beloved is as human as mine.' Having tried in vain for centuries to convince the Muslim of the beauty of his own beloved (the Bible), he now resorts to telling the Muslim how ugly his (i.e., the Muslim's) beloved is. Another species in this category is one that is alarmed by the supposed rise and political influence of the lover and assumes that his doings are the result of the whisperings of the lover.

The blame-it-on-the-woman character asks rhetorically, 'Doesn't the Qur'an tell Muslims to kill?' 'And, so,' he reasons, 'The beloved should be unmasked and cut down to size so that she would no longer be able to exercise such a pernicious hold over her lover.' The methodology of the revisionists are never seriously discussed by this polemicist – of this he is incapable – for if he were to seriously consider the methodology of the revisionists then his own fundamentalist mindsets would probably collapse. All that matters to the polemicist are the conclusions of the revisionists, however disparate and tentative (Wansbrough refers to his own work as "conjectural," "provisional," "tentative," and "emphatically provisional"), of the utterly human and fallible nature of these Muslim's beloved. Pamphlets, tracts, the internet, and Prometheus Books are where these polemicists hang out.

The adversarial nature of the relationship between Muslims and others is noteworthy. With some noteworthy exceptions, it often appears as if we are simply incapable of hearing what critical outsiders have to say about our text. This ability to listen, even if only as a prelude to subsequent rejection, is a condition for surviving in the world of scholarship today.

One of the notions that the world of confessional scholarship shares with modernist scientific thinking is the putative ahistoricity of the scholar. Referring to commentators of the Qur'an, Jane McAuliffe notes, "the reader searches in vain for such reference [to their current political, social and economic environment]. It is frequently difficult to determine from internal evidence alone whether a commentary was written in Anatolia or Andalusia, whether its commentator had ever seen a Mongol or a Crusader or had ever conversed with a Christian or conducted business with one." Both confessional Muslim scholarship as well as those who claim scholarly disinterest are loath to acknowledge their own histories for fear of suggesting that the truths that they write about may be relative to those histories. Like other progressive scholars such as liberation and feminist theologians, scholars do have inescapable histories of class, gender, race, and period.

Wansbrough

Wansbrough presents his work as tentative, and yet proceeds to make assumptions premised on those very tentative conclusions. His demarcation of categories of *tafsīr*, for example, besides depending on a very limited number of *tafsīr* works for each genre, presents them in neat chronological order. For his category of Haggadic Tafsir he depends nearly entirely on the work of Muqātil ibn Sulaymān (d. 150/767) and Muḥammad al-Kalbī (d.763). We will recall his view that in this category, the text really followed and was subject to the narrative, and he cites these two works as examples thereof. When however, he runs thin on Ibn Isḥāq as actually being an example thereof, he casually resorts to unsubstantiated claims of editorial intervention: "I am tempted to ascribe this to editorial intervention." Referring specifically to Ibn Isḥāq's inability to fit squarely into his categorization, he says "That this is less true of Ibn Isḥāq's work could be the result of its having been drastically edited by a scholar fully conversant with the methods of and principles of masoretic exegesis." Wansbrough, of course, uses his typology to argue that the text evolved over nearly ten generations without offering any idea why this could not be accomplished in one generation. As William Graham has argued, "The identification of various periscopes, older prescriptural motifs, and language taken from Judaic usage is suggestive of many new interpretative possibilities, but it is not clear that it necessitates the radical conclusion that there was no generally recognized fixed Qur'anic text before AH 200."

Curiously, many of the terms Wansbrough readily applies to the Qur'anic *Tafsīr* tradition (haggadic, halakhic, masoretic, etc) are explained in *The Shorter Oxford English Dictionary* exclusively in terms of Jewish tradition. In other words, there is little or no meaning to them outside this tradition. Wansbrough's persistence in the employment of this terms, in addition to the intended point that the Qur'an is a product of Jewish scriptural tradition, also has the effect of highlighting the Qur'anic tradition's supposed emptiness, with the message, 'On your own, you are nothing.' Like all of us, Wansbrough is also the child of a particular milieu. He belongs to a generation of scholars wedded to a political and cultural worldview that sees subjected people as mere borrowers and inheritors from the dominant classes. The Arabs could thus not possibly produce something remotely coherent on their own.

Not that they made these claims; Instead they readily acknowledged the interconnectedness of the Qur'an with other scriptures. In Makkah, Muhammad was accused of having learnt the Qur'anic messages from a non–Arab, probably a Jew or a Judeo-Christian. "They say that it is only a man who teaches him. But the tongue of the man they allude to is foreign while this is in Arabic plain and clear" (16:103). The Qur'an does not deny that Muhammad was in contact with Christians or Jews; in fact, it claims an affinity with their scriptural traditions and describes itself as a verifier of those scriptures.

> Oh Children of Israel, Remember those blessings of Mine with which I graced you, and fulfill your promise unto Me, [whereupon] I shall fulfil My promise unto you; and of Me, of Me stand in awe. Believe in that which I have bestowed from on high, confirming the truth already in your possession and be not foremost among those who deny its truth; and do not barter away my messages for a trifling gain; and of me, of Me be conscious. And do not overlay the truth with falsehood and do not knowingly suppress the truth (2:40-42).

The Qur'an and Hermeneutics

The term 'hermeneutics' refers principally to textual interpretation and the problems surrounding it. The problem of hermeneutics emerges from the fact that human expressions, or divine expressions in a human language (texts in particular) are simultaneously familiar and alien to the reader. Taking into account this seeming paradox, the reader, if the text is to be understandable, has the task of transposing the meaning of text into his/her own system of values and meanings. Derived from the Greek verb *hermeneuein* ("to interpret") hermeneutics is defined as the "intellectual discipline concerned with the nature and presuppositions of the interpretation of expressions." As an interpretative activity, its essential concern is the written text and can be described as "the theory of the operations of understanding in their relation to the interpretation of written texts." Hermeneutics deals with three major conceptual issues: the nature of a text; what it means to understand a text; and how understanding and interpretation are determined by the presuppositions and assumptions (the horizon) of both the interpreter and the audience to which the text is being interpreted.

The term hermeneutics does not seem to be employed in the Arabic language. The compound *fiqh al-tafsīr wa al-ta'wīl* – 'the understanding of exegesis and interpretation' – however, is appealing. The absence of a definitive term for hermeneutics in the classical Islamic disciplines, or its non-employment on a significant scale in contemporary Qur'anic literature, does not imply the absence of definite hermeneutical notions or operations in Qur'anic studies. While the term 'hermeneutics' dates only to the seventeenth century, the operations of textual exegesis and theories of interpretation, religious, literary, and legal, date back to antiquity.

Traditional *tafsīr* activity has, however, always been categorized, and these categories – Shiite, Muʿtazilite, Abbasid, Ashʿarite, etc – are acknowledged to say something about the affiliations, ideology, period, and social horizons of the commentator. Connections between the subject of interpretation, the interpreter, and the audience are rarely made. When this is the case, it is usually done with the intention of disparaging the work or the author, or they are made to underline the theological prejudices of the author. To date, little has been written about these connections in a historical or literary critical manner or about the explicit or implicit socio-political assumptions underlying their theological orientations, the central concern of contemporary hermeneutics.

In contemporary Muslim scholarship, Fazlur Rahman, Nasr Hamid Abu Zayd, and Muhammad Arkoun are among the rare exceptions who deal with hermeneutics. Rahman insists that "the Qur'an is the divine response...to the moral and social situation of the Prophet's Arabia." He thus pleads for a "hermeneutical theory that will help us understand the meaning of the Qur'an as a whole so that both the theological sections of the Qur'an and its ethico-legal parts become a unified whole." Arkoun emphasizes the need "to reconstruct the historical background of each [Qur'anic] text or period" and for greater consideration to be given to "the aesthetics of reception: how a discourse is received by its listeners and readers." He suggests a critical re-evaluation of the interpretative methodology "elaborated by jurists-theologians based on rationality as founding the true knowledge and excluding the constructions of imagination." In its place he offers the "hope that semiotics and linguistics can create the possibility of reading religious texts...in a new way."

While both Rahman and Arkoun emphasize the historical context of the Qur'an's revelation, Abu Zayd stresses the Arabic nature of its origin and the need to approach it as an Arabic literary work. While he does not deny the divine origin of the Qur'an, he argues that it is futile to delve into this because the divine is beyond the realm of scientific inquiry:

> The Qur'an is a communicative relationship between sender and recipient that arose through the means of a code or a language system. Because, in the case of the Qur'an, the sender cannot be the subject of scientific inquiry, the study of the text must proceed from the premise of the verifiable / observable reality of the culture of the community addressed by the text as well as its primary, the recipient, the Messenger. Culture is expressed in language. The study of the text must thus proceed from the reality and culture as empirical givens. From these givens we arrive at a scientific understanding of the phenomenon of the text. The idea that the text is a product of culture [*muntaj thaqafi*] is so obvious that it does not have to be argued any further.

For Abu Zayd, the text is larger than the Qur'an, which he describes as the "primary text" from which all other Islamic texts sprang forth. By text in the broader sense, he refers to "that reservoir of knowledge of the Arabs at a time when they had no science; only poetry." While at a superficial glance, his methodology resembles that of Wansbrough and others who have adopted a literary approach to Qur'anic studies, his emphasis on the Arabicity of the text places him firmly in the camp of Arabists rather than in Islamic studies.

While Wansbrough saw interpretation as so thoroughly interwoven with the text that they have become indistinguishable, Abu Zayd regards interpretation of the text as 'the flip side of the text' – irrevocably tied to each other and argues that only though interpretation can the text be comprehended. For this to take place, the Qur'an needs to be decoded in the light of its historical, cultural, and linguistic milieu. Furthermore, the results of this decoding must be decoded in the code of the cultural and linguistic milieu of the interpreter. Unlike Arkoun, he regards his own work as part of an Islamic renewal-cum-reform project and has utilized the results of his work to argue for human rights and gender justice, saying that in these matters the spirit of the text must take precedence over its letter.[25]

We have in these writings the beginnings of the emergence of hermeneutics as a discipline in Qur'anic studies. If previous patterns in Islamic scholarship are indicative, then considerable time will pass before its direction and nature becomes evident. Clearly though, in societies where Muslims are desperate to make contemporaneous sense of the speech of God in the midst of active struggles for justice, a significant contribution to this discipline will emerge.[26]

NOTES

1. In general, my description of these positions should be regarded as descriptive rather than evaluative. I am thus not suggesting that the first level is the 'highest' or 'lowest' level.

2. Any literature scan or bibliographical selection is invariably arbitrary on a subject as vast as the Qur'an. In general, I have confined my references in this section to sources that I have frequently consulted. My sample range is also confined to English and Arabic with a few others in Urdu and German.

3. Mawdudi, originally from India, is one of the most influential activist-scholars of the twentieth century whose work inspired two generations of Islamic activists. His six volume exegetical work is in Urdu, titled *Tafhim al-Qur'an* (Understanding the Qur'an) (Lahore: 1949-1972).

4. Islahi was an Indian scholar who wrote *Tadabbur-i-Qur'an* (Reflections on the Qur'an), an exegetical work in Urdu based on the ideas of Hamid al-Din Farahi (d.1930) which strongly emphasizes the Qur'an's structural cohesion and harmony. Various parts of *Tadabbur-i Qur'an* were published in Lahore by three publishers over the period 1967-80. It is currently being reprinted in nine volumes (Lahore: Faran Foundation).

5. Muhammad Husayn Tabataba'i, one of the great contemporary Shiite theologians, is the author of a twenty-volume work, *Al-Mīzān fī Tafsīr al-Qur'ān* (Beirut: Mu'assasah al-ʿIlm li al-Maṭbuʿāt, 1997), which is a comprehensive philosophical, mystical, linguistic, and theological exposition of the Qur'an.

6. Muhammad Asad, a Polish scholar, translated the Qur'an in 1980 (Gibraltar: Dar al-Andalus). Titled *The Message of the Qur'an* and dedicated to 'people who think,' his translations, which have extensive comments, are widely used by modernist and progressive English-speaking Muslims.

7. Among the few women Qur'an scholars is the Egyptian Aishah Abd al-Rahman, who has distinguished herself by her literary and exegetical studies of the Qur'an, of which the most important are *Al-Tafsīr al-Bayānī li al-Qur'ān al-Karīm*, 2 vols. (Cairo: Dār al-Maʿārif, 1962-69); *Al-Qur'ān wa al-Tafsīr al-ʿAṣrī* (Cairo: Dār al-Maʿārif, 1970). Another noteworthy Egyptian woman Qur'an scholar is Zaynab al-Ghazali al-Hubayli who authored *Naẓarāt fī Kitāb Allāh* (Glimpses into the Book of Allah) (Cairo: Dār al-Shurūq, 1994).

8. Al-Dhahabi, a professor in Qur'anic Sciences at the University of Al-Azhar in Cairo, has produced an exhaustive four-volume account of the development of Exegesis (*tafsīr*) and commentators from the earliest period until today. His *'Tafsīr wa al-*

Mufassirūn' (Exegesis and Exegetes) was first completed in 1976 and has since seen four subsequent editions (Cairo: Maṭbaʿah Wahbah, 1989).

9   Muhammad Abd al-Azim al-Zarqani's four-volume *Manāhil al-ʿIrfān fī ʿUlūm al-Qur'ān* (Springs of Knowledge in the Sciences of the Qur'an) (Cairo: Makatabah Wahbah, 1989) follows the traditional format of most works on Qur'anic sciences.

10 Abu al Qasim al-Khui 's *Al-Bayān fī Tafsīr al-Qur'ān* (The Elucidation of the Exegesis of the Qur'an) is a brilliant contribution to the area of Sunni-Shiite polemics around the Qur'an and its beginnings as a canon. I have made use of the translation of part of this work into English by Abdulaziz Sachedina appearing as '*The Prolegomena to the Qur'an*' (Oxford: Oxford University Press, 1998).

11 Rudiger Lohker has published an extensive overview of a number of English and German articles on the Qur'an. This appears on the internet at http://www.sub.uni-goettingen.de/ebene_1/orient/koran1.htm.

12 Rahman was a Pakistani scholar and the doyen of contemporary modernist Muslim scholarship. His views on the Qur'an are represented in numerous articles and books. His *Major Themes of the Qur'an* (Minneapolis: Bibliotheca Islamica, 1989) is a significant contribution to thematic Qur'anic exegesis.

13 Arkoun is a Sorbonne-educated Algerian scholar who has done pioneering work on the Qur'an, revelation, and semiotics. He does, however, distance himself from the more reformist orientation of other scholars that I have placed in this category.

14 Abu Zayd was condemned as an apostate by conservative Muslims scholars in his native Cairo for his views on the Qur'an expressed in *Mafhūm al-Naṣṣ: Dirāsah fī ʿUlūm al-Qur'ān* (*Interpreting the Text: Studies in Qur'anic Sciences*). (Cairo: Al-Hay'ah al-Maṣriyyah al-ʿĀmmah li al-Kutub, 1993) and is currently (2002) based in the Netherlands.

15 Cf. Fuat Sezgin, *Geschichte des Arabischen Schriftums*, 6 vols. (Leiden: Brill, 1967). Sezgin's work is a compilation of mostly manuscripts from the first four centuries of Islam which is used to validate hadith (the traditions of Muhammad) transmission.

16 His views on the Qur'an as scripture are covered in his series of articles: "The True Meaning of Scripture: An Empirical Historian's non-Reductionist Interpretation of the Qur'an," *The International Journal of Middle Eastern Studies* (1980).

17 Graham's views on the Qur'an must be seen within the context of his notion of "humane scholarship" which recognizes that to reduce another person's faith to purely psychic, social, or genetic determinants alone, and to consider it eccentric, is to pass judgment on matters to which the historian at least has no ability to penetrate with any kind of final assurance (1983, p.25). His views are dealt with in, among others, *Divine Word and Prophetic Word in Early Islam* (The Hague and Paris: Mouton, 1977) and several articles, the most relevant here being "The Earliest Meaning of 'Qur'an'," *Die Welt des Islams* (1984), vol.23-24, pp.361-377.

18   Cf. Montgomery Watt, "Early Discussions about the Qur'an," *Muslim World* (1950), vol.40, pp. 27-40; *Companion to the Qur'an* (Oxford: Oneworld, 1994); and *Islamic Revelation in the Modern World* (Edinburgh: University Press, 1969).

19   Kenneth Cragg has written a large number of books on the Qur'an and responses to it as well as numerous articles. His most important works are *The Event of the Qur'an: Islam and its Scripture* (Oxford: Oneworld, 1994); *Readings in the Qur'an* (London: Collin, 1988); and *The Pen and Faith: Eight Modern Muslim Writers and the Qur'an* (London: George Allen and Unwin, 1985).

20   Wansbrough's *Qur'anic Studies: Sources and Methods of Scriptural Interpretation* (Oxford: University Press, 1977), is still the leading work on the Qur'an for all subsequent revisionist scholars although nearly all of them arrive at different and even conflicting conclusions which is probably due to their emphasis on method. Wansbrough argues that all of Islamic scripture was generated in the midst of sectarian controversy over a period of two centuries and then fictitiously projected back to an Arabian point of origin.

21   While I am unfamiliar with Syriac or Aramaic and can therefore not comment authoritatively on Luxenberg's work, from a superficial perusal though, it does seem set to become at least as significant as Wansbrough's *Qur'anic Studies* and Crone and Cook's *Hagarism* for revisionist scholarship.

22   Christoph Luxenberg, *The Syro-Aramaic Reading of the Koran: A Contribution to the Decoding of the Language of the Koran* (Berlin: Hans Schiler Publishers, 2007).

23   Crone and Cook combine early Muslim accounts with that of Greek and Syriac sources in their inquiry into the early history of Islam. They conclude that the whole of Islamic history up to the period of ʿAbd al-Malik (d.86/705) is fabrication and, in reality, the product of identity struggles among peoples united only by their common status as conquered communities.

24   Muslims have often viewed much of non-Muslim Qur'anic scholarship as part of an onslaught against Islam and the origins of critical Qur'an scholarship dating back to Peter the Venerable (d.1156) certainly bear this out. Contemporary Qur'an criticism, regardless of whose anti-Islam polemics it may serve, is, however, essentially a combination of the post-Enlightenment critique of all religious thinking and the colonialist project rather than an 'anti-Islam' or 'anti-Qur'an' undertaking. In the words of David Tracy, "We are in the midst of a deconstructive drive designed to expose the radical instability of all text and the inevitable intertextuality of all seemingly autonomous text." See David Tracy, *Plurality and Ambiguity: Hermeneutics, Religion, and Hope* (Chicago: University of Chicago Press, 1987), p.12.

25   He believes that studying the Qur'an from its historical-linguistic perspective will necessarily yield progressive results for a number of social questions. He distances himself from the methodologies of the likes of Tantawi Jawhari, Rashid Rida, and Muhammad Abduh, who attempted to interpret the Qur'an from the perspective of then new theories of exact sciences and or understandings of a society dealing with

questions such as democracy, human rights, and gender equality. They, he argues, took contemporary values as their basic premises rather than the socio-historical context of the Qur'an.

26 See my *Qur'an, Liberation and Pluralism: An Islamic Perspective of Interreligious Solidarity Against Oppression* (Oxford: Oneworld, 1997) as an example of this contribution to Qur'anic hermeneutics.

Islam and Gender in Muslim Societies: Reflections of an Anthropologist[1]

SABA MAHMOOD

THE follow study focuses on key debates within the discipline of anthropology that have been crucial to how the concept of gender is debated and discussed in literature on Islam. Even though many of the examples cited in this essay draw on anthropological work, key tropes within this literature also pertain to how the topic of gender and Islam has been discussed within the humanities and the social sciences generally.

As is well-known, the turn to the study of "gender," when it first emerged in the 1960s, was not specific to any single discipline but cut across a number of fields. Its key contribution lay in showing how an analytical focus on gender is crucial to understanding the operation of culturally specific systems of religious, economic, political, and social inequality. Since this analytical intervention was first launched, there now exists a rich scholarship on Islam and gender that poses new challenges that are important to consider. First is a short synopsis of key turns within the anthropological literature around the issue of gender in Muslim societies before addressing the critical challenges that face us today.

The Question of Gender

Early anthropological scholarship produced on Muslim societies, not unlike ethnographies of other non-western cultures, tended to be largely devoid of analysis of women's activities or gender relations.[2] This was in part due to the male bias that has historically characterized the academic enterprise and in part due to the absence of female anthropologists and scholars in the academy. As more women academics entered the discipline, they began to focus on women's activities and lives in an unprecedented manner. During the sixties, within anthropology there emerged a respectable tradition of ethnographic documentation of women's lives in Muslim societies that focused both on urban and rural contexts.[3] It was not until the 1970s, however, that gender as an analytical category emerged in the study of Muslim societies, substantially transforming the conceptual presuppositions of the literature produced on Islam.

During the 1970s, a number of feminist anthropologists argued that it was not enough to simply document women's lives and activities but to focus instead on how relations of gender inequality are produced and sustained in various religious, economic, social, and cultural systems. Notably, these scholars proposed that gender is a relational category that marks the difference in power between men and women.[4] Gender in this formulation is not simply synonymous with women, but elucidates the broader production of social inequality in a variety of social domains, including politics, economics, law, and religion. Cynthia Nelson's 1974 work is well-known for introducing this argument into the anthropology of the Middle East. Since then a number of sensitive studies have emerged that examine, for example, how a focus on gender transforms scholarly understandings of property relations,[5] political culture,[6] and tribal discourse and authority.[7] Similarly, there now exists a rich body of scholarship on Muslim societies outside of the Middle East that elucidates how an analysis of gender relations is crucial to the operation of modern capitalism and market economies,[8] the sustenance of ideological boundaries such as public/private, production/reproduction,[9] and the valuation of religious and spiritual practices.[10] The recent work of historians Leslie Pierce (1993) and Judith Tucker (2000) continues this tradition by showing, respectively, how an analysis of gender relations elucidates the operation of law and politics in the Ottoman imperial court and Islamic law in the Ottoman-controlled Levant.

Critique of Orientalism and Reflexive Anthropology

The anthropology of gender had already been established as a robust field of inquiry when two critical currents swept the discipline of anthropology in the 1980s, introducing a new set of debates that have been central in shaping the discipline. The first of these two currents addressed the intertwined character of anthropological knowledge and colonial domination, drawing attention to the power that western disciplines like anthropology have historically commanded in representing "other" cultures in reductive and essentialist ways.

From within the discipline of anthropology, Talal Asad's *Anthropology and the Colonial Encounter* (1973) was one of the first publications to address this issue, later followed by Edward Said's *Orientalism* written from the perspective of a literary critic (1978). Edward Said exposed how the scholarly tropes used to describe non-western societies were not only misrepresentations of the social reality they purportedly captured but were also premised on assumptions of western superiority that helped facilitate projects of imperial and colonial rule.

Talal Asad, on the other hand, emphasized how the power of western forms of knowledge lies not only in their ability to represent social reality but also to intervene and remake non-western traditions, practices, and institutions, thereby transforming what it means to live as a Muslim subject in the modern world. In the last forty years since the publication of these two books, a number of scholars have expounded and written on these themes, heralding a new era within anthropology that has focused on the production of cultural difference as a site of colonial and post-colonial hegemony and power.[11]

A second intervention that changed the terrain of anthropology in the 1980s focused more specifically on the discipline's claims to "objective" knowledge, drawing attention to those aspects of fieldwork and ethnographic writing that entail ambiguity, approximation, subjective judgment, and inequality of relations between the observer and the observed.[12] A number of influential anthropologists responded to this critique by coining a new genre of ethnographic writing glossed as "reflexive anthropology" in which the anthropologist foregrounds her privileged position as a researcher, drawing attention to the problems of reductionism, reification, ventriloquism, and essentialism that are endemic to any anthropological enterprise.[13]

Asad and Said's work provided analytical vocabulary for the disease many scholars had felt with essentialist and ahistorical depictions of Islam was an ideational system largely insulated from forces of political, economic, and social change.[14] This propensity was particularly evident in the scholarship produced on Muslim women, wherein an ahistorical concept of "patriarchal Islam" was held responsible for women's inequality, often ignoring the socioeconomic and political arrangements productive of historically-specific forms of gender subordination.[15] Critics charged that the trope of "the oppressed Muslim woman" had served as a convenient tool for colonial powers to justify the superiority of western civilization, allowing them to couch their imperial interventions in the benign language of "saving Muslim women."[16] Not only was this disingenuous, these scholars argued, but such an approach made gender inequality appear as if it was a consequence of religious tenets, scriptural authority, and native culture, rather than a product of complex social and cultural factors in which religion as much as colonial rule had played a key role.

Following this critique, subsequent scholarship on gender and Islam has helped displace the stereotype that women in the Muslim world are passive victims of patriarchal oppression, drawing attention to the myriad ways in which they create complex life worlds, at times resisting and at times colluding in the reproduction of hegemonic norms and values.[17] This work also makes the important point that Islam is only one among many religious traditions practiced within Muslim societies, a fact that requires scholars to pay adequate attention to the specificities of social, economic, and political contexts in which Muslim, as well as non-Muslim, men and women lived in these societies.

The tradition of "self-reflexive anthropology" (introduced in the 1980s as a response to the critique of anthropology's claim to "objective knowledge") has had a particularly robust career in works on the Middle East. As an increasing number of Arab and Arab-American women have entered the field of anthropology, they have reflected upon the kinds of complicated alliances and challenges their position engenders in the field, which are quite distinct from when the researchers were primarily male and often Euro-Americans.[18] Anthropologists writing in this vein have emphasized how their own ethnic identity, as well as their location in the western academy, tends to inevitably affect the kind of knowledge they produce about Muslim societies. Questions of authenticity, identity and hierarchy have been central to these accounts. In summary, what must be clear by now is that within a short span of about fifty years, the scholarship on gender and Islam has undergone substantial changes and reformulations. Some of the developments are internal to the discipline of anthropology, while many of these cut across the disciplinary divide in the U.S. academy and are generally characteristic of the work produced on the topic of Islam and gender.

Post-Orientalist Scholarship

These important transformations notwithstanding, the history of the scholarship on gender cannot be represented simply as a march of progressive improvement wherein incorrect ways of thinking have been replaced by more enlightened modes of analysis. Old ways of thinking are often hard to discard, but also new scholarship tends to generate fresh conceptual problems reflective of shifting historical realities. It is important therefore to trace some of the new questions generated by the "post-orientalist" scholarship on Muslim societies and the lacunae and dilemmas that characterize it, and to reflect upon the different ways these may be addressed.

One of the striking features of the scholarship on gender and Islam is the problematic persistence of the term "Muslim women." One would have thought that once the idea of gender as a relational category was established, any analytic work on gender relations would require a simultaneous engagement with the lives of men and women. This is seldom the case: with few exceptions, studies produced on gender in Muslim societies tend to focus solely on the lives of women.[19] The problems entailed in the collectivity that the term "Muslim women" indexes immediately become apparent when we compare it to the term "Christian women." Clearly, the latter term, while used to describe activist or devout Christian women, is rarely used to designate women who live in countries as diverse as South Africa, Tanzania, the U.S., Poland, France, Italy, and Australia, all of which have majority Christian populations. In fact, it is more common to refer to women living in predominantly Christian societies by their nationality, rather than by their relationship to a faith. (For example, even though France is predominantly a Catholic country, one refers to women living in France as French rather than Christian.) In other words, the term "Christian women" often refers to women who actively profess the Christian faith and seldom includes those who do not abide by such an allegiance. No parallel distinction, however, seems to hold regarding "Muslim women."

The problem is further compounded if we consider that large non-Muslim populations inhabit many of the regions comprising the Muslim world (such as Indonesia, Malaysia, India, Egypt, Lebanon, Sudan, and Palestine). A quick survey of anthropological literature shows that while studies on the topic of "Muslim women" abound, there are few ethnographies about non-Muslims living in Islamic societies.[20] This lacuna is especially problematic given that large non-Muslim populations have historically inhabited Muslim lands. These non-Muslim populations have had an enormous impact not only on the kind of Islam that is practiced in these areas, but their own identity and self-image has been fundamentally shaped by the sociopolitical form Islam has taken. (For example, since the inception of the post-colonial nation-state, the Egyptian Coptic community has often defined itself as part of "Islamic civilization.") In light of the recent ascendance of Islamic movements, some of which support the adoption of Islamic law and a robustly Islamic public ethic, it has become all the more important to interrogate how non-Muslim men and women have been affected by such developments in the Muslim world.

Some of these problems are manifest in the title of the recently published multi-volume *Encyclopedia of Women in Islamic Cultures* that documents, with utmost rigor and copiousness, the complex and variegated issues pertaining to women's lives, both Muslim and non-Muslim. While dropping the qualifier "Muslim" from women acknowledges the religious diversity constitutive of the Muslim world, problems persist in the use of the term "Islamic culture." A perennial anthropological question haunts the term: can any culture be described by virtue of the religion practiced by its inhabitants? How do we describe a cultural practice as Islamic when Muslims and non-Muslims alike observe it, and when its origins cannot be grounded in sources of religious authority? How do we analyze other forms of belonging – nationalist, ethnic, religious – that are not encompassed by Islam, and whose modes of existence are only tangentially related to Islam? In other words, how does one give equal analytical weight to various aspects of social life encompassed by the term "culture" without reducing one to the other?

The issue gets even more complicated when one takes into account the presence of large groups of Muslim minorities living in non-Muslim countries. For example, does it make sense to say that Indian Muslims, who comprise the largest minority Muslim population in the world today, live in an "Islamic culture," or are they the inhabitants of a "Hindu culture?" Can the two be separated, and if so, on what basis, and by whom? Given the long history of Muslim rule in India and the vast cultural heritage this legacy commands, this question points to the complicated ways in which the ideology of nationalism has forced questions of religious belonging through the narrow spectrum of majority and minority populations.

As is clear from the communal riots that have swept India in the last three decades and the increasing anti-Muslim violence, these are not simply academic questions. It is crucial for scholars interested in these issues to ask how the rubric of "Islamic cultures" articulates with the narrow discourse of nationalism that reduces heterogeneous forms of religious and ethnic belonging into the simplistic calculus of minority and majority cultures. Recall here that the project of nation-building is dependent upon a singular and unified conception of culture, language, and ethnicity (that of the "majority population") that necessarily places those who do not fit this construction as outside the narrative and history of the nation.

Anthropologists have tried to avoid the problems entailed in hegemonic constructions of community and nation by letting "native voices" speak to provide a "true account" of the heterogeneity of life in the Muslim world, making these voices speak against the confines of received cultural and political categories.[21] The idea is that insomuch as the anthropological method of research – participant observation and field work – allows unmediated access to the immediacy of people's daily lives, the ethnography can sidestep the reductionism entailed in conceptual categorizations.

This work, while salutary in its aims, is not free of problems. Part of the problem resides in assuming that a "thick cultural description," or an untainted record of "native voices," helps the scholar avoid the use of conceptual categories altogether. Any descriptive form (anthropological or otherwise) inevitably entails selection, translation, and organization, all of which impose, in one form or another, the analyst's system of classification on the data. Thus, the problem of finding appropriate analytical categories and theoretical frameworks cannot be avoided in the name of description or unmediated native voice. Rather, thorny questions about how one defines culture, religion, and the category of women must be addressed to produce analytically insightful scholarship on the Muslim world.

Is Economic Transformation to Women as Islamic Culture is to Men?

The political force that religion has come to command in the last century raises further analytical dilemmas for the study of gender and Islam. Contrary to modernist predictions that religion will decline in importance in the twentieth century, there has been a sharp rise in popular interest in religion all over the world. The last five decades have witnessed a dramatic ascension of Islamic movements (often referred to as the "Islamic Revival") all over the globe. These movements are comprised not only of Islamist political parties but also a range of social networks and activities that are organized around Islamic precepts, principles, and practices. Indeed, no contemporary discussion about the Muslim world would be complete without paying adequate attention to this phenomenon given its wide sweep (from South East Asia and Central Asia to the Middle East and Africa), and the challenge it poses to nationalist and socialist ideologies that had held sway in the Muslim world from the 1930s until the 1970s. Notably, the phenomenon of the Islamic Revival is also currently flourishing among Muslims living in North America and Europe, a development that has increasingly become the focus of a number of dissertations produced on Europe and America in recent years.

Regarding gender, a key paradox haunts the participation of women in Islamic movements. While the Islamic Revival has facilitated the entry of women into vast domains of life that were hitherto the provenance of men (such as religious pedagogy, scriptural interpretation, charity, and social welfare work), these movements are predicated upon a discursive logic that upholds many principles of gender inequality central to the Islamic juristic tradition. As the work of a number of anthropologists shows, Muslim women are one of the major driving forces behind the Islamic Revival, even if they do not hold formal leadership positions in it.[22]

Scholars have analyzed this paradoxical aspect of the Islamist movement in a variety of ways. A notable number argue that the patriarchal character of the Islamic movement may be explained by the threat men feel by the inroads women have made into public domains in the modern period (such as education, employment, and public office) from which they were previously excluded. This argument has been made in the context of the rise of Islamic politics in countries as disparate as Morocco, Malaysia, and Bangladesh, to take just a small sample.[23] The argument is simple: while modern opportunities have transformed women's lives by opening the door to education and employment, male members of these societies have resorted to longstanding patriarchal Islamic values to punish and exclude women for their intrusion. Muslim men, these scholars argue, regard women's entry into the public domain as an "erotic aggression," as a threat to their own ability to flourish socioeconomically, to which they respond either by meting out Islamic punishments to women (hence the support for the institutionalization of Islamic law) or aggressively instituting conservative religious norms (hence the popularity of modest dress styles and the resurgence of traditional role models).[24]

This argument is problematic in that it compartmentalizes women's and men's ideological worlds: while Islamic patriarchy appears to govern male identity in this analysis, women's identity, in contrast, is seen to emerge in relation to economic transformation, role changes, and modern lifestyles. Furthermore, this line of argument seems to suggest that while men suffer from anxiety brought about by socio-economic transformations (hence their attacks on women's mobility), women embrace these changes quite comfortably, the only impediment to this accommodation being the opposition they face from their male counterparts. Given that men and women living in Muslim societies *both* have been subject to Islamic patriarchal values as well as modern socio-economic transformations, is it not wrong to assume that only men are invested in preserving Islamic ideology and women remain antithetical to it?

Moreover, recent research on Islamist movements suggests that many of the Islamic practices associated with patriarchal forms of Islam (such as wearing the veil) are not forced upon women by men, but are the result of women's increasing conviction that this is the "correct" interpretation of Islam.[25] If one does not want to revert to the exhausted and widely criticized trope of "false consciousness,"[26] then the question that any scholar of contemporary Islam must address is: how does one adequately account for the emphasis Muslim women and men have come to place on Islamic juristic interpretations and orthodox mores? What are the discursive and historical conditions that have given rise to this social phenomenon, with what sorts of social and political effects? What kinds of challenges does this emphasis on orthodox tradition pose for the future of Muslim and non-Muslim relations in the Muslim world?[27]

This critique of the above-mentioned approach is not meant to single out authors for their faulty reasoning, but to point to the analytical difficulties entailed in maintaining a critical balance between a perspective that gives adequate attention to Islamic ideological formations and one that is attentive to processes of material and socioeconomic change that have transformed the Muslim world (as well as the interpretation of Islamic scripture and law) in the modern period. While clearly the intent of many scholars writing in this vein is to avoid presenting a temporally frozen picture of Islam, they tend to treat Islamic ideology as homologous with male interests and economic change with women's wellbeing. Consequently, this framework compartmentalizes the analysis of ideology from material change and the analysis of social forces that shape the world of women from those that affect men.

This problem surfaces repeatedly in the scholarship on gender and Islam is because it is assumed that all women, regardless of which discursive formation they are a product of, hold the desire for freedom from relations of domination and male subordination as their coveted goal. As a result, this scholarship tends to naturalize the desire for freedom from male domination, and ignore those desires and aspirations that are either indifferent to the goal of freedom or simply inattentive to it.[28] Yet, if we concede that all forms of desires are socially constructed, as a number of feminists have argued for some time now, then it is crucial that scholars inquire into a range of different kinds of desires (even those for subordination to male authority), and not naturalize those that are more conducive to certain kinds of political projects over others. Such an approach would require the analyst to *not* assume that while men are motivated by the desire to uphold relations of gender inequality as enshrined in Islam, women are constitutionally predisposed to oppose such a system. Rather, such an approach requires that we pay adequate attention to specific kinds of social and religious projects, variable conceptions of the self and their relationship to social authority, as well as structures of hierarchy (economic, gender, and social) that bind women and men to the very forces that subordinate them.

Importantly, such an analytical approach would have to be careful not to commit the mistakes made by the Orientalist scholarship wherein the desire for freedom, equality, and autonomy was equated with "western values," and its absence was held to be synonymous with "Islamic cultures." It is important to realize that the project of developing an analytically appropriate language that captures different kinds of collective and social commitments is not the same as finding an essential cultural essence that defines all people living in a given society, regardless of their historical and social location. It would be just as wrong to say that all women live by a commitment to freedom and equality in Islamic cultures as it would be to assume that none do.

One of the key challenges facing scholars today is to develop a conceptual language that analyzes different kinds of social and collective projects that do not follow any single cultural logic but are products of different kinds of discursive and political formations that inhabit a single cultural space simultaneously. Just as scholars have been attentive to the multiplicity of commitments, ideals and goals that coexist in any given western liberal society, it is equally important to be attentive to the variety of projects, conceptions of selfhood, structures of authority, and discourses that animate the lives of Muslims across the globe. Careful analysis of the ways in which ordinary people inhabit the world differently is perhaps the strongest insight that anthropology can bring to the study of women who live in Muslim societies.

Secularism and Islam

One of the most exciting areas of research that has opened up recently is the study of secularism and what it means for societies where Muslim and non-Muslim populations live in close proximity. This pertains not only to Muslim minority populations living in Europe, America, Central Asia, Africa, and Southeast Asia but also to non-Muslims living in Muslim majoritarian societies. It is important to draw a distinction between the more descriptive literature that exists on the topic of how Islam is diversely practiced around the world given a particular context, and an emergent, more analytical scholarship that unpacks the history and conceptual category of modern secularism.

There is a vast amount of scholarship that shows the distinctly different ways in which Islam is practiced among populations, for example, living in Euro-American cities versus India or Central Asia. These dramatically different histories and contexts reveal very different articulations of gender and religion, gender and polity, and gender and community. A different set of issues emerges when one focuses on non-Muslim populations living in majoritarian Islamic cultures wherein historical proximity has produced distinct models of co-habitation and co-existence. Consider, for example, the key role Christian Palestinians have played in the struggle against Israeli occupation in the modern period, or the history of anti-colonial struggle that Indian

Muslims shared with Indian Hindus and Christians, a history further cemented with the founding of the postcolonial secular state in India. This cooperation across religious lines owes, in part, to the secular history of these struggles wherein Palestinians and Indians shared a political vision that de-emphasized their religious identity. This history of political solidarity has come under some strain in the last three decades as religious movements have gained ground both in Palestine and India (Islamist and Hindutva respectively), and the secular values that provided the ideological glue for collective projects have become undone. The same set of developments may be observed, to varying degrees, in countries like the Sudan, Malaysia, Indonesia, and Egypt.

Faced with these challenges, it is important to inquire into different traditions and models of secularism that characterize the regulatory life of modern societies both western and non-western. It is often assumed that secularism is an ideological principle that demarcates a separation between religion and state. In the past decade, there has emerged a distinct body of scholarship that argues secularism is not simply the opposite of "religion" or its abandonment, and refers to a gradual and shifting process through which traditional religious structures and sensibilities have been rearticulated to fit the requirements of liberal governance. This historically variegated process has produced different accommodations between religion and state and entailed vast socio-cultural transformations that have changed how ordinary adherents practice and understand their religious traditions.[29]

The history of this process has been particularly contentious in Muslim societies. To understand what exactly is entailed in this process, it is important not to assume a single normative definition of secularism drawn from western European history, but instead to explore the indigenous language and grammar through which the concept of secularism has historically emerged in postcolonial Muslim societies.[30] Rather than treat the historical development of secularism in the Muslim world as an aberration from the Protestant trajectory followed by western liberal societies, it is crucial that we understand the historically and culturally specific character of secularism while being attentive to the structural logic of modern governance within which the specificity of the Islamic tradition has unfolded. This in turn might help elucidate why secularism has become such a contested site of struggle within diverse Muslim communities and how gender configures this struggle in specific ways.

NOTES

1   This is a modified version of a review essay that appeared in the *Encyclopedia of Women in Islamic Cultures* (Leiden: Brill Publishers, 2003), pp.307-314.

2   For example, Fredrik Barth, "Political Leadership among Swat Pathans," *London School of Economics Monographs on Social Anthropology Series* (Oxford: Berg Publishers, 1965), vol.19; Clifford Geertz, *Islam Observed: Religious Development in Morocco and Indonesia* (Chicago and London: University of Chicago Press, 1968); Ernest Gellner, *Saints of the Atlas* (Chicago: University of Chicago Press, 1969).

3   B. Aswad, "Key and Peripheral Roles of Noble Women in a Middle Eastern Plains Village," *Anthropological Quarterly* (1967), vol.40, pp.139-152; Elizabeth Fernea, *Guests of the Sheik: An Ethnography of an Iraqi Village* (New York: Anchor Books, 1969); Hilma Granqvist, *Marriage Conditions in a Palestinian Village: Vol. 1* (Helsingfors: Societas Scientiarum Fennica, 1931); S. Mohsen, "The Legal Status of Women Among Awlad Ali," *Anthropological Quarterly* (1967), *vol.*40, pp.167-183; L. Sweet, "The Women of 'Ain ad Dayr," *Anthropological Quarterly* (1967), vol.40, pp.167-183.

4   Michelle Rosaldo, and Louise Lampher, eds., *Women, Culture, and Society* (Stanford: Stanford University Press, 1974); Carol MacCormack and Marilyn Strathern, eds., *Nature, Culture and Gender* (Cambridge, New York and Melbourne: Cambridge University Press, 1980); Sylvia Yanagisako, and Jane Collier, eds., *Gender and Kinship: Essays Toward a Unified Analysis* (Stanford: Stanford University Press, 1987).

5   Vanessa Maher, *Women and Property in Morocco: Their Changing Relation to the Process of Social Stratification in the Middle Atlas* (New York: Cambridge University Press, 1974).

6   S. Joseph, "Working-class Women's Networks in a Sectarian State: A Political Paradox," *American Ethnologist* (1983), vol.10, pp.1-22; Soraya Altorki, *Women in Saudi Arabia: Ideology and Behavior Among the Elite* (New York: Columbia University Press, 1988).

7   Lila Abu-Lughod, *Veiled Sentiments: Honor and Poetry in a Bedouin Society* (Berkeley: University of California Press, 1986).

8   Aihwa Ong, *Spirits of Resistance and Capitalist Discipline* (Albany: SUNY Press, 1987); Margaret Strobel, *Muslim Women in Mombasa: 1890-1975* (New Haven: Yale University Press, 1979).

9   Carol Delaney, *The Seed and the Soil: Gender and Cosmology in Turkish Village Society* (California: University of California Press, 1991); H. Papanek, "Purdah: Separate

Worlds and Symbolic Order," *Comparative Studies in Society and History* (1973), vol.15, pp.289-235.

10 Janice Boddy, *Wombs and Alien Spirits: Men and Women in the Zar Cult in Northern Sudan* (Wisconsin: University of Wisconsin Press: 1989).

11 James Clifford, *The Predicament of Culture: Twentieth-Century Ethnography, Literature and Art* (Cambridge: Harvard University Press, 1988); Nicholas Dirks, ed., *Colonialism and Culture* (U.S.: University of Michigan Press, 1992); George Marcus and Michael Fischer, *Anthropology as Cultural Critique: An Experimental Moment in the Human Sciences* (Chicago: The University of Chicago Press, 1986); David Scott, *Formations of Ritual: Colonial and Anthropological Discourses on the Sinhala Yaktovil* (Minneapolis: University of Minnesota Press, 1994).

12 James Clifford and George Marcus, eds., *Writing Culture: The Poetics and Politics of Ethnography* (California: University of California Press, 1986); Ruth Behar and Deborah Gordon, eds., *Women Writing Culture* (California: University of California Press, 1995).

13 Vincent Crapanzano, *Tuhami: Portrait of a Moroccan* (Chicago: Chicago University Press, 1980); Kevin Dwyer, *Moroccan Dialogues: Anthropology in Question* (U.S.: Waveland Press, 1987); Kristin Koptiuch, *A Poetics of Political Economy in Egypt* (Minneapolis: University of Minnesota Press, 1999); Smadar Lavie, *Poetics of Military Occupation* (U.S.: University of California Press, 1990).

14 For example, Geertz, *Islam Observed*; and Gellner, *Saints of the Atlas*.

15 L. Ahmed, "Western Ethnocentrism and Perceptions of the Harem," *Feminist Studies* (1982), vol.8, pp.521-534; R. Hammami and M. Reiker, "Feminist Orientalism and Orientalist Marxism," *New Left Review* (1988), vol.170, pp.93-106; M. Lazreg, "Feminism and Difference: The Perils of Writing as a Woman on Women in Algeria," Marianne Hirsch and Evelyn Fox Keller, eds., *Conflicts in Feminism* (New York: Routledge Press, 1989); Chandra Mohanty, et al, eds., *Third World Women and the Politics of Feminism* (Bloomington: Indiana University Press, 1991).

16 Lila Abu-Lughod, *Veiled Sentiments: Honor and Poetry in a Bedouin Society* (California: University of California Press, 1986); Leila Ahmed, *Women and Gender in Islam: Historical Roots of a Modern Debate* (U.S.: Yale University Press, 1992); Malek Alloula, *The Colonial Harem* (Minneapolis: University of Minnesota Press, 1986); Marnia Lazreg, *The Eloquence of Silence: Algerian Women in Question* (New York: Routledge, 1994). Since the events of 9/11, this older civilizational discourse about the inferiority of Islamic cultures vis-à-vis Islam's treatment of women has resurfaced with a vengeance. For recent responses and critiques of this resurgent trope, see L. Abu-Lughod, "Do Muslim Women Really Need Saving? Anthropological Reflections on Cultural Relativism and its Others," *American Anthropologist* (2002), vol.104, pp.783-790; C. Hirschkind, and S. Mahmood, "Feminism, the Taliban, and Politics of Counter-Insurgency," *Anthropological Quarterly* (2002), vol.75,

pp.339-354; and S. Mahmood, "Feminism, Democracy, and Empire: Islam and the War of Terror," *Women Studies on the Edge* (North Carolina: Chapel Hill University of North Carolina Press, 2007).

17   Lila Abu-Lughod, *Writing Women's Worlds* (California: University of California Press, 1993); Barbara Callaway, *The Heritage of Islam: Women, Religion, and Politics in West Africa* (Boulder: Lynne Rienner Publishers, 1994); Erika Friedel, *Women of Deh Koh: Lives in an Iranian Village* (Harmondsworth: Penguin, 1991); M. Hegland, "Political Roles of Aliabad Women: The Public-Private Dichotomy Transcended," *Women in Middle Eastern History: Shifting Boundaries in Sex and Gender*, N. Keddie and B. Baron, eds. (New Haven: Yale University Press, 1991); Maria Mies, *Lace Makers of Narsapur* (London: Zed Books, 1982); Nayereh Tohidi and Herbert Bodman, eds., *Women in Muslim Societies: Diversity within Unity* (Boulder: Lynne Rienner Publishers, 1998).

18   Soraya Altorki, and Camillia El-Solh, eds., *Arab Women in the Field: Studying Your Own Society* (Syracuse: Syracuse University Press, 1988).

19   Anthropologists might argue that in many Muslim societies, researchers are often restricted in their access to the opposite sex. While this is quite true, it does not account for the lack of any discursive analysis of public contestations and representations of sex and gender relations that are equally accessible to male and female researchers. For an exception in this regard, see Kamran Asdar Ali, *Planning the Family in Egypt: New Bodies, New Selves* (Austin: University of Texas Press, 2002).

20   For exceptions, see Julie Peteet, *Gender in Crisis: Women and the Palestinian Resistance Movement* (New York: Columbia University Press, 1991).

21   Daisy Dwyer, *Images and Self Images: Male and Female in Morocco* (New York: Columbia University Press, 1983).

22   Saba Mahmood, *Politics of Piety: The Islamic Revival and the Feminist Subject* (New Jersey: Princeton University Press, 2005); Ziba Mir-Hosseini, *Islam and Gender: The Religious Debate in Contemporary Iran* (New Jersey: Princeton University Press, 1999); A. Najmabadi, "Feminism in an Islamic Republic: Years of Hardship, Years of Growth," *Islam, Gender and Social Change*, Yvonne Haddad and John Esposito, eds. (New York: Oxford University Press, 1997).

23   Dina Siddiqi, "Taslima Nasreen and Others: The Contest over Gender in Bangladesh," *Women in Muslim Societies*, H. Bodman and N. Tohidi, eds. (London: Lynne Rienner Publishers, 1998).

24   A. Ong, "State Versus Islam: Malay Families, Women's Bodies, and the Body Politic in Malaysia," *American Ethnologist* (1990), vol.17, pp.258-275.

25   S. Brenner, "Reconstructing Self and Society: Javanese Muslim Women and 'the Veil,'" *American Ethnologist* (1996), vol.23, pp.673-697; F. El-Guindi, "Veiling Infitah with Muslim Ethic: Egypt's Contemporary Islamic Movement," *Social Problems* (1981), vol.28, pp.465-483; Nilufer Gole, *The Forbidden Modern* (U.S.: University of Michigan Press, 1996); Sondra Hale, *Gender Politics in Sudan:*

Islamism, Socialism, and the State (Boulder: Westview Press, 1997); Arlene MacLeod, *Accommodating Protest: Working Women, the New Veiling and Change in Cairo* (New York: Columbia University Press, 1991); Sherifa Zuhur, *Revealing Reveiling: Islamist Gender Ideology in Contemporary Egypt* (Albany: SUNY Press, 1992).

26   See my Introduction to *Politics of Piety*, 2005.

27   For different kinds of answers to this question, see Charles Hirschkind, *The Ethical Soundscape: Cassette Sermons and Islamic Counterpublics* (New York: Columbia University Press, 2006).

28   See M. Strathern, "An Awkward Relationship: The Case of Feminism and Anthropology," *Signs* (1987), vol.12, pp.276-293.

29   Talal Asad, *Formations of the Secular: Christianity, Islam, Modernity* (Stanford: Stanford University Press, 2003); Rajeev Bhargava, ed., *Secularism and its Critics: Oxford in India Readings, Themes in Politics* (New York: Oxford University Press, 2005); Hugh McLeod, *Secularisation in Western Europe, 1848-1914* (New York: Palgrave Macmillan, 2000); and Brinkley Messick, *The Calligraphic State: Textual Domination and History in a Muslim Society* (California: University of California Press, 1993).

30   Saba Mahmood, "Secularism, Hermeneutics, and Empire: Politics of Islamic Reformation," *Public Culture* (2006), vol.18, no.2, pp.327-343.

The Academic Studies of Sufism at American Universities

MARCIA HERMANSEN

THE following article provides an overview of the history and current situation of the academic study of Sufism (Islamic mysticism) at American universities. It will examine the place of Sufism within the broader curriculum in Islamic studies as well as some of the main themes and approaches to this subject taken by western scholars. In addition, it will explain both the academic context where Sufi studies are located and the role of contemporary positions in Islamic and western thought in shaping the academic study of Sufism.[1] Due to the nature of this volume, topics and issues of particular interest to a Muslim audience will be raised in the course of the essay, in addition to strictly academic observations on the topic at hand.

In comparison to its role at academic institutions in the traditional "Muslim world,"[2] Sufi studies has played a larger role within the western academic study of Islam during the twentieth century, especially the later decades. The reasons for this are manifold and will be discussed under the following contexts: institutional, intellectual, "political," and pedagogical.

Institutional Context

A clear distinction should be made between the institutional contexts of the study of Islam in Muslim societies and in the U.S. Most departments of Islamic studies at western-style universities in the Muslim world might be comparable to theology departments at American Catholic universities or to seminaries for the education of American Protestants. That is, these faculties employ a large and diverse faculty in subfields or areas such as Shari'ah, 'aqīdah, hadith, da'wah, and so on, who teach and examine the diverse aspects of the religious Islamic tradition academically and at the same time from a largely "confessional" perspective.

Another aspect of the institutional background of Sufi studies is the difficulty of defining what is specifically "American" in terms of scholarship and scholars. A previous generation perceived this issue as fraught with complexity because so many of the "greats" in the field of Islamic studies were European immigrants to the U.S. in the wake of World War II. For example, Hamilton Gibb moved from Oxford to head the Center for Middle Eastern Studies at Harvard in the mid-1950s, Gustave von Grunebaum headed the Center at UCLA, and Franz Rosenthal was hired by Yale in 1956.3 This, according to one scholar, made for an implicit transfer of a continental "Orientalism" to the American context.4 One aspect of this Orientalism was the sense of "Islam" as constituting a unifying, essential, and somewhat static factor unifying disparate cultural, intellectual, and social realities in Muslim societies. This debate continues with vigor in the field of Islamic studies as a whole and within Sufi studies, as will be discussed later.

In American universities today, the study of Islam will most likely be found in either area studies or religious studies programs. In fact, the location of the academic study of Islam in American universities shifted during in the 1970s from their centers in departments or institutes of Oriental or Near Eastern Studies to becoming components of courses offered in religious studies programs.5 Within the American academy, Near Eastern studies departments are relatively rare today, for generally only major research institutions can offer the range of languages and specialties to support serious work in this area. In addition, area studies programs have been criticized for training specialists who speak to a narrow range of issues and are unable to engage in the broader theoretical debates and employ the cross-disciplinary methodologies that would make their work accessible and relevant to a broad range of scholars.[6] By the 1960s and 1970s the majority of American MAs and Ph.Ds in non-western traditions were awarded by disciplines in the social sciences and humanities rather than area studies departments.[7]

Religious studies, on the other hand, has during the last forty years become recognized at many institutions as a central component within a liberal arts curriculum and is therefore offered at a greater number and broader range of universities. This is especially the case at religious and private liberal arts institutions. For these reasons institutionally, and therefore ultimately economically, there is a broader scope for offering courses on Sufism, a topic that engages student interest, within the undergraduate curriculum. Consequently, training in such an area would seem more likely to lead to employment for the prospective graduate with interests in a humanities or social scientific approach to the study of Islam.

It would be a distortion, however, to attribute the crest of interest in the academic study of Sufism to economic pragmatism alone, for the study of Islamic mysticism has proven particularly appealing to western academics attracted to the study of Islam as well as to the western general public.

Language Training and Its Role

Viewed in historical context, increased government support for the study of the Muslim world and Islamic languages emerged in the U.S. during the post-World War II period of Cold War contestations over the developing nations in Asia and Africa. Previously, internationally-oriented teaching and research in American colleges rarely extended beyond Europe.[8] Government programs such as the Title VI part of the National Defense Education Act (NDEA), established in 1958, provided scholarships at major research institutions for students pursuing advanced study related to these security and defense interests.[9] This support improved the extent and quality of appropriate language instruction in many fields, including Islamic studies.

Title VI supported "language development" especially that of less commonly taught languages such as Arabic, Persian, Turkish, and Urdu, through initiating language area centers for the expansion of instruction in these languages and related subjects.[10] Scholars trained during this period were the first cohort to have the possibility of government subsidies for research not directly tied to military objectives. However, the Cold War was definitely part of the background that sustained the need to promote American expertise in critical defense languages.[11] Additional resources were provided through Public Law (PL) 480, a program where from 1966-1980, U.S. foreign aid in food and agricultural assistance was reciprocated by having recipient nations provide copies of all books published locally to the Library of Congress and selected major research universities. In 1980, libraries had to begin paying for these materials.[12] As a result, library collections in languages and scholarship of the Muslim world were greatly enhanced in various parts of the U.S.

Language training immersion programs at sites such as the Center for Arabic Studies Abroad in Cairo (CASA), the Berkeley Urdu program in Pakistan, and Bogazici University in Turkey were established for American students. Consequently, American scholarship about the Muslim world became increasingly vigorous, and even social scientists were expected to develop competence in regional languages.

The recipients of these scholarships for the study of "critical defense languages" were the most capable students, and in the initial phases they did not have to repay the government through any particular service or internship. Since 1992, a limited element of programs funded through the National Security agency has required a commitment to try to find employment in security agencies for a certain period at the completion of relevant studies.[13]

Ironically, many of the students attracted to Islam and religious studies during the 1970s could be characterized a part of the "generation of seekers"[14] who pursued personal edification as well as intellectual depth in graduate programs. For the first time, large numbers of American students from non-privileged backgrounds were provided the resources to study abroad for extended periods and were subsidized in mastering the classical Islamic languages requisite for serious study. The greatest growth in American scholarship on Sufism, then, has arisen from the work done by scholars trained during the 1970s. As Alexander Knysh notes, "in the decades after World War II the majority of western experts in Sufism were no longer based in Europe, but in North America."[15]

Training in American graduate schools in Islamic studies normally requires reading knowledge of at least four additional languages: two languages of the Muslim world and two European languages at the "reading knowledge" level. These are usually French and German although another language, such as Spanish or Dutch, may be substituted if there is a compelling rationale related to the topic of the student's research. In practice the use of European, especially German sources, is relatively limited on the part of American scholars. This is perhaps because so few American secondary schools prepare students with an adequate base in these languages, so that the graduate student might really achieve some ability to use sources and continue using them once the dissertation is completed. There is also some skepticism as to whether reading European scholarship is as essential as it was in the era of the Orientalists. An additional concern is that this European language requirement has been a stumbling block to some students from Muslim societies who were attempting to pursue graduate degrees in the U.S.

The "two language" requirement from the Muslim world also tends to limit the exposure to the secondary language, in many cases Persian or Turkish, so that the majority of American scholars of Islam work primarily in sources from one language of the Muslim world. This, of course, would also be common in Arab Muslim societies. In terms of scholars of Islam from the non-Arab Muslim world, non-Arabs would have mastery of their own language as well as Arabic, giving them an edge in comparative work if they were interested in local as well as classical issues. In previous times, South Asian Muslim scholars of Islam would probably have known Arabic, Persian, and Urdu at high degrees of mastery. In this case, the issue would be one of the value of the secondary or tertiary language (Urdu, for example) in scholarly work. Today, significant secondary scholarship, including both translations from Arabic and Persian and analytic studies of Islam, exists in the vernaculars. For this reason, South Asians and American scholars of pre-modern South Asian Islam usually master Urdu and Persian, which are in any case both Indo-European languages and therefore easier for English speakers to learn, and then to a lesser degree learn to read sources in Arabic.

In previous decades, scholars of Islam who did not have at least a basic reading knowledge of Arabic tended to be passed over for academic jobs due to a bias that "real scholars of Islam" work in Arabic sources. Scholars of Sufism in a non–Arab local context would have been affected by this perception, and this often included individuals with stronger theoretical interests in religious studies theory such as ritual or in the social sciences generally, rather than in the philological model inherited by Near Eastern studies programs. In terms of South Asian studies in the U.S., the important Muslim presence in the subcontinent has historically been under-represented since scholars of Islam were expected to be specialists in the Middle East, while the South Asian area studies centers were dominated by scholars of India and Hinduism.[16]

Unlike the European experience, area studies in the U.S. was not focused on colonial or ex-colonial territories and thus featured more comparative and varied interests in aspects of Islam, and therefore in Sufism. Therefore, one could argue that American scholarship was more likely to be able to encompass the new "global" Islam of the end of the twentieth century. In fact, the Social Science Research Council established a Committee on the Comparative Study of Muslim Societies in 1986. The Council of American Overseas Research Centers (CAORC) also established a special category of grants for comparative studies and the Fulbright program has developed a Middle East, South Asian and North Africa comparative research grant. In addition, the growth of the Muslim population in the U.S., especially after the 1980s, made the topic of diaspora Islam and transnational migration accessible to American scholars in a more direct way.

Intellectual Context

The prevailing methodological orientation of western scholars of religion during most of the twentieth century was "phenomenology," a term used within the study of religion with less than technical philosophical rigor. One definition holds that "the phenomenology of religion is that method of religious studies which is characterized by a search for the structures underlying comparable religious data that does not violate the self-understanding of the believers." In addition, the search for similarity is premised on an assumption of similar underlying structures rather than on the dynamics of any historical interaction.[17] Such an approach privileges Sufism among the sub-fields of Islamic studies, as will be discussed later in this essay.

In fact, the position of the study of Islam within the academic study of religion shifted dramatically over the twentieth century. In the late nineteenth century, the project of developing a scientific study of religion was framed in a quest for origins. As a latecomer on the religious scene, Islam was much less germane to the quest than primal religion or even Hinduism and the Sanskrit corpus of texts. The phenomenological approach to religious studies that emerged and remained dominant during most of the twentieth century flowered after the carnage of World War I in Europe. It derived from a philosophical endeavor to shift from neo-Kantian abstractions to the religious things, and the religious subjects themselves. Here again, Islam was generally at the periphery rather than the center of interest for phenomenologically-oriented scholars.

For example, among the dominant approaches to comparative religion during the 1960s and 1970s was the "Patternist school," inspired by the works of the Romania scholar, Mircea Eliade (d. 1986). This method was characterized by the assumption that there were universal patterns underlying human religiosity, somewhat analogous to the Jungian archetypes. Eliade's work posited a homo religiosos; i.e., that humans were by nature religious, although the disenchantment of the modern world had resulted in a rupture from the meaningful and sacralized cosmos that had existed in primal religious traditions. All this made Islam less interesting for patternists, some of whom espoused the view that Islam was born in "the full light of history" and thus had minimal space for myth and other "real" religious elements of interest to the phenomenologist of religion. Still, among all aspects of Islamic studies, Sufism was probably the most interesting topic for patternists and phenomenologists.[18]

Mircea Eliade was a scholar of religion and taught at the University of Chicago Divinity School from 1957 until his retirement. His approach to comparative or history of religion dominated the study of religion in the U.S. in the 1970s. While Eliade was not particularly interested in Islam, his favoring the search for the sacred as displayed in archetypal symbols had a certain affinity for approaches to Sufism. Some members of the earlier cohort of influential European scholars in Sufi studies including Henri Corbin (1978) and Fritz Meier (1998) shared Eliade's interest in religion and spirituality. Together they participated in the annual meetings of the Eranos Society, a Jungian gathering held near Ascona, Switzerland,[19] and made important contributions to the study of Islam, especially its mystical and esoteric elements. There is a fair amount of secondary scholarship on Corbin's methodology, at the time criticizing his interpretation of Sufi writings and those of related esoteric Islamic traditions, particular ones in Shiism, as privileging the "batin" and superimposing a template of finding repeating archetypal themes. The fact that Corbin presents particular authors through his own appreciation and affinity with them possibly obscures elements of the texts themselves.

A further characteristic prominent among a number of the earlier cohort of European scholars of Sufism such as Miguel Asin Palacios (1871-1944), Louis Massignon (1883-1962),[20] and his student Paul Nywia (1925-1980) was their affiliation with Catholic religious orders. One might argue that this led to a particular perception of and approach to Sufism on the part of these researchers who were similarly committed to a religious vocation. It also lead to a search for sympathetic parallels and, according to some critics, a "Christianization" of some aspects of Sufi thought.[21]

Later in the 1970s, however, major theoretical shifts occurring in the broad theoretical debates within the human and social sciences were to influence the study of Islam and Sufism in the western academy. There was an increased role of theory derived from anthropology and literary theory as well as new critical initiatives such as feminism, post-modernism, and post-colonial theory that interrogated the very foundations of the production of authoritative knowledge. Central to this watershed was the work of Edward Said, *Orientalism*,[22] which took aim in particular at the way that Islam and the Muslim world had been constructed within the canons of supposedly neutral gathering and dispassionate interpretation of knowledge.

This work had a broad impact across the humanities and social sciences disciplines and laid the basis of post-colonial theory. Sufism, in terms of these new theoretical paradigms, was generally less central to the political aspects of these debates and yet very central to the discussion of what constitutes Islamic normativity and the critique of essentializing Islam as a static and monolithic entity. Ironically, while many Muslims welcome the critique of Orientalism, the marginalization of the study of Sufism in university departments of Islamic studies in the Muslim world and even in Islamic organizations, institutions, and schools in the West is an example of a similarly exclusionary approach to representing what is normatively "Islamic."

In a review article on Seyyed Hossein Nasr's contribution to Islamic studies, noted historian John Voll delineated three major movements in theory of the study of Islam during the latter part of the twentieth century:

- An initial post-WW2 phase was dominated by modernization theory that postulated a diminishing public role of religion. According to modernization theory, vestigial Islamic behaviors such as Sufism were represented as fading and temporary resistance to the inevitable secularization process.

- A period of revisionism that entailed a recognition that religion remains important. However, at this point religion is studied in its exotic or extreme forms such as New Religious Movements and cults or fundamentalist and extremist movements.

- Finally, there emerged an appreciation for the "normalcy" and persistence of aspects of religion such as its role in conveying meaning, embodiment, and expressing emotion.

Within the context of his argument Voll associates S.H. Nasr's concept of "tradition" with the possibility of recognizing the substrata of "everyday" religion permeating Muslim life.[23] While these developments in theorizing about religion are shared across the social sciences, it is unlikely that Voll's validation of Nasr's concept of "tradition" would be universally accepted by either academics or Muslim intellectuals.

Sufi Studies and Scholarly Debates

The pervasive hypothesis or trope of "decline" with regard to Islam in general and Sufism in particular continued from the days of the colonial administrators through modernization theorists, as we have already indicated.

The British Orientalist and Sufi specialist, A.J. Arberry, stated in the 1950s that "the age of Ibn al-Farid, Ibn Arabi and Rumi [twelfth and thirteenth centuries AC] represented the climax of Sufi achievement both theoretically and artistically. Thereafter...the signs of decay appear more and more clearly."[24]

Thus, even in the 1960s both the older Orientalism as well as the new area studies scholarship seemed to agree that Sufism as a living expression of Islam was anachronistic and would fade away. The resurgence of religion in the West began in the 1960s with the New Age and countercultural embrace of exotic religious experience and the emergence of new religious movements. The challenge to modernization theory might have been ignored or explained away, but an event in the Muslim world, the Iranian revolution of 1979, compelled social scientists to try and account for the resurgence and vitality of religion on a world scale.

Scholars of Islamic thought and movements and studies of contemporary Islam generally, would frame the ongoing contestation for the "soul" of Islam in terms of a debate between Islamic modernists/liberals and fundamentalists/Islamists. In some sense Sufism falls between the cracks of such a binary model, although it can be related to either term of the equation, or presented as a third and mediating force. For example, John Voll's portrayal of Nasr's traditionalism as representing such an alternative of a normal daily "traditional" routine that could be embraced by conservatives and moderates alike.[25]

Among more recent trends in cultural theorizing, Sufism has come to play a more important role since it is the expression of Islam that most incorporates local cultural elements and embodies "local" Islams. Sufism is also amenable to be studied in terms of "globalization" and negotiations of identity and practice in "the modern" and "post-modern." This meshes with the theoretical interests of the late twentieth-century academy in the "local," the embodied, and multiple articulations of normativity. Muslim scholars of Islam such as Fazlur Rahman were initially troubled by the anthropological, or post-modern, formulation of multiple "Islams" in the sense that the corollary would be "that there is in fact, no real Islam."[26]

The "Politics" of Sufi Studies

During the 1970s, graduate students interested in the study of Islam in American graduate programs came overwhelmingly from white middle class and upper middle class backgrounds. There were few foreign students, students from Muslim societies or backgrounds, or African Americans. A good number of these American students eventually converted to Islam and pursued Sufism as a personal commitment in addition a subject for academic research. Therefore, currently in terms of personal attitude, many scholars of Sufism in American universities are themselves Sufis, crypto-Sufis, or religious persons from other traditions who are sympathetic to Sufism. This would be in contrast, for example, to the case of American scholars of Islamic law or Qur'anic studies. This is interesting because at universities in the Muslim world Sufism is generally considered marginal to Islamic studies and issues of the Qur'an and Islamic law are so sensitive that serious academic work and critical studies are more difficult to undertake.

Sufi studies in North America may be characterized as the sub-field of Islamic studies most engaged in bridge-building and dialogue between the "West" and "Islam"[27] whereas some other sub-fields tend to be perceived by Muslims as the home of those who wish to "chip" away at confidence in Islam. The role of the critical historical textual scholar is not necessarily politically motivated. In the approach to the study of religious texts established by nineteenth-century

Biblical criticism, the quest for textual and redactive anomalies and the investigations of authorship, multiple sources and the identification of their polemic or other motivations became recognized as the primary methodology for studying scripture. It is therefore only natural that scholars shaped by this tradition would find it necessary and appropriate to subject Islamic scriptures, the Qur'an, and hadith, to the same scrutiny.

The fact that such historical critical methodologies are tabooed in much of the Muslim world reflects negatively on the intellectual integrity and objectivity of scholarship there and ultimately ensures that the leading academic work in Muslim primary sources will be done elsewhere and later filter back to Muslim societies. This will ultimately have an even more deleterious impact than had this project been undertaken by Muslims themselves, since in this case Muslims will be relegated to the roles of editors and compilers of the past rather than interpreters and molders of the present.

Broadly speaking, the tone of studies of Sufism, even in American academic settings, may vary from "Sufism is true," "Sufism is nice," to "Sufism is a topic worthy of study for social, historical, or any number of analytic reasons within a humanities or social science framework." Post-9/11, a political trope emerged in American public discourse of Sufism as the "moderate" or "good" Islam but this seems to have remained largely the purview of neo-con think tanks[28] and government policy, rather than impacting the patronage or research agenda of academic studies in any substantive way.

Scholars interested in how Sufi ideas might speak to larger social or political issues are developing a liberatory theology of Sufi activism or "engaged Sufism" which may be associated with the idea of an emerging progressive Islam movements among scholars who are Muslim or Muslim sympathizers. Examples are certain articles in Gisela Webb's *Windows of Faith*[29] and the South African *Journal of Islamic Studies*[30] dedicated to "Engaged Sufism."

Gender in Sufism and Sufi studies is also emerging as a more prominent topic. Is the Islamic practice of Sufism more welcoming of female participation, and do female scholars of Sufism find themselves more warmly received if they work on popular topics, leaving the

"Orientalist" excavation of texts to male scholars who consider that they do the more "serious" work of finding out what Sufis really say?

Approaches to Sufism: Discipline or Discipleship

Reviews of approaches to the study of Islam within American academia in the 1990s tended to highlight the approaches of three expatriate academics from the Muslim world as emblematic of ideological and methodological diversity: Fazlur Rahman (d.1988), Ismail al-Faruqi (d.1986), and Seyyed Hossein Nasr (b.1933).[31] Of the three Nasr definitely represented the Sufi tendency. Each of these three individuals could be characterized as being an "engaged Muslim scholar" in his own way. Rahman's commitment was to Islamic modernism,[32] Faruqi's to Muslim intellectual nativism (Islamization of knowledge)[33] and political Islam, and Nasr's to a specific interpretation of Sufism known as perennialism or traditionalism.[34] This gives Nasr's work on Islam a coherence and at the same time an advocacy of a particular interpretation of Islam that has proven sympathetic and acceptable to a broader American public, although it has achieved less centrality and even garnered some suspicion within the academic study of Islam.[35] Nasr has received the most prominent recognition within academic circles of any Muslim public intellectual. He was invited to offer the prestigious Gifford Lectures in 1992,[36] is the only Muslim accorded a volume in the "Living Philosophers" series, and appeared frequently in American documentaries and television interviews regarding Islam.[37]

Traditionalists such as Nasr are influenced by the interpretations of Rene Guenon (d.1951) and Fritjhof Schuon (d.1998), both independent scholar/practitioners of Sufism whose interpretations stressed a transcendent unity of religions, esotericism, and a condemnation of the modern desacralization of the world. Through Nasr, his students, and academic disciples this interpretation has come to play an important, if not a dominant role, in certain sub-fields of Sufi studies, for example, the interpretation of the works of Ibn al-ʿArabī and the Akbarian school[38] by scholars such as James Morris,[39] William Chittick,[40] and Sachiko Murata.[41]

The Royal Institute of Islamic Philosophy provided Seyyed Hossein Nasr and his students a base in Tehran from the 1970s until the Iranian revolution. This was the first academic institution to be conducted in accordance with the intellectual principles of the Traditionalist School. Nasr's co-followers of Schuon whose publications addressed Sufism from a religious studies/theological aspect include Martin Lings (d.2005),[42] Victor Danner (d.1990),[43] and Huston Smith[44] who popularized Sufism through his work in religious studies, including a film, "The Sufi Way."[45] Another film used in religious studies courses that represents Sufism from a perennialist perspective is "The Inner Life."[46] A marked contrast is the video "I am a Sufi: I am a Muslim,"[47] produced some 25 years later by a Belgian film crew. This video shows much more of the local cultures and actual Sufi rituals in diverse cultural contexts such as Pakistan and the Balkans. It also illustrates the more sensational aspects of Sufi ritual such as Balkan *Rifai* Sufis sticking skewers through their bodies and South Asian Sufis thrashing around in ecstasy.

Perennialism may play a continuing role in the academic study of Islam through the next generation of students of Nasr, who approach Islamic studies from a perennialist philosophical perspective and to engage in theological reflection on topics such as Islam and environmentalism or peace studies. This group includes many young scholars from the Muslim world and the new cohort of born or raised in America children of Muslim immigrant families.[48]

The academic culture of Sufi studies with the most similarity to the U.S. is probably that of France where an Akbarian school of Sufi studies is represented by the works of Michel Chodkewitz, Denis Gril, and others. A Moroccan branch of the *Shādhiliyyah* Sufi Order, known as the *Bouchichiyyah*, is the prevalent *ṭarīqah* affiliation of many French Sufi academics. A common lineage runs through Michel Valsan (1974), a Romanian student of Mircea Eliade and Schuon who settled in Paris and attracted his own circle of French convert disciples. He published a journal, *Etudes Traditionelles*, that featured a perennialist approach to Sufism and other fields of religious studies.

The perennialist school influences academic publishing on Islam through Nasr's editing of a series from SUNY Press and the efforts of the Islamic Texts Society/Fons Vitae, which concentrates on translations of Sufi classics and Islamic and other spiritualities in a Traditionalist mode.

In the American (immigrant) Muslim community outside of the academic world, the most sympathy would have been felt for Ismail al-Faruqi's approach to Islamic thought, which, like that of the modern Islamist movements such as the Muslim brotherhood (*Ikhwān al-Muslimīn*) and *Jamaat-e-Islami*, would have seen Sufism as decadent, deviant, and superstitious. Contemporary Islamist discourse tends to view cultural adaptations with suspicion, for example, the use of music in some Sufi traditions, and the general sense is that western or academic interest in Sufism is largely irrelevant to the concerns of Muslims. More recently, an interest in elements of sober Sufism such as teachings of righteousness (*iḥsān*) and the purification of the soul (*tazkiyyah al-nafs*), have managed to bridge some of the gap between diaspora Muslims interested in spirituality and puritan elements in the leadership of the community.

Interestingly, current academic approaches to Sufism and some of its more recent inroads into Muslim discourse in North America share certain intellectual roots. These would be the teachings of the Algerian *Shādhily* Sufi, Shaykh al-Alawi (d. 1934) and his interpreters,[49] popularized among academics and non-Muslims through Schuon, Lings, and Nasr in one lineage.[50] Among diaspora Muslims these teachings have been disseminated through contemporary Sufi-related groups with *Shādhily* backgrounds such as the *Murābiṭūn*, the Zaytuna Institute (Hamza Yusuf), and the *Hāshimī-Darqawy* under Nuh Ha Mim Keller.[51]

The Pakistani-American scholar, Fazlur Rahman's, relationship to Sufism was quite complex. He seems very much to have been the heir to the rationalism of the modernists such as Muhammad Abduh (d. 1905) and Muhammad Iqbal (d. 1938) in finding the superstitious and fantastic claims of Sufism and its popular manifestations in folk practices distasteful. In his comprehensive overview of the tradition from a Modernist perspective, *Islam*, Rahman coined the expression "neo-Sufism."[52] This spawned about two debates of intellectual debate about whether Sufism had in fact changed its focus in a significant way during the eighteenth-century reform movements to emphasize hadith studies and the role of the Prophet Muhammad rather than the gnostic monism of Ibn al-ʿArabī.[53]

At the same time Rahman's erudition in Islamic philosophy provided readings of Sufis such as Ahmed Sirhindi (d. 1625)[54] and Ibn al-ʿArabī (d. 1240)[55] that inspired interest in Sufism among his students. One may even speak of a "Chicago" school of literary readings of Sufism by scholars such as Michael Sells,[56] Tom Emil Homerin,[57] and later Franklin Lewis,[58] influenced in turn by other Chicago faculty in Near Eastern languages such as Jaroslav Stetkeyvich (Arabic literature) and Heshmat Moayyad (Persian literature).[59]

Other of Fazlur Rahman's students who worked on aspects of Sufism ironically became interested in popular forms and the role of local cultures, although with reference to classical texts and teachings. These include studies on Sufi musicians in Egypt and Morocco by one of the first figures trained in both religious studies and Islam at the University of Chicago Divinity School, Earle Waugh,[60] and Fazlur Rahman's later students in Near Eastern languages and civilizations, Valerie Hoffman[61] and Marcia Hermansen.[62]

Another of the academic lineages of American scholars of Sufism descends from Annemarie Schimmel (2003) who taught at Harvard from 1967 until her retirement in 1992.[63] Schimmel's forte was a deep acquaintance with the Muslim world, especially Turkey and South Asia, and her interest in classical and vernacular languages and poetry. She wrote entire monographs on such individual Sufis such as Iqbal (*The Sound of Gabriel's Wing*), Rumi (*The Triumphal Sun*), and Mir Dard (*Pain and Grace*). She also authored an encyclopedic work on Sufism entitled *Mystical Dimensions of Islam*.[64] Schimmel's approach was linguistic and thematic, stressing translation and interpretation as well as historical description. Carl Ernst, Schimmel's student, also follows the course of a sympathetic presentation of Islam and Sufism with an emphasis on South Asian materials. Ernst discusses the roots of the academic study of Sufism[65] in the West.[66]

According to Ernst, western perceptions of Sufism were shaped by the colonial experiences of the eighteenth and nineteenth centuries. Early colonial administrators perceived Sufis as deceptive *faqīrs* and mendicant dervishes and exaggerated their exotic nature. Later colonial officials intellectually embraced Sufis as kindred spirits in an era when religion's hold was loosening in Europe. In their writings, largely based on Persian mystical verses, Sufis were understood as poets, wine-drinkers, and freethinkers whose "pantheism" and "theosophy" were not associated with official Islam.[67] Other of Schimmel's students who have worked on various aspects of Sufism include Peter Awn, James Morris, Ali Asani and Arthur Buehler.

Among other scholars of Sufism based at U.S. universities whose students have proceeded in the field are Hamid Algar at Berkeley who trained Alan Godlas and Barbara Schlegell. Interestingly, in terms of intellectual cultures, Princeton, despite have a strong program in Islamic studies, has produced only one American scholar of Sufism, Jonathan Katz. UCLA, despite not having a Sufi specialist, has graduated scholars of Sufism such as Vincent Cornell and Qamar al-Huda.

Gerhard Bowering at Yale and his colleagues were the mentors of Jerry Elmore, Jamal Elias, Shehzad Bashir, Joseph Lumbard, and Amina Steinfels, whose careful studies of classical Sufis follow a tradition of strong philological training and historical and hermeneutic interests.[68] Bowering worked at the McGill Institute of Islamic Studies in Montreal with Landolt, as did Ahmet Karamustafa of St. Louis University.

In his review article on the historiography of Sufi studies, Alexander Knysh observes the existence of "intellectual dynasties" descending from the great European scholars Massignon to Nwyia (1925-1980) and Corbin (1903-1978); from Nicholson (1868-1945) to Arberry (1905-1969); in Germany from Richard Hartman (1881-1965) to Helmut Ritter (1892-1971) and Fritz Meier (1912-1998), and then from Meier to Richard Gramlich (1925-2006) and Bernd Radtke.[69] We note the development of a similar process of scholarly "silsilas" in the American context. It is interesting and instructive to note which scholars studied with which mentors and from which institutions they graduated. While not absolutely determinative, it is clear that only major universities specialized in the field of Islamic studies have produced career scholars of Sufism and that the methodological perspectives and commitments of the mentors have often profoundly affected the research agendas and choices of their pupils.

An academic program with a strong initial record in Sufi studies is the Research Triangle consortium in North Carolina where Bruce Lawrence, Carl Ernst, and for a time, Vincent Cornell, and more recently Ebrahim Moosa, directly worked in this field. Among their graduates in Sufi studies over the past decade or so have been Omid Safi, Scott Kugle, Rob Rosehnal, and Zia Inayat Khan.

Teaching Sufism / Islamic Mysticism

The author of this paper conducted an informal survey on the teaching of Sufism through a broadcast e-mail to the list of scholars of Islam in the American Academy of Religion. Total responses came to about 30, to which was added some 20 more based on personal acquaintance. The results of the survey, roughly speaking, indicate that about 90 percent of the faculty teaching courses on Sufism are in the departments and programs of religion, religious studies, or theology, and less than 10 percent are in area studies programs.

Introductory courses of Islam were offered at all institutions that responded to the survey. During a typical 14-week term, more than two weeks on average were spent on Sufism within such courses. About half of the survey respondents identified themselves as having a primary interest and expertise in Sufism within the sub-fields of Islamic studies.

The first survey of Sufism in English was Arberry's *The Mystics of Islam*. Some 30 years later (1975), Annemarie Schimmel published *Mystical Dimensions of Islam*. This demonstrates how far the field developed by that point, with translations, critical editions, and studies of individual mystics and regional mystical sub-cultures available so that a much more detailed presentation of Sufism's history could be made. Now, some thirty more years after Schimmel's work, we find quite a selection of works that introduce Sufism for an undergraduate or popular audience, including Carl Ernst's *Shambhala Guide to Sufism*, Alexander Knysh's *Islamic Mysticism: A Short History*[70] and William Chittick's *Sufism: A Short Introduction*.[71]

An introductory text used in many introductory courses on Islam is *The Vision of Islam* by William Chittick and Sachiko Murata. This could be considered the first textbook on Islam written from a perennialist "Sufi" perspective that focuses on philosophical or theological doctrines rather than on historical events and the activities of prominent individuals within the tradition.

NOTES

1   Earlier review articles on Sufi studies include R. Caspar, "Muslim Mysticism: Tendencies in Recent Research" (originally published in 1962 in French), *Studies in Islam*, ed. Merlin L. Swartz (New York: Oxford, 1981), pp.164-181 and Seyyed Hossein Nasr, "Studies in Sufism in the 1950s and 1960s," *Hamdard Islamicus* (1989), vol.xii, no.2, pp.1-9 (with almost no American contributions noted). Each of these early review articles concluded that most work to date had focused on the edition and dissemination of the basic texts of Sufism, noted the preponderance of work on Ibn al-ʿArabī and the role of "traditionalist" scholars. Each author expressed a certain optimism that exposure to works of classical Sufism would prove valuable in the Muslim world in countering the influence of literalists such as Wahhabis.

    Later in the 1970s David P. Brewster published an article, "The Study of Sufism: Towards a Methodology," *Religion* (1976), vol.6, pp.31-47. The recent article by Alexander Knysh, "Historiography of Sufi Studies in the West" *A Companion to the History of the Middle East,* ed. Youssef M. Choueiri (Oxford: Blackwell, 2005), pp.106-131 largely refrains from commenting on recent (post-1970s) American scholarship and developments and is heavily slanted towards the philological approach.

2   Here I am referring to universities and research institutes that follow a "modern" western model of disciplinary scholarship, although the situation in traditional *madrasahs* would probably not include much scope for the study of Sufism in a historical critical or even in a practical sense.

3   Timothy Mitchell, "The Middle East in the Past and Future of Social Science," *The Politics of Knowledge: Area Studies and the Disciplines*, ed. David L. Szanton (Berkeley: University of California Press, 2004), p.82.

4   Ahmad Dallal, "The Study of Islam in American Scholarship: the Persistence of Orientalist Paradigms," http://francestanford.stanford.edu/Conferences/Papers/Dallal.pdf. (At the time of going to the press, the referenced webpage was no longer available).

5   Timothy Mitchell argues that the established programs of "Oriental Civilizations" at major American universities focus on archeology and museums may have ultimately impeded the study of later Islamic civilization in the region. Mitchell, "The Middle East in the Past and Future of Social Science," p.78.

6   Rashid Khalidi, 1994 MESA presidential address, "Is there a Future for Middle Eastern Studies?," http://fp.arizona.edu/mesassoc/Bulletin/Pres%20Addresses/khalidi.htm, addresses Richard Martin's volume.

7   David L. Szanton, "The Origin, Nature, and Challenges of Area Studies in the U.S.," *The Politics of Knowledge: Area Studies and the Disciplines*, ed. David L. Szanton (Berkeley: University of California Press, 2004), p.7.

8   Ibid., pp.5-6.

9   For a history of Title VI see "The History of Title VI and Fulbright-Hays: An Impressive International Timeline," http://www.ed.gov/about/offices/list/ope/iegps/history.html.

10 In addition to the National Research Centers, Foreign Language and Area Studies Fellowships (FLAS), and International Research and Studies (IRS), Title VI today supports other interrelated programs including: the Undergraduate International Studies and Foreign Language Program (UISFL); Language Resource Centers (LRCs); and American Overseas Research Centers (AORCs), http://www.ed.gov/about/offices/list/ope/iegps/title-six.html.

11 Richard D. Brecht and William P. Rivers, *Language and National Security in the 21st Century: the Role of Title VI/Fulbright-Hays in Supporting National Language Capacity in the U.S.* (Dubuque, Iowa: Kendall/Hunt Pub. Co., 2000).

12 http://www.library.uiuc.edu/administration/collections/tools/development statement/south_and_west_asian_studies.htm.

13 Jeffrey J. Kuenzi, *Foreign Language and International Studies: Federal Aid under Title VI of the Higher Education Act*, http://digital.library.unt.edu/govdocs/crs//data/2005/upl-meta-crs-7881/RL31625_2005Jun21.pdf?PHPSESSID=aef02ba92c72ceb1f12c6889b7497d2b.

14 Wade Clark Roof, *A Generation of Seekers: the Spiritual Journeys of the Baby Boom Generation* (San Francisco: Harper Collins, 1993).

15 Alexander Knysh, "The Historiography of Sufi Studies," p.122.

16 Nicholas B. Dirks, "South Asian Studies: Futures Past," *The Politics of Knowledge: Area Studies and the Disciplines*, ed. David L. Szanton (Berkeley: University of California Press, 2004), p.361.

17 Arvind Sharma, "Towards a Definition of the Phenomenology of Religion," *Milla wa Milia* (1976), vol.16, p.17, as summarized in Mujiburrahman, "The Phenomenological Approach in Islamic Studies: An Overview of a Western Attempt to Understand Islam," *Muslim World* (2001), vol.91, no.3/4, pp.425-449.

18 David P. Brewster wrote in 1976, "Sufism, together with Islamic art and architecture, represents one of the more 'immediate' and accessible aspects of Islam for the western student," in "The Study of Sufism," p.31.

19 Steven M. Wasserstrom, *Religion after Religion: Gershom Scholem, Mircea Eliade, and Henry Corbin at Eranos* (Princeton: Princeton University Press, 1999).

20 Louis Massignon has been studied as a scholar in several scholarly treatments and articles, for example by Jacques Waardenberg, Julian Baldick, and Herbert Mason.

Notes

21 Asin Palacios titled one of his books, "El Islam Christianizado" and Massignon identified al-Hallaj with Christ and his doctrines with the entry of incarnation theology into Islam through Sufism. Brewster mentions Caspars work as well as the works (in French) of Anawati and Gardet *Mystique Musulmane: Aspects et Tendances*, 2nd edn. (Paris, 1968) in this regard. Some aspects of this phenomenon are discussed in Knysh, "Historiography of Sufi Studies in the West," pp.116-117,123.

22 Edward Said, *Orientalism* (New York: Vintage, 1979).

23 I find Voll's thesis problematic and refer to it again later in the essay.

24 A.J. Arberry, *Sufism: An Account of the Mystics of Islam* (London: Georger Allen and Unwin, 1950), p.119. Cited in John Voll, "Changing Western Approaches to Islamic Studies and Seyyed Hossein Nasr's Vision," *Beacon of Knowledge*, eds. Mohammad H. Faghfoory and Huston Smith (Louisville, KY: Fons Vitae, 2003), p.83.

25 John Voll, "Changing Western Approaches to Islamic Studies," pp.78,87-88.

26 Fazlur Rahman, "Islamic Studies and the Future of Islam," *Islamic Studies: A Tradition and Its Problems*, ed. Malcolm H. Kerr (Malibu, CA: Undena Publications, 1980), p.131.

27 See Waardenburg, *L'Islam dans la miroir*, pp.77-78.

28 Cheryl Bernard, "Civil Democratic Islam: Partners, Resources, Strategies," *Rand Report* (2004), http://www.rand.org/pubs/monograph_reports/MR1716/index.html.

29 Gisela Webb, *Windows of Faith: Muslim Women Scholar-Activists in North America* (New York: Syracuse University Press, 2000).

30 *Journal of Islamic Studies*, Centre for Contemporary Islam, University of Cape Town, Vol. 26, 2006.

31 Yvonne Haddad, *Muslims of America* (New York: Oxford University Press, 1993).

32 Fred M. Denny and Earle H. Waugh, eds., *The Shaping of an American Islamic Discourse: A Memorial to Fazlur Rahman* (Atlanta: Scholars Press, 1998).

33 For a discussion of the Islamization of Knowledge Project, see Faruqi's own pamphlet *Islamization of Knowledge* (Herndon, VA: International Institute of Islamic Thought, 1982); and Leif Stenberg, *The Islamization of Science: Four Muslim Positions Developing an Islamic Modernity*, Lund Studies in History of Religions, no.6 (New York: Coronet Books, 1996).

34 Mark Sedgwick, *Against the Modern World* (New York: Oxford, 2004); and Carl Ernst, "Traditionalism: The Perennialist Philosophy in Islamic Studies" *Middle East Studies Association Bulletin* (1994), vol.28, no.2, pp.176-81, http://www.unc.edu/~cernst/Traditionalism.htm.

35 Jane Smith, "Seyyed Hossein Nasr: Defender of the Sacred and Islamic Traditionalism," *The Muslims of America*, ed. Y.Y. Haddad (New York: Oxford University Press, 1993), pp.80-95.

36 Published as *Knowledge and the Sacred* (Edinburgh University Press, 1981). Annemarie Schimmel was also invited to give the lectures in 1991-1992, which is notable given the emphasis on Sufi studies as representing Islamic theology in this series. Muhammad Arkoun was the only Muslim intellectual besides Nasr to be invited thus far.

37 For example, Bill Moyers, "Islam and Nature" as well as the "Traditional World of Islam" series that was created for the "World of Islam" festival in London in 1976.

38 Ibn al-ʿArabī was known as "al-shaykh al-akbar," the greatest shaykh, and thus his teachings are said to constitute an Akbarian school transmitted through intellectual and spiritual successors.

39 James Morris was among the group that studies at the Iranian Academy with Nasr.

40 William Chittick is a noted translator and interpreter of Sufi thought, in particular works of the school of Ibn al-ʿArabī.

41 Murata, like her husband Chittick, studied at the Iranian Academy with Nasr during the 1970s. She is the author of *The Tao of Islam* and works on Sufism and Chinese thought.

42 Martin Lings was Schuon's deputy in England and authored *The Book of Certainty* and *A Sufi Saint of the Twentieth Century*.

43 Victor Danner was Professor of Islamic Studies at Indiana University Bloomington, and authored *Ibn Ata Allah, the Book of Wisdom* (Paulist Press, 1978).

44 Huston Smith is a major figure in the study of world religions from a philosophical and "traditionalist" perspective.

45 Hartley Films, 1979.

46 "The Inner Life" was part of a series "Traditional World of Islam" prepared on the occasion of the World of Islam festival in 1976.

47 "I am a Sufi: I am a Muslim," 52 min., 1996.

48 For example, Waheed el-Ansary, Ibrahim Kailn.

49 On Alawi, see Martin Lings, *A Sufi Saint of the Twentieth Century* (Cambridge, U.K: Islamic Texts Society, 1993).

50 The *Shādhiliyyah Maryamiyyah*.

51 Marcia Hermansen, "The 'Other' Shadhilis of the West" *The Shadhiliyya*, ed. Eric Geoffroy (Paris: Maisonneuve et Larose, 2005), pp.481-499.

52 Fazlur Rahman, *Islam* (New York: Anchor, 1968), pp.239-240.

53 On the Neo-Sufism debate, see the extensive critique of the concept in R.S. O'Fahey and Bernd Radtke, "Neo-Sufism Reconsidered," *Der Islam*; and the discussion in R.S. O'Fahey, *Enigmatic Saint: Ahmad ibn Idris and the Idrisi Tradition* (Evanston, IL: Northwestern University Press, 1990), pp.1-9.

54 Fazlur Rahman edited and commented on some of his writings in selected letters of Shaykh Ahmad Sirhindi.

Notes

55 Rahman did not produce scholarly work on Ibn al-ʿArabī but often taught courses on his thought due to student demand. He did produce a monograph on the more philosophical elements of the thought of Mulla Sadra Shirazi that could be considered an alternative to the more "perennialist" reading of Seyyed Hossein Nasr.

56 Michael Sells, *Early Islamic Mysticism: Sufi, Qur'an, Miʿraj, Poetic and Theological Writings* (New York and Mahwah: Paulist Press, 1996). He translated some of Ibn al-ʿArabī's poetry in *Stations of Desire*.

57 Homerin has worked extensively on Egyptian Sufi poet, ʿUmar ibn al-Farīd in *Sufi Verse, Saintly Life* (New Jersey: Paulist Press, 2001).

58 Franklin Lewis, *Rumi Past and Present: East and West* (Oxford: Oneworld, 2000).

59 *Reorientations: Studies in Arabic and Persian Poetry*, ed. Suzanne Stetkevych (Bloomington: University of Indiana Press, 1994).

60 Waugh is Canadian and has spent most of his career at the University of Alberta. *The Munshidin of Egypt: Their World and Their Song* (University of South Carolina, 1989); and *Memory, Music and Religion: Morocco's Mystical Chanters* (University of South Carolina, 2005).

61 Valerie J. Hoffman, *Sufism, Mystics, and Saints in Modern Egypt* (Columbia: University of South Carolina Press, 1995).

62 Author of the present article who works on South Asian Sufism and Sufis in America, among other topics.

63 A brief autobiography is available at http://www.acls.org/op21.htm. Also see Stefan Wild, "In Memoriam of Annemarie Schimmel," (in German) *Die Welt des Islams* (2003), vol.43, no.2, pp.131-142.

64 Annemarie Schimmel, *Mystical Dimensions of Islam* (U.S: University of North Carolina Press, 1978).

65 Carl Ernst, *Shambhala Guide to Sufism*, (Boston: Shambhala, 1997), pp.1-18.

66 Annemarie Schimmel. Another treatment of the influence of Sufism on the premodern West is Michel Chodkiewicz, "La réception du Soufisme par l'occident: conjectures et certitudes," *The Introduction of Arabic Philosophy into Europe*, eds. Charles Butterworth and Blake Kessel (Leiden: E.J. Brill, 1994), pp.136-149.

67 Carl Ernst, *Shambhala Guide to Sufism*, (Boston: Shambhala, 1997), pp.1-18.

68 http://www.yale.edu/religiousstudies/fields/islamic.html#graduates.

69 Alexander Knysh, "Historiography of Sufi Studies in the West," *A Companion to the History of the Middle East,* Youssef M. Choueiri (Oxford: Blackwell, 2005), pp.106-131,122.

70 Leiden-Boston-Köln: E.J. Brill, 2000.

71 Oxford: Oneworld, 2000.

Teaching Islam in American Theological Schools

JANE I. SMITH

The Struggle for Globalization

GLOBALIZATION has been a recognized goal of theological education in North America for over a quarter of a century. In the late
1970s, under the leadership of Union Theological Seminary's Donald
Shriver, the Association of Theological Schools in the U.S. and
Canada developed a small task force to begin thinking how its member
schools could broaden their curricula to include the study of both
global Christianity and other world religions beyond Christianity and
Judaism. By 1996, the revised standards of the ATS mandated that
member theological schools and seminaries report progress toward the
goal of globalization.

Under this initiative, a few institutions began to offer courses in
world religions, although many looked to fulfill the requirement of
globalization by fortifying their study of Christianity and Christian
institutions in other parts of the world. Schools of theology associated
with universities generally had, and continue to have, access to the
offerings in world religions that are available to undergraduate and
graduate institutions. Yet for the most part, students wishing to learn
more about the religion of Islam in most seminaries and theological
schools had difficulty finding anything beyond the minimal offerings
in comparative religions, if that. An exception could be found in the

seminaries that had developed programs in Christian mission, especially those that focused on mission work in Islamic countries.

By the 1990s, however the situation began to change significantly, due to both the impetus toward globalization and international politics. World events dictated the necessity in the minds of some theological school administrators for changing the curriculum by adding courses or segments of courses, and introducing students to the basics of Islamic faith. Seminaries offer a range of degrees, but their bread and butter courses are those designed to fill the requirements of the Master of Divinity (generally three-year) degree that prepares students for pastoral ministry, and some kind of Master of Arts or Master of Theological Studies (generally two-year) degree offering more specialized study in one of the theological disciplines. A few schools of theology in the ATS, even those not university-affiliated, have offered programs focused on the study of Islam for a long time. Such institutions, however, continue to be rare among the more than 250 member schools of the ATS.

There is little question the Twin Tower attacks of 9/11, a defining moment for America, had an impact on theological education. All evidence is that efforts by conservative and evangelical Christian denominations to bolster the missionary presence in Muslim countries have increased as a result of 9/11, and the seminaries and theological schools providing the training for that missionary presence have reinforced their curricular offerings. Other schools have responded to the need that they recognize for their students, future pastors, and teachers, to have at least some rudimentary exposure to who Muslims are, what they believe, and, in some cases, how Christians can begin to think theologically about a religion that claims nearly as many members worldwide as Christianity. Some have filled this gap by creating new faculty positions in world religions or comparative theology and ethics. Others have hired adjunct teachers, occasionally Muslims but usually Christians with some training in Islam, to help fill the educational gap. The few existing programs in the study of Islam have been maintained or strengthened, and a few new programs featuring Islamic studies in the context of general comparative studies have been developed.

Despite these efforts, the majority of schools affiliated with the ATS do not offer any specific instruction about Islam. Many state they are eager to do so but constrained by budgetary concerns, while others do not believe that there is room in their already full curricula for the study of any faith outside of the Judeo-Christian fields.

The Nature of the Project

The general study, which addresses the ways in which seminaries, schools of theology, and divinity schools who are part of the member-ship of the Association of Theological Schools[1] teach about Islam, has not been a comprehensive, scientific, questionnaire-blanketing kind of project. It rather was carried out through a series of conversations with colleagues who teach, or might be interested in teaching, about the religion of Islam in their particular ATS-related institutions. The information is "soft," specific in some cases, and generalized in others. Many of the persons who contributed, both in person and in written communication, were not known personally to the author, while oth-ers were friends and colleagues over the years who worked together to communicate accurate information about Islam to audiences of stu-dents preparing for some kind of religious vocation. In all but a few exceptional cases, the students who take courses at ATS institutions are working at the graduate level.

No two institutions that offer anything about Islam look exactly alike, and the most fair approach might simply be to list the approxi-mately 40 institutions that reported back on their Islamic offerings one by one, showing the relationship of the coursework on Islam to the mission and direction of the school and the nature and constituency of the study body. Instead, this study clusters the responding institutions into five different groupings, suggesting some patterns to the ways institutions respond to the perceived need to teach about Islam. More schools than those represented here probably do offer some instruction in Islam as a religion, a historical force, a reality in the multicultural West, or a field of Christian service. Those faculty members and administrators who have provided responses to inquiries, however, suggested the ways Islam is taught, the reasons participating institutions support such teaching, and issues of most concern to the students who take these courses. Suggested groupings are:[2]

- Programs to train students for Christian ministry in Islamic contexts

- Segments on Islam as part of general (usually introductory) courses on comparative religion or comparative ethics

- One or two courses on Islam dealing with the basics of the faith and/or the relationship of Islam and Christianity (historically, doctrinally)

- Courses or parts of courses devoted to the study of Islam as part of interfaith studies

- A developed curriculum or program in the study of Islam

Generalizations are unavoidable, and may be justified to the extent they suggest a broad picture of a field of study that is changing rapidly. A similar study ten years hence might reveal that significant changes have taken place and that many more Christian theological institutions have taken up the study of Islam. Quotations in the material to follow are taken directly from e-mail communications from these teachers and administrators, and thus are not referenced in the endnotes.

Programs to Train Students for Christian Ministry in Islamic Contexts

Training candidates for service on the mission field has been an important commitment of many seminaries and schools of theology from their founding until today. Taking seriously what they believe to be the mandate of Jesus in chapter 28 of the book of Matthew, to go into all nations making disciples, many have instituted strong programs of mission training. Often the mission field has been a Muslim country, from the Middle East to the Islamic countries of Africa to Indonesia and other areas of South and Southeast Asia. On the reasonable assumption that the more missionaries know about the religion and culture of the people to whom they are to minister the more effective they will be, such institutions have sometimes offered specific training in the faith and practice of Islam, as well as in methods by which Muslims might be introduced to Jesus Christ.

The creation of the World Council of Churches in 1948 led to the beginnings of serious discussions (sometimes disagreements) between those who supported the enterprise of evangelization and those who felt that the time had come rather for conversation and better interfaith understanding. Since that time, some theological schools have undergone long processes of interpretation leading to the view that the original call to train men and women to bring Muslims to Christ is now better understood as the call to train future religious leaders – Christian and Muslims – to know enough about Islam to be able to engage in serious dialogue and interaction.

Many schools, however, remain firm in their conviction that the work of the church, and the preparation provided for training religious leaders, must be for the purpose of spreading the gospel. A few examples illustrate this continuing effort.

Professor George Martin, Associate Dean of the Billy Graham School of Missions, Evangelism and Church Growth at Southern Baptist Theological Seminary in Louisville, KY, who himself served with the International Mission Board in Indonesia, acknowledges that Islam is a major world religion that graduates must know how to address in their ministries. Students taking courses on Islam at SBTS typically are interested in vocational ministry in an Islamic context, and particularly looking in their courses for effective ministry strategies among Muslims. When asked whether his own theological position influenced his teaching, he professed a double intent: objectivity in describing Islam historically and phenomenologically, but at the same time making evident his evangelical concern for the effectiveness of Christian ministry among Muslims.

On two of Gordon Conwell Seminary's three campuses, Professor of World Missions Timothy Tennent teaches a regular course on Introduction to Islam. His class at the main Hamilton, MA campus attracts some 70 students. While the course is not billed as an introduction to mission, the texts reflect an orientation of preaching God's message of salvation for the purpose of mission.3 The fall 2006 syllabus proposes as a goal "to demonstrate...how the gospel can be most effectively communicated to members of the Islamic faith..." Tennent, who has a Th.M. degree in Islamic Studies from Princeton, gives his students the option to interview a Muslim and discuss their faith with that person, spend at least five hours witnessing to Muslims, or provide a theologically informed apologetic to challenges Islam poses to the Christian faith.4

Similar purposes are served in the teaching of Islam at Southern Baptist Theological Seminary in Wake Forest, NC. "...Students take the courses primarily with missions in mind," says Assistant Professor of Missions and Islamic Studies Ant Greenham. "They are evangelicals who wish to win Muslims to Christ." SBTS's mission statement refers specifically to the "Great Commission" of Matthew 28, and Greenham affirms the importance of students knowing how to interact meaningfully with Muslims with a view to fulfilling this mandate. He is clear that his own theology does affect his teaching about Islam, and draws on his experience as a diplomat in the Middle East. While he strongly advocates friendship between Muslims and Christians as the best way to introduce people to Jesus Christ, whom he calls "the greatest friend of all." Greenham also warns that Christians must not fool themselves into thinking that Muslims are not mounting serious efforts today "to bring the world under the sway of Islam."

Dallas Theological Seminary and Southwestern Baptist Theological Seminary in Ft. Worth, TX share the services of Southwestern's Associate Professor of Missions Tony Maalouf. His Dallas course, "Ministry in Muslim Context," puts forth the objectives of a serious study of Islamic history, doctrine and practice, as well as "...developing a strategy to win the Muslim person to the love of Christ in an attempt to achieve the Great Commission among the nations." Maalouf is from Amman, Jordan, and a member of the Evangelical Free Church. At Southwestern he teaches "Christian Inquiry into Islamic Faith and Practice."5

Several other institutions identify their work in Islam as mission-oriented. Asbury Theological Seminary's Dale Walker, for example, says that the one course they offer on Islam carries the central theme of mission along with a basic survey of the religion.[6] Walker is on the faculty of Asbury's E. Stanley Jones School of World Mission and Evangelism. The program in the study of Islam at Fuller Seminary in California, one of the largest evangelical seminaries in the world, will be detailed in the last category below.

Segments on Islam as Part of Courses on Comparative Religion/Ethics

Some schools that teach about Islam in the context of other courses may still do so with an emphasis on training students for Christian service (otherwise called mission work). At Pittsburgh Theological Seminary, for example, Associate Professor of Mission and Evangelism Scott Sunquist is the only faculty member trained to teach Islam, and he does so as part of general courses on religion and Christian mission. No specific study of Islam is currently required, although that may change as the curriculum is reviewed. Evolving contexts of ministry, in which the school is interested, as Sunquist says, "can seldom avoid relating to Islamic communities and local Muslims in our communities." Sunquist says that "objective" approaches to religion have proven to be a myth, and that the task of a seminary instructor is to help students understand their own theological development in light of religious pluralism.

Many institutions favor training for dialogue over preparation for mission. Openness to learning from other religious traditions, for example, is one of the stated goals of Professor Richard Randolph's course entitled "Engaging World Religions through Ethics" at St. Paul School of Theology in Kansas City, MO. In this course, which covers Hinduism, Buddhism, Judaism, and Islam, students are encouraged to develop basic tools for interacting dialogically with members of other religious traditions. Also part of the St. Paul curriculum is "Engaging World Religions at Home," offered by Vern Barnet, which contains a segment on Islam. The course concludes with a consideration of how Christians can understand their faith in relation to others. Barnet also writes about Islam and his Muslim friends in a column for the *Kansas Star Weekly* called "Faiths and Beliefs."

Many institutions profess interest in moving toward full courses on the study of Islam, but are not yet ready in terms of curricular vision or budgetary allotments. Academic Dean Lester Ruiz at New York Theological Seminary regrets the lack of "dedicated" courses on Islam, but says that the school often collaborates with Auburn Seminary to take advantage of their programs on Islam. NYTS faculty often touch on Islam as part of their regularly offered courses in history, theology, and ethics, he says, "as constitutive for any theological education enterprise." Professor Wesley Ariarajah of Drew University Theological School of Theology regrets that no one at the Seminary deals specifically with Islam, although he includes reference to it in his course "Challenge of World Religions to Christian Faith and Practice." One session of the course covers Christian reflection on non-Christian religions.7

Andover Newton Theological School in Newton Centre, MA, offers a basic course on "Hinduism, Buddhism and Islam," taught by Samuel Abbot Professor of Christian Theology S. Mark Heim. The course includes interaction with one of the Islamic centers of Boston. Heim also includes reflection on Islam in his courses on Christian theology of religions.8

Courses Dealing with the Basics of Islam and / or the Relationship of Islam and Christianity

A small but growing number of schools offer one or more courses specifically about Islam, often in the context of the ways Islam has interacted with Christianity over history and in the current context. In his course "Christianity and Islam, Points of Intersection," for example, Paul Fitzpatrick, SM, of Blessed John XIII Seminary in Weston, Massachussetts, looks at personalities and spiritual practices common to the Bible and the Qur'an: Adam, Cain and Abel, the major prophets, Jesus and Mary, prayer, fasting, almsgiving, and loving one's enemies. The more highly motivated students, he says, take the course because they realize the importance of openness to Islam in light of the growing Muslim presence in the U.S. Fitzpatrick reports that students are often interested in learning from the religion of Islam, and are impressed, for example, by the seriousness with which Muslims undertake their disciplines of prayer, fasting, and care for the poor.

Union Theological Seminary in New York City has typically offered little in the area of Islamic studies. Recently it added Roman Catholic theologian Paul Knitter, Emeritus Professor of Theology at Xavier University in Cincinatti, OH, to its faculty. Knitter, who has written extensively about issues of religious pluralism,[9] affirms Union's conviction that to be religious today is to be so inter-religiously. He also acknowledges the particular importance of studying Islam in today's world. "It is the geo-political situation of our world, and especially the politics of the present Administration in Washington," Knitter said, "that make it important, if not urgent, to provide students with a correct understanding and appreciation of Islam." In his classes, he promotes a theology that will enable Christians not just to tolerate but to actively affirm the religion of Islam.

A number of courses try to balance the objective imparting of facts with some attempt to orient Christian students to a personal understanding of the religion. Typical of this genre is the basic "Introduction to Islam" course taught by adjunct faculty member Robert Douglas at Beeson Divinity School of Samford University. Beeson students have a heavy Evangelical orientation, says Douglas, so the course has a certain confessional stamp. Douglas attempts to be balanced, open, and fair, but acknowledges that his approach must be understood contextually: "...one that seeks to be respectful yet stands four square for basic traditional core beliefs of the Church" (the deity and uniqueness of Christ, the reality of the crucifixion and resurrection, and the reality of salvation in and through Christ). The course ends with a consideration of Islamic values and their impact on Christian ministry, and a discussion of how Christians might view Islam.

In other instances, courses introducing Islam to seminary students attempt to present the elements of the faith without presuming any kind of Christian framework. "Basics of Islam," for example, offered by Scott Steinkerchner at Aquinas Institute of Theology in St. Louis, MO, presents the history, development, major divisions, and basic teachings of Islam without expecting students to do any personal theological reflection. The purpose of the course is to understand Islamic teachings and discover some of the ways that Islam is lived out in different world cultures.

At Columbia Theological School in Decatur, GA, Carlos Cardoza-Orlandi, Associate Professor of World Christianity, argues it would be deceitful to deny that his own position as a Christian does not affect the way he teaches about Islam. Nonetheless, he says that while he is not an expert in Islam, and there has been no institutional incentive to teach a course on the topic, he does so with the hope of teaching his students as objectively as possible about such issues as Qur'anic authority, the Crusades, colonialism, and inter-religious relationships. As he demonstrates the variety of interpretations within Islam itself, he presents a range of voices regarding the theological aspects of Muslim-Christian encounter and inter-religious experience. Cardoza-Orlandi is particularly interested in minimizing the effects that stereotypes of Islam produced by American media can have on the public.

Princeton Theological Seminary in NJ has only one faculty member offering a course on Islam. Associate Professor of History of Religions Richard Fox Young, a historian of religion trained as an Indologist rather than an Islamicist, teaches on Islam in America from what he calls a more sociological approach. He identifies Princeton Theological Seminary students as of two types: those who are convinced that members of other faiths are "unsaved" and those who believe that they are. While this question may be of particular interest to some students in relation to Islam, Young makes it clear that in this course it is important to set the salvation question aside and work rather for a deep inter-religious respect.[10] The Seminary's president Iain Torrance specifically encourages this respect. For a long time, Young says, Princeton has not seen itself as preparing students for mission, but faculty increasingly see Islam as a religion that needs to be understood and addressed. This is true not only because of issues of religious violence, but because Islam brings up the whole matter of Abrahamic religions and whether we worship the same God. Young himself says that he is a bit cynical about why Islam seems so important to his colleagues: "It is less Islam itself that interests them than the opportunity Islam presents of asking a new set of questions about ourselves."

One of the few Methodist institutions with a faculty member whose primary task is teaching about Islam is Perkins School of Theology, part of Southern Methodist University in Dallas, TX. According to Robert Hunt, Director of Global Theological Education, Perkins intends to train its students for pastoral ministry that includes enough knowledge about Islam to be able to guide congregations toward good relationships with the Muslim community. "By no means secondary to our concern in teaching Islam," he says, "is to counter the virtual tidal wave of dangerously virulent anti-Islamic and anti-Muslim propaganda being peddled to the Christian public, particularly here in Dallas." A large number of students, he argues, are eager to be given a biblical and theological justification for an essentially pluralist theology of religions, despite their otherwise conservative theological views. Hunt is explicit that his main purpose in teaching is to help students learn to love Muslims as they are in all their diversity as much as to instruct in the basics of Islamic history and doctrine. "In the end, abstract theologies of religion are usually inadequate to the complex reality of relations between religious communities."

Among the most prominent Christian scholars and interpreters of Islam involved in theological education is Professor of Comparative Religion Charles Kimball, who serves both at Wake Forest University Divinity School in Durham, NC, and at the University itself.[11] He teaches one course on Islam specifically in the divinity curriculum. Acknowledging the school's commitment to Christian encounters with people of other traditions, Kimball said, "Islam is the tradition that most students wish to understand better, both because of contemporary events in the Middle East, Pakistan, and Afghanistan and because of the global reach of Islam as the world's second largest religious tradition." Kimball addresses what he calls the "hard issues" in class, such as treatment of Jews in Medina, women in Islam, and violent extremism, trying to show similar ways that Christians have reflected the good and the bad in their own actions. Part of his requirement is for students to interview Muslims in the Durham area and interact with Muslims he brings to class.

Among the few Muslims teaching in ATS-related theological schools is Amir Hussain, Associate Professor of Theological Studies in the Loyola Marymount University Department of Theological Studies.[12] Hussain's special area of interest is contemporary Muslim societies in North America, particularly in Canada. A student of the late Wilfred Cantwell Smith, former Director of Harvard's Center for the Study of World Religions and eminent scholar of Islam, Hussain has helped the school inaugurate the Wilfred and Muriel Smith Collection at the Oviatt Library of CSUN. In his course "Islam and Interreligious Dialogue" Hussain honors Smith, reflecting his style and orientation in his own teaching. In an article, "An Accidental Theologian: Thoughts on Islam in Public and Private Religious Universities,"[13] Hussain discusses the interesting circumstance of teaching Islam as a Muslim in a Catholic school of theology.[14]

Courses or Parts of Courses Devoted to Study of Islam as Part of Interfaith Studies

Partly in response to the ATS insistence that member schools attend to the matter of globalization in their curricula, and also with an awareness of the increasing plurality of American society, some theological institutions are in the process of developing more intentional programs of interfaith or inter-religious studies, of which Islam is inevitably a part. One interesting venture, for example, is led by Paul Numrich at the Theological Consortium of Greater Columbus, OH, whose constituent member ATS schools include the Methodist Theological School, Pontifical College Josephinum, and Trinity Lutheran Seminary. Here an already ecumenical organization takes the next step of going interfaith.

Numrich, who is Associate Professor and Chair of the Program in World Religions and Inter-Religious Dialogue, says the program is "cutting-edge seminary education for an informed clergy in today's complex multi-religious world." He believes that the fact that his is the only joint faculty appointment in the Consortium shows the institutional investment of the three schools in this interfaith venture. Numrich's teaching on Islam, as on other religions, explores the variety of

Christian perspectives on interfaith issues, encouraging students to develop their own perspectives. "We need to train seminarians to be humble, reverent, and charitable to Muslims," says Numrich, stressing the importance of bringing more evangelical and non-pluralist Christians into theological dialogue with Islam.[15]

In a few cases, including that of Amir Hussein above, Muslims serve as members of ATS institution faculties.[16] (Increasingly, though not widely, Muslims are being asked to teach an occasional course in an adjunct status.) One of those faculty members is Ibrahim Abdurrahman Farajaje, Director of the Starr King Luce Project for Multi-Religious Theological Education. Farajaje, an African American, is Dean of the faculty at the Unitarian Universalist Starr King School for the Ministry in Berkeley, and serves on the core doctoral faculty of the Graduate Theological Union. He brings to the project his expertise in the African American Muslim experience and in Moroccan, Caribbean, and Latin American Islam, especially Sufism.

Another African American, a Christian, who has spent much of her life bringing a better understanding of Islam to Christian theological education, is Marsha Snulligan-Haney of the Interdenominational Theological Center in Atlanta, GA.[17] "Our ecumenical Christian institution has a long history of valuing religions of the African Diaspora," she says, "which includes Islam as well as Judaism." Snulligan-Haney argues that Islam in many variations has historically been part of the African–American social context. ITC therefore considers offering courses on Islam to be part of its mission to educate Christian leaders to be informed and involved in local communities. As ordained clergy in a mainstream Protestant denomination where interfaith dialogue and witness is encouraged and resourced, Snulligan-Haney often finds that her students come new to these ideas and discover that openness to Islam or other faiths is a discipline to be examined and learned.

In contrast to some programs in inter-religious studies that are fairly new to the theological curriculum of their host schools, Austin Presbyterian Theological Seminary boasts a commitment to the study of world religions for some 20 years. Professor Whit Bodman, Assistant Professor of Comparative World Religions and a specialist in the study of Islam, holds a position that has been established for nearly that long, although he is relatively new to the institution. Bodman explains that this faculty position is distinct from one in mission and evangelism, also present in the school. According to Bodman, he was hired particularly due to his concentration in Islamic studies, underscoring the institution's recognition of Islam "as the most important coming issue."

Austin Presbyterian intends that Bodman will work in a very public way on relations between Muslims/Islam and the church. Bodman acknowledges that his own theological position clearly affects the way he teaches about Islam, but calls it not so much a doctrinal as an attitudinal stance. "I describe my theology as a pilgrim theology, one that is explorative and takes no doctrine as the final word," he says, insisting that Austin Presbyterian is ultimately an academic and not a religious institution. Students should enter the study of Islam with an attitude of free inquiry that, if done right, will challenge many of their beliefs.

A Developed Curriculum or Program in the Study of Islam

Here we move to consider attention given in a few seminaries and schools of theology to the study of Islam with more than one faculty member and a range of courses offered in the school's curriculum. A few institutions in the ATS have for some years worked on developing a series of courses related to the understanding of Islam, which in some cases have full degree or program status.

Some schools related directly to universities have depended on the offerings of the larger institution to cover the needs of their students. A few others have developed programs of Islamic study within their own curricula. Of the latter, Harvard Divinity School offers the widest range of courses related to Islam. The Dean himself, William Graham, has an appointment in the department of Middle Eastern Studies. Graham thus holds the double title of John Lord O'Brian Professor of Divinity and Murray A. Albertson Professor of Middle Eastern Studies.[18] Since 1999, Victor S. Thomas Professor of Divinity Leila Ahmed, a Muslim, has taught at the school as Professor of women's studies in religion; many of Ahmed's courses include aspects of the study of Islam, including feminism and Islam, and Islam in America.[19] Baber Johansen has served as Professor of Islamic Religious Studies at HDS since 2005, and offers a wide range of courses on Islam including history, Islamic law, religious texts, Qur'an, and theology.[20]

Three visiting faculty also taught there in the 2006-2007 academic year. French political scientist Jocelyne Cesari is Visiting Associate Professor of Islamic Studies and coordinates the Provost Interfaculty Program on Islam in the West.[21] South African Muslim scholar Farid Esack and Moroccan Muslim scholar Fatima Sidiqi served as Visiting Professors during 2006-2007. Harvard Divinity School, while maintaining a Master of Divinity among the several degrees it offers, approaches the study of Islam from a history of religions perspective, influenced to a great extent by the legacy of Wilfred Cantwell Smith. The Divinity School enjoys the resources of the Center for the Study of World Religions, located adjacent to its campus.

Two Roman Catholic institutions have taken the lead in their denominations in providing curricular resources in the study of Islam. One is the University of Notre Dame Department of Theology. Assistant Professor Gabriel Said Reynolds has taken up the mantle of retired Professor David Burrell, one of Notre Dame's most renowned scholars of Islam. Reynold's course "Regarding the Islamic Challenge to Christian Theology," which discusses the Islamic critique of various Christian theological and ecclesiological doctrines, is geared for undergraduate students. Advanced undergraduate and graduate courses, such as "Reading the Qur'an" and "Islamic Origins," primarily attract students in Theology or Middle Eastern Studies from the University.

A number of Ph.D. students have an interest either in Muslim-Christian relations/dialogue today or the mutual influences/interaction of Islam and Christianity in history. For a Catholic institution, says Reynolds, the question of other religions is central to theological reflection. Notre Dame is committed to being an active partner in religious dialogue, and emphasizes Christian-Muslim dialogue. Reynolds believes the environment at Notre Dame leads students to have a more profound interest in Islam. His own theological orientation persuades him that not only should the Qur'an always be read together with the Bible, but that it should also be appreciated as an important part of the biblical tradition.

Another ATS Roman Catholic institution with a considerable history of interest in Islam, one not part of a university, is the Catholic Theological Union in Chicago. CTU was formed immediately after Vatican Council II, firmly rooted in the Council's vision of a Church with a mission to serve humanity in all its diversity. It is now the largest Roman Catholic school of theology and ministry in North America. Associate Professor of Islam Scott Alexander serves as instructor and Director of the Catholic-Muslim Studies Program, assisted by two adjunct professors, both Muslim. According to Alexander, "CTU is dedicated to educating leaders who clearly hear the call of the Council to cooperate, especially with our Muslim sisters and brothers, in the struggle for social justice, the preferential option for the poor, and the upholding of human dignity." Alexander insists, "the privilege of studying Islam and forging relationships of dialogue and love with Muslims has taught me to be a much better Christian than I would have ever been without this opportunity."[22]

Of CTU's student body of about 500, half are men studying for the priesthood and half are lay men and women, as well as some already ordained priests and a few Protestants. A few Muslim students participate in the program. The great majority of the Christian students who take courses on Islam are convinced that dialogue is an important part of the mission of the church, says Alexander, although their personal theologies may differ in terms of openness to pluralism. They recognize that Islamic literacy and facility in Christian-Muslim dialogue will constitute a critical component of pastoral competency in the coming decades. Chicago, the students generally find, is a congenial and convenient place for "getting their feet wet in the dialogue," especially if they come from home contexts in which Christian-Muslim relations are particularly strained.

One particular Islamic studies program has longstanding credibility, and could also have been mentioned in the first category related to programs that train students for Christian ministry in Islamic contexts – that offered by Fuller Seminary. Self-described as evangelical, multi-denominational, international, and multiethnic, Fuller, whose main campus is in Pasadena, CA, is one of the largest evangelical seminaries in the world. Two members of the faculty teach full-time in its program in Islamic Studies and intercultural relations: Assistant Professor Evelyne Reisacher and Professor of Islamic Studies J. Dudley Woodberry. Coordinator of the concentration on Islamic Studies in Fuller's School of International Studies, Woodberry is a senior interpreter of Christian-Muslim relations with many years of missionary experience in Pakistan, Afghanistan, and Saudi Arabia. Woodberry reports that since 9/11, a growing number of students have enrolled in the program from the School of Theology, and that police officers and even the head of the Shura Council of the Islamic Center of Southern California have taken Islamic Studies courses. The theological orientation that characterizes the school, he says, is a broad evangelicalism of over 100 denominations, the largest block from the Presbyterian Church USA.[23]

In Summer 2006 a federally-funded multi-year conflict transformation project was concluded, shared by Fuller and the Salaam Peace and Justice Institute of American University in Washington D.C., a Muslim center for research and practice in mediation and peace-making. Considered the first of its kind to feature interfaith collaboration between Muslims and evangelicals and to develop models for interfaith dialogue, the project was entitled "Creating Collaboration and Reducing Conflict in Muslim-Christian Relationships." It began by interviewing 50 Muslim and Christian leaders as to their views about their own faith and that of the other, and moved through a series of local training sessions designed to give leaders communication skills and models for joint action projects between Christian and Muslim groups. One of the products is a small book entitled *Interfaith Dialogue: A Guide For Muslims*.[24]

Hartford Seminary in Connecticut has an interest in the study, along with an understanding of Islam that extends well over a century. Since 1893, the School has provided curricular offerings designed to teach students about the complex relationship between Christianity and Islam throughout history and in the contemporary world. After the 1910 missionary conference in Edinburgh, Scotland, Hartford Seminary was designated a premier institution for training missionaries to go to Islamic countries. Much of the literature of earlier editions of

The Muslim World journal, begun in 1911, was dedicated to spreading the Gospel to Muslims. As the Protestant church in general began to rethink the distinction between mission and dialogue around the middle of the twentieth century, Hartford Seminary also changed the focus of its Islamic studies from preparation for the mission field to interfaith understanding.

The Seminary's Macdonald Center for the Study of Islam and Christian–Muslim Relations was started in 1973, and is now responsible for the Islamic studies component of the Seminary's M.A. and Doctor of Ministry programs, and its collaborative Ph.D. programs with the University of Exeter. *The Muslim World,* which reaches subscribers in over 65 countries, is now dedicated to the dissemination of scholarly research on Islam and Muslim societies and on historical and current aspects of Christian–Muslim relations.

The Macdonald Center is the only one of its kind among ATS institutions that is co-chaired by a Muslim male, Ibrahim Abu-Rabi,[25] and a Christian female, Jane Smith,[26] both Professors of Islamic Studies and Christian–Muslim Relations. As the faculty in Islamic studies they are joined by Professor Ingrid Mattson,[27] who currently serves as President of the Islamic Society of North America, and Steven Blackburn, Professor of Arabic. Together this faculty provides offerings in Islamic history, law and doctrine; contemporary Islamic societies and communities; Muslim religious life; the study of Qur'an and Arabic, and Christian–Muslim relations. In the last five years, the Macdonald Center assumed another first initiative – developing the only accredited program for Muslim leadership training in the country. The Muslim Chaplain Training program now services over 40 students, preparing both men and women for positions in universities, hospitals, prisons, and the military.

Finally, two Lutheran Seminaries built on their own heritage of training for Christian ministry in Muslim countries. One is Luther Seminary in St. Paul, MN, described by Charles Amjad-Ali, Martin Luther King, J. Professor for Justice and Christian Communities and Director of Luther's Islamic studies program, as an institution with very clearly defined confessional borders and commitments. The Islamic Studies Program was initiated to fulfill an evangelical missionary need of the Evangelical Lutheran Church of America, and was thus mainly focused on the missionary task. "Over the years," says Amjad-Ali, "we have moved towards a combination of that initial concern now mitigated with a dialogical and neighborly concern. We have vacillated between the high missionary calling/enterprise of trying new approaches to conversions and the quest for, and teaching of, transcendent 'eidectic' commonalities approaches." Amjad-Ali teaches advanced/graduate level courses on Islamic theology, Qur'an, history and civilization, religion and politics, and Islam in the modern world.[28] When asked whether his own theology influences the way he teaches about Islam, Amjad-Ali responded, "Of course! This question for me is so obvious that it has almost tautological and even a non-sequitur quality about it." We will always be influenced by our theology, he insists, and will always have a certain anxiety about Islam as the only major post-Christian religion. His students seem fascinated by how Islam deals with the same existential questions that preoccupy western Christian understanding of mission, witness, and faith praxis, yet arrive at very different conclusions. They wonder how these conclusions might have pedagogical values for their own Christian vocation and witness.

At the Lutheran School of Theology in Chicago a team of faculty teaches Islam and Christian-Muslim relations. LSTC has long taken this task seriously, moving itself in much the same direction as Hartford Seminary. The ELCA as a denomination has taken interfaith studies seriously since the late 1960s, and church leaders identified LSTC as one of the schools where they wanted to integrate interfaith concerns with the core curriculum. Interfaith has now become of the "marks" of the seminary, and one of the five "emphases" from which students may choose. Faculty members believe that the challenge of interfaith is so important that to neglect this kind of training would be detrimental to Christian ministry today. Within that interfaith context, the study of Islam is offered by Mark Swanson, Harold S. Vogelaar Professor of Christian-Muslim Studies and Interfaith Relations, and by Ghulam Haider Aasi, a Muslim, and several other adjunct faculty members. Courses in Muslim faith, Islam in the modern world, Qur'an and Christian engagement with Muslims are now being arranged in a two-year cycle, allowing students to move from basic to more advanced courses in Islamic religion and Christian-Muslim relations.[29]

Also deeply involved in the project of teaching Islam at LSTC is the namesake of Swanson's position, Harold Vogelaar, Emeritus Professor of World Religions and Interfaith Dialogue, and now Director of the new Center of Christian-Muslim Engagement for Peace and Justice. Vogelaar, who along with Swanson served many years in the mission field in the Middle East, emphasizes the practical nature of the education that students receive in Islam. He noted that for the past few years, Muslim students lived in the dorms along with other students, and social and practical issues are on the School's agenda. Religious practices such as Muslims performing *wudu'* (ritual washing before prayer), or cultural preferences such as Christian students having dogs for pets, can sometimes present challenges.

In the classroom, Muslim students tend to ask different questions, Vogelaar says, and this can spark lively discussion. "Most difficult for the Muslim students is the critical approach we take toward our sacred texts and traditions. Gradually they have become accustomed to the fact that being critical does not mean being disrespectful." Meanwhile, Christian students find they learn much from their Muslim colleagues about the disciplines of prayer and fasting, and the importance of the oral recitation of sacred texts. Vogelaar says that in his own teaching he tries to model a kind of intellectual and spiritual hospitality that he believes has very deep roots in Christian tradition. Rather than simply rising above the particularities of individual traditions, Vogelaar is convinced "that the intentional vulnerability of interfaith dialogue can only lead to new mutually-comprehensible language and understanding."

Conclusion

We have looked at some of the reasons ATS seminaries and schools of theology support the teaching of Islam in their institutions, the philosophies underlying those decisions, and the pedagogical approaches taken by those who undertake such instruction. Following are some of the reasons students in these schools want to include the study of Islam in their own programs of study, or more specifically the kinds of topics they want to investigate: Muslim scripture, tradition, theology and law; theological pluralism, specifically similarities and differences between Christians and Muslims; Christian theological approaches to religious diversity in general and Islam in particular; religious pluralism in the West: the reality of, and possible reasons for, the rise of Islam in America and Europe; Islam and violence: Islamic theology and interpretations of jihad; the role of Islam in post-colonialism; the welfare of Christians in Muslim states; the welfare of Muslims in an increasingly "Islamophobic" West; gender issues: women in Qur'an and Islamic tradition; changing roles for Muslim women; and potential for cooperation between Christians and Muslims in everything from local projects to global peacemaking.

It remains true that many American seminaries and schools of theology offer no courses or programs in the study of Islam and evince little interest in wanting to change this circumstance. Others "would if they could," or at least indicate such an interest, and may be moving to institute new offerings. Moreover, students at seminaries and divinity schools increasingly want to know more about Islam, and schools are responding both to those interests and to the reality of a world in which educated religious leaders need to know something about this major world religion that is becoming a partner in the American religious scene.

Some faculty members teach with a hope of advancing the cause of the Christian mission, some out of concern for furthering the dialogue, and some with an interest in the academic study of religion. These lines clearly are not distinct, and as circumstances change and new theologies and pedagogies are being advanced, theological schools are trying to stay ahead in formulating their own mission statements as well as in developing new course offerings and re-thinking new faculty position descriptions.

Added to this interesting mix is the fact that a few institutions now have full faculty positions in the study of Islam that are filled by Muslims, and more Muslim students are finding their way into seminary classrooms. This study presents one moment in an evolving scene as American theological education struggles to adapt itself to changing demographics, politics, and theological interpretations.

NOTES

1   Each institution described below is listed as a member on the ATS website.

2   Although the Association of Theological Schools represents institutions in the U.S. and Canada, this study deals primarily with schools located in the U.S.

3   For example, Joshua Massey, "God's Amazing Diversity in Drawing Muslims to Christ," *International Journal of Frontier Missions* (Spring, 2000), vol.17, no.1, pp.5-14.

4   Tennent is the author of *Theology in the Context of Global Christianity: How the Global Church is Influencing the Way We Think About and Discuss Theology* (Michigan: Zondervan, 2007).

5   See Maalouf's *Arabs in the Shadow of Israel: The Unfolding of God's Prophetic Plan for Ishmael's Line* (Michigan: Kregal Publications, 2003).

6   The M.A. Missions Program at Oral Roberts University, says Program Coordinator Chin Do Kham, currently has no course on Islam but is being evaluated with an end to adding such instruction.

7   Wesley Ariarajah's, *Not Without my Neighbour: Issues in Interfaith Relations* (Geneva: World Council of Churches, 1999) has been used as a text in many seminaries in courses on theology and/or world religions.

8   Heim is the author of several works on religious pluralism, including *Salvations: Truth and Difference in Religion* (U.S.: Orbis, 1995) and *Grounds for Understanding: Ecumenical Resources for Responses to Religions Pluralism* (Michigan: Erdmans, 1998).

9   Paul Knitter, *The Myth of Christian Uniqueness* (New York: Orbis, 1987); *Jesus and the Other Names: Christian Mission and Global Responsibility* (New York: Orbis, 1996); *Introducing Theologies of Religion* (New York: Orbis, 2002); and *The Myth of Religious Superiority: Multifaith Explorations of Religious Pluralism* (New York: Orbis, 2005).

10   Young says, "While I cannot say that my classroom is 'theology-free,' I make a concerted effort to put on the brakes and prevent my students from rushing into normativity."

11   See Charles Kimball, *Striving Together: A Way Forward in Christian-Muslim Relations* (New York: Orbis, 1991); *When Religion Becomes Evil* (San Fransisco: Harper, 2002).

12   In some cases, such as this, a university department has status as a member school of the ATS.

13   Amir Hussain, "An Accidental Theologian: Thoughts on Islam in Public and Private Religious Universities," *Crosscurrents* (2006), pp.364-372.

14 See also Hussain's *Oil and Water: Two Faiths, One God* (Kelowna: CopperHouse, 2006).

15 Paul Numrich is the co-author of *Sacred Assemblies and Civil Society: How Religion Matters for America's Newest Immigrants* (New Jersey: Rutgers University Press, 2007).

16 In most cases Muslim faculty hold appointments at non-ATS related institutions, although they occasionally teach at seminaries and schools of theology. Hamid Mavani, for example, a Shiite Muslim, became a faculty member at Claremont Graduate University School of Religion on July 1, 2005, specifically to teach courses on Islam in their M.A. program in Islamic Studies.

17 See Marsha Snulligan-Haney, *Islam and Protestant African American Churches: Responses and Challenges to Religious Pluralism* (U.S.: International Scholars Press, 1999).

18 Among Graham's publications are *Divine and Prophetic Word in Early Islam* (The Netherlands: Mouton & Co.,1977); *Beyond the Written Word: Oral Aspects of Scripture in the History of Religion* (Cambridge: Cambridge University Press, 1987); and *Three Faiths, One God*: The Formative Faith and Practice of Judaism, Christianity, and Islam (Boston: Brill Academic Publishers, 2002).

19 Leila Ahmed is the author of *Women and Gender in Islam: Historial Roots of a Modern Debate* (Connecticut: Yale University Press, 1992).

20 Among Baber Johansen's many publications is *Contingency in a Sacred Law: Legal and Ethical Norms in the Muslim Fiqh* (The Netherlands, Brill, 1999).

21 Jocelyne Cesari's publications include *When Islam and Democracy Meet: Muslims in Europe and the U.S.* (New York and Hampshire, U.K.: Palgrave Macmillan, 2004); and *European Muslims and the Secular State* (Hampshire, U.K. and Burlington, U.S.: Ashgate, 2005).

22 Scott Alexander is editor of *Sisters, Women, Religion and Leadership in Christianity and Islam* (Lanham, MD: Sheed and Ward, forthcoming).

23 Among J. Dudley Woodberry's publications are *Muslims and Christians on the Emmaus Road* (Monrovia, U.S.: MARC Publication, 1989); *Where Muslims and Christians Meet* (California: Zwemer Institute of Muslim Studies, 1989); and *Muslim and Christian Reflections on Peace: Divine and Human Dimensions* (Maryland, U.S., Oxford, U.K.: University Press of America, 2005).

24 Muhammad Shafiq and Mohammed Abu-Nimr, *Interfaith Dialogue: A Guide for Muslims* (Herndon: The International Institute of Islamic Thought: 2007).

25 Among many publications are Ibrahim Abu-Rabi's *Contemporary Arab Thought: Studies in Post-1967 Arab Intellectual History* (London, U.K., Sterling, U.S.: Pluto Press, 2004); *The Blackwell Companion to Contemporary Islamic Thought* (Malden, U.S., Oxford, U.K., Victoria, Australia: Blackwell, 2006).

26 Jane Smith's publications include *Islam in America* (New York: Columbia University Press, 1999); *Muslim Women in America: The Challenge of Islamic Identity Today* (with Y. Haddad and K. Moore) (Oxford: Oxford, 2006); and *Muslims, Christians, and the Challenge of Interfaith Dialogue* (New York: Oxford University Press, 2007).

27 *The Qur'an and its Place in Muslim Societies* (Blackwell, forthcoming).

28 See Amjad-Ali's *Liberation Ethics* (Notre Dam, IN: Center for the Scientific Study of Religion, 1985); *Passion for Change: Reflections on the Healing Miracles of St. Mark* (Rawalpindi, Pakistan: Christian Study Centre, 1989).

29 Mark Swanson is the author of *The Encounter of Eastern Christianity with Early Islam* (The Netherlands: Brill, 2006).

The Constitutionality of Teaching Islam: The University of North Carolina Qur'an Controversy[1]

CHRISTOPHER BUCK

Introduction

THE terrorist events of 9/11 sparked public interest in Islam across the U.S. The attacks riveted world attention on Islam (albeit radical Islamism). Sales of the Qur'an and texts on Islam skyrocketed.

To truly understand Islam, one should begin with the Qur'an, the holy book of Islam. Although there are at least five distinct "responses to modernity" in the Muslim world today,[2] one starts with the Qur'an in the same way that reading the Bible is necessary to understand Christianity. The study of the Qur'an at the university level is a hot topic. One national academic and legal controversy in particular has raised a number of legal and pedagogical issues in academic settings. In summer 2002, the University of North Carolina (UNC) at Chapel Hill initially required incoming freshmen, as part of its Summer Reading Program, to read and discuss Michael Sells's *Approaching the Qur'an: The Early Revelations*.[3] This text, a fresh translation and elucidation of the early Makkan surahs of the Qur'an, was recommended by UNC Islamicist Carl Ernst to promote an understanding of Islam, especially in the wake of the events surrounding the 9/11 terrorist attacks.[4]

Alleging that UNC violated the Establishment Clause of the First Amendment and abridged students' rights to free exercise of religion by obliging incoming freshmen and transfer students to study Islam against their will, a conservative-Christian activist group, the Family Policy Network (FPN), filed suit in the U.S. District Court, Middle District of North Carolina, on July 22, 2002, seeking a preliminary injunction to keep UNC from conducting its summer program. The case was captioned *Yacovelli v. Moeser* (after James Yacovelli, an FPN spokesman, and James Moeser, UNC Chancellor). When the FPN lost, it immediately appealed to the 4th Circuit Court of Appeals, but lost again. This case was widely reported,[5] nationally and internationally, but was not judicially "reported;" that is, the district and appellate decisions were not published.

As Sells commented: "Behind the lawsuit is an old missionary claim that Islam is a religion of violence in contrast to Christianity, a religion of peace. In effect, the plaintiffs are suing the Koran on behalf of the Bible."[6] While America was involved abroad in Afghanistan and Iraq in the aftermath of 9/11, a clash of religions was occurring at home.

What the national press appears not to have covered yet is a later challenge filed in 2004, which also lost on appeal. The Court applied technicalities of the *Lemon* test along with the endorsement and coercion tests, and the challenge failed. In his decision, Chief Judge N. Carlton Tilley, Jr. ruled:

> *Approaching the Qur'an* simply cannot be compared to religious practices that have been deemed violative of the *Establishment Clause*, such as posting the Ten Commandments, reading the Lord's Prayer, or reciting prayers in school. The book does include surahs, which are similar to Christian Psalms. However, by his own words, the author endeavors only to explain Islam and not to endorse it. Furthermore, listening to Islamic prayers in an effort to understand the artistic nature of the readings and its connection to a historical religious text does not have the primary effect of advancing religion.[7]

This ruling is consistent with the U.S. Supreme Court's endorsement of the academic study of religion in public schools and universities, when Justice Tom C. Clark in 1963 declared, "one's education is not complete without a study of comparative religion or the history of religion and its relationship to the advancement of civilization."[8] The secular approach makes the academic study of religion constitutionally permissible: "Nothing we have said here indicates that such study of the Bible or of religion, when presented objectively as part of a secular program of education, may not be effected consistently with the First Amendment."9

Of course, this is purely dicta, but dicta are often construed as holdings by those outside the legal profession. As Justice Powell has said more recently: "Courses in comparative religion of course are customary and constitutionally appropriate."10 Based on Justice Clark's statement as it applies to the Qur'an specifically, university officials now argue that, in addition to being *constitutionally permissible*, one's education is not *complete* without a study of the Qur'an (as well as the history of Islam) and its relationship to the advancement of civilization.11

Religion in general is a controversial topic within higher education, and demands inevitably arise to know why the Qur'an should (or even can) be taught in a state university. The situation in the U.S. has provoked legal discussions and challenges, chiefly: Does the study of the Qur'an in the University violate the Establishment Clause of the First Amendment by breaching the wall of separation of church and state? Academic experts in the study of religion think they know the answer, and for legal scholars the answer may be the same: Religion is a proper object of study, just like any other topic, but the explanations may and do differ.

To gain a proper perspective on the rationale behind teaching the Qur'an in the University, this article provides an introduction to the Qur'an, its world-historical significance, a brief history of its revelation, collection, and editing, and its salient themes. This is followed by a review of Michael Sells's *Approaching the Qur'an*, then a detailed analysis of the cases brought against the University of North Carolina at Chapel Hill, with a conclusion after a brief look at some parallel cases.

Introducing the Qur'an12

The Qur'an, the holy book of Islam, may well be the most powerful book in human history, with the arguable exception of the Bible. Both in world history and contemporary affairs, it is doubtful that any other book now commands, or has in the past exerted, so profound an influence. Objectively, one of every five people on earth today is Muslim, and thus subjectively believes the Qur'an supersedes the Bible, and that the Qur'an is unsurpassed. Since Muslims see Islam as the last of the world's religions, they view the Qur'an as the latest and greatest book. Even if one does not share this view, the sheer magnitude of its influence commands respect, and one cannot be cross-culturally and globally literate without some understanding of this monumental text.

The Qur'an is nothing less than an attempt to reorder civilization: to rescue it, Muslims would say, from the appetites and turpitude that threaten the moral fiber of human society. Islam offers to fill a spiritual vacuum to which western society has largely turned a blind eye. Islamic spirituality can be harmonized with the best of western – Christian as well as contemporary secular – traditions of civic virtues, moral decency, and family values, informed by the West's traditional Judeo-Christian ethic. Just as the Ten Commandments are still relevant, the Qur'an still has much to say, although even some Muslims say it needs to be understood anew within the changed circumstances of modernity and post-modernity.

The real heart of the Qur'an is its message. One useful way of approaching the Qur'an is to see it as the vehicle for expressing profound truths regarding God and the universe, and humankind and its civilizations. God is the creator, and humankind the created (physically dependent) and the creative (morally independent). The themes of the Qur'an, therefore, are the organizing principles of Islamic religion and civilization. Whether the Qur'an is informed by previous sources is a vexing question. To suggest that the Qur'an somehow derives from predominantly Jewish or Christian sources is tantamount to discrediting the Qur'an as a document of revelation. For Muslims, the question should be the other way around. The Qur'an is the gold standard of divine truth. Since it is pure and unadulterated, previous scriptures should be measured against the Qur'an, not the other way around. Indeed, the Qur'an comprehends all previous scriptures.

Within itself, the Qur'an provides Muslims with a view of the Bible. Mention is made of the "scrolls" of Abraham and Moses, the

Tawrāh (Torah) of Moses, the *Zabūr* (usually understood as the Psalms) of David, and the *Injīl* (Gospel) of Jesus, all conceived as direct revelation from God to the prophet concerned: "Surely we sent down the Torah wherein is guidance and light" (5:44); "And we sent, following in their footsteps, Jesus son of Mary, confirming the Torah before him; and we gave to him the Gospel, wherein is guidance and light" (5:46). In this way, these (and, by implication, all) previous scriptures are pictured within the revelatory and compositional image of the Qur'an itself.

The Qur'an, Muslims believe, is a revelation from God, pure and simple, communicated through a series of revelations imparted to the Prophet Muhammad over the course of twenty-three lunar years. Thus, it would be error and sacrilege to speak of Muhammad as the "author" of the Qur'an. Furthermore, to say that Muhammad was "influenced" by his religious world and that the Qur'an is a hodge-podge of intermixed influences is not only highly reductionist, but also suggests that the Prophet, not God, was himself the author of the Qur'an. The tension between traditional Muslim and western academic approaches is perhaps nowhere more intense than on this issue. Theologically, to concede that the Qur'an is a text revealed by God is to obligate a believer in God to abide by it.

Just as the Qur'an cannot be read from cover to cover in quite the same way that one reads a novel or a textbook, the Qur'an was not written from cover to cover. Just as writers have flashes of inspiration, Muhammad experienced flashes of revelation. These cumulatively became the Qur'an. Tradition is unanimous that Gabriel was the agent of revelation, even though he is mentioned only twice in the Qur'an and such a role is never explicitly given to him. The Qur'an itself explains how God reveals: "It belongs not to any mortal that God should speak to him, except by revelation, or from behind a veil, or that He should send a messenger and he reveal whatsoever He will, by His leave; surely He is All-high, All-wise" (42:51). In other words, while the Prophet revealed the Qur'an, God authored it, according to Muslim belief. *Wahy* is the technical term for revelation in the Qur'an. The fundamental sense of *wahy* seems to be what those steeped in the European romantic ethos would call a "flash of inspiration" that it is sudden and unpremeditated, although Muhammad's revelations were sustained for over two decades.

The Qur'an itself claims that it is modeled on an archetypal *lawḥ maḥfūz*, or "preserved tablet" (85:22), having been sent down to the nearest heaven on the "night of power" (surah 97) in the holy month of Ramadan, for Gabriel to transmit it to Muhammad. The text of the Qur'an is from God, Muslims believe, while the recording and editing of the Qur'an is by men. It is important to understand the implications of the Qur'an being originally revealed over a period of time, and thereafter collected and edited.

It was Muhammad's practice to meditate prayerfully in a cave on Mount Hira. He was practicing some sort of pious exercise (*taḥannuth*) when he first encountered a mysterious entity later identified as the archangel Gabriel, who revealed the Qur'an to him over the next twenty-three years. The hadith literature provides many anecdotes as to how revelations would come upon Muhammad. The descriptions vary. Gabriel, the agent of revelation, taught Muhammad to recite the first passages of the Qur'an. Most frequently, the accounts speak of revelations "descending" upon Muhammad, such that he would hear the sound of buzzing, or of bells, or would feel a great weight come upon him, or would enter a trance, after which the words of the Qur'an would become indelibly inscribed in his heart, and subsequently dictated to scribes. The revelations of the Qur'an were first recorded by scribes who wrote down the verses on whatever writing materials were available: leaves and branches of palm trees, white stones, leather, shoulder blades of sheep, ribs. One early account states that a revelation was actually eaten by a domestic animal, because it had been recorded on something organic and edible.

After Muhammad's death in 632 CE, there was no authoritative record of the revelations. They had to be collected. The process of assembling, collating, and codifying the Qur'an was not informed by a great deal of available information as to dating and other historical information on which to base the traditional form the Qur'an eventually took. According to tradition, the decision to preserve the Qur'an was taken after hundreds of reciters were killed in Battle of Yamāmah (12/633). ʿUmar (who was to become the second Caliph) suggested to Abū Bakr that the Qur'an be collected and written down. Zayd ibn Thābit, one of Muhammad's secretaries, was commissioned to do so. He wrote it on sheets (*ṣuḥuf*), handed it to ʿUmar when completed, then passed it to the caliph's daughter. Finally, the text was fixed under ʿUthmān, in dialect of the Quraysh tribe (that of Muhammad), said to be the clearest of dialects, according to tradition. Where difficulties in establishing the text arose, the Quraysh dialect was given preference. Written texts required attestation from reciters, who had heard and memorized the Qur'an by heart. Thus, the canon of the Qur'an was fixed around twenty years after the Prophet's death, as well as the order of the surahs and the integrity of the consonantal text. The vocalization was not firmly established until around 300 years after Muhammad.

The urgency with which the text became fixed under the decree of Caliph ʿUthmān afforded precious little opportunity for a systematic, much less "scientific," ordering of the text. Its preservation was more important than its sequencing, and it was left to later Muslim scholars to provide a critical apparatus for more fully appreciating the pieces that made up the larger whole. How much editing and how intrusive or interpretive such editing may have been is largely a modern question that has occupied much of western scholarship on the Qur'an.

Soon after the Qur'an was revealed, it spread like wildfire, racing with the Arab conquerors during the first two centuries of Arab expansion. The rapidity and breadth of that expansion was dramatic. At this stage, the Qur'an had not yet achieved its status as a world text, for the simple reason that it was considered an "Arab" book (or, rather, "the" Arab book, since the Qur'an is the first book in Arabic). Non-Arab converts were at first obliged to attach themselves to various Arab tribes, in a kind of process of spiritual and social adoption.

Soon, non-Arabs, especially Persians, took umbrage with this. How could a scripture with a universal message, they argued, be restricted to just a single ethnicity? And, if not, on what grounds were Arabs justified in relegating to non-Arabs a secondary status, when the category of "Muslims" constitutes a spiritual and social "nation" that embraces all races and nations, yet transcends them? Was not the Prophet Abraham a Muslim ("one who surrenders" to the will of God)? And is not anyone who professes belief in the oneness of God and in the authenticity of the Prophet Muhammad to be accounted as a believer, on equal footing with every other? And so it came to be: the appeal to the Qur'an's universalisms, expressive of its egalitarian ethic, prevailed. Thus Islam, although based on a message revealed in Arabic, was transposed to other cultures and climes, although it took centuries before the Qur'an itself was actually translated into other languages. This singular revelation became a universal scripture.

In its final form, the Qur'an consists of 114 surahs, customarily arranged by the longest surah first, except for the short "opening" surah. Generally, a traditional dating of these surahs has emerged, with the so-called "early Makkan surahs" spanning the first thirteen lunar years (with Early, Middle, and Final periods), shifting to the period of "Madinan surahs" in 622, coinciding with the first year of the hijrah or migration of the early Muslim community from Makkah to Madinah, followed by the "Later Makkan surahs" on the Prophet's triumphal return to his native city of Makkah shortly before the end of his life in 632.

Taking what has become Montgomery Watt's classic, two-part division of Muhammad's life, the early Makkan surahs exemplify Muhammad's role as "Prophet" while the Madinan and later Makkan surahs present Muhammad's vocation as "statesman." Thus, the earlier revelations are intended to strike the fear of God into the heart of the listener by the promise of heaven and the threat of hell. Accordingly, the Prophet's role is that of a "warner" who has come to make people alive to the threat of impending doom and death unless they repent and surrender to the will of God.

First warned, later guided is the basic purpose of the revelations and the logic of their sequence. The later Qur'anic revelations enshrine laws and principles for Muslims to follow. Once a Muslim community had formed (the migration of Muslims to Makkah in 622 effectively created the first Muslim state), laws were needed. Accordingly, Muhammad became a statesman in addition to his role as prophet, and began revealing the laws and ethical principles that later became the foundation for the Muslim schools of law and way of life.

As the recipient of revelation, the Prophet Muhammad was commissioned with a divine mission to present the Qur'an as the voice of

God, calling the entire world to righteousness and justice, to morality and decency, to a life of prayer and fasting, and to surrender to the will of God. That Muhammad was commissioned with a divine mission does not make Muhammad himself divine, as the Qur'an itself states: "He would never order you to take the angels and the Prophets as Lords" (3:80). This idea may be seen in an early Christian text: "Neither is there salvation in believing in teachers and calling them lords" (Homilies 8:5).

This concept of the Qur'an as a revealed scripture is basic to an appreciation of why Muslims both revere the Qur'an and orient their entire lives according to its dictates, for the Qur'an and the hadith (oral traditions that report the sayings and actions of the Prophet Muhammad) are the two principal sources of authority for Muslim doctrine and praxis. A deeper walk with God on the "straight path" of Islam can come about through spiritual growth and transformation. How does one do this? What can serve as an infallible spiritual guide?

For Muslims, the way to bring one's life into greater conformity with God's will is to follow the laws of the Qur'an and the example of Muhammad. The truest sign of one's transformative faith is conformity and dedication to the principles and teachings of Islam that are preserved, first and foremost, in the Qur'an itself. The single most important act of piety is to surrender one's own will to that of the will of God. The word "Muslim" means "one who has submitted" or committed themselves to the civilizing will of God. "Surrender" is not the best translation, because following God's will is an act of free will, a vigilant choice, and a matter of strength through commitment and practice.

Salvation then, for Muslims, consists of much more than simply being forgiven for one's past sins and transgressions. The act of repentance itself affects much of this, and the true test of one's sincerity is a matter of public record in terms of one's actions. However, Islam sees a spiritual life beyond forgiveness. Salvation is not a change of status that magically and suddenly averts God's wrath. Salvation is a process, a refinement of one's character over time.

A nineteenth-century mystic once said that the Qur'an eclipses all of the miracles of all of the previous prophets, for the miracle of the

Qur'an, alone, remains.[13] That is to say the staff of Moses may have turned into a serpent and swallowed up the magicians' snakes in Pharoah's court, but that prophetic sceptre has vanished. Moses may well have parted the Red Sea, as Muslims themselves believe, but that prodigy is long gone. No empirical evidence of either miracle remains today. What alone abides is the "miracle" of the Qur'an – its prodigious ability to transform the lives of those who believe and accept the Qur'an as the best guide for their lives. This transformation is spiritual alchemy, taking the base appetites that most of us are born with and transmuting these into the pure gold of a refined moral and spiritual character. The Qur'an can transform a pair of horns into a set of wings, changing the pious believer from a devil into an angel. Such is the nature of Muslim belief about the Qur'an.

Approaching the Qur'an

Reading the Qur'an is far easier said than done. The Qur'an is a challenging text. To the uninitiated, the Book is both simplistic and enigmatic. To the untrained eye, the Qur'an, on first impression, may strike one as arcane, florid, repetitive, or otherwise impenetrable to westerners wholly unprepared to study the text dispassionately. However, there is a deeper hermeneutical issue involved, one of attitude and assumptions as to the authority and nature of the text. The Qur'an may be a difficult text for non-Muslims, but it is not unfathomable. Sells's *Approaching the Qur'an* has probably done more to render the Qur'an accessible to a western audience than any other book in the past few years.

The Qur'an makes its own particular truth-claims, which are quite audacious. It tells the reader that its source is an archetypal "mother of the book" (*umm al-kitāb*) in heaven. The Qur'an is therefore of divine origin. It is not only authorized but is actually authored by God Himself. This is an extraordinary claim, indeed. As such, from a Muslim perspective, the element of divine revelation is of paramount importance. God wrote the Qur'an, Muslims believe, and thus the book commands their respect. Yet should it command the respect of those who have not been raised in its culture, who might consider it in the university? Absolutely. So where does one begin? There are methodological considerations that must first be addressed.

The predominantly Christian West may have serious misgivings regarding the truth of such claims. They may view the Qur'an as an ersatz version of the Bible, as a derivative imitation. This very assumption largely biased the western reception of the Qur'an from the very start, and affected and infected its study until now. As a result, polarities in the study of the Qur'an have emerged, although these are beginning to disappear. The great divide in Qur'anic studies has historically been the tension between traditional Muslim approaches and western academic approaches.

Although problematic for gaining a coherent understanding and appreciation of the Qur'an, these two competing paradigms are somewhat synergistic. If you combine the two, you get what Wilfred Cantwell Smith regarded as the insider-outsider dynamic. In principle, he suggested that the best approach to the study of the Qur'an and Islam is to be able to enter into a believer's (emic) perspective while maintaining some degree of relative objectivity (etic perspective). Indeed, Smith's canon of believer intelligibility requires that "no statement about a religion is valid unless it can be acknowledged by that religion's believers" (although in later writings he reversed this somewhat). This "creative principle" offers the best of both worlds, for it "provides experimental control that can lead" scholars "dynamically towards the truth." However, unless one adheres to Smith's principle, polarities will inevitably arise. The following table highlights the nature of these polarities.

Polarities in the Study of the Qur'an

Western	Muslim
Secular academic	Traditional academic
Analytic	Synthetic
Tendency to over-differentiate	Tendency to harmonize
Use of reason and bias	Use of reason and faith
Sometimes offensive	Sometimes defensive

Here we see a complement of productive and reductive approaches. The method of reading largely determines what is read and how it is understood. The Muslim approaches the Qur'an reverentially and with full faith in the truth it enshrines. The western secular approach can be just the opposite: it is skeptical and analytic, yet it does not have to be. Where there are apparent difficulties and even apparent contradictions in the text, the Muslim will try to resolve those anomalies by harmonizing them on a higher plane of understanding, while a person approaching the text from a secular perspective (the westerner) may be dismissive of the Qur'an as simply a human enterprise where inconsistencies and errors are to be expected. Such a conclusion is not only misguided, according to any knowledgeable Muslim, it is also an attack upon the integrity of a sacred text that is divinely revealed.

Returning to *Approaching the Qur'an* itself, Professor Sells makes his objective clear: "The purpose of this book is neither to refute nor to promote the Qur'anic message. Rather, the goal is to allow those who do not have access to the Qur'an in its recited, Arabic form to encounter one of the most influential texts in human history in a manner that is acceptable."[14]

Critics see the book as presenting a glorified image of the Qur'an, and thus of Islam itself, through a process of favorable selectivity. This, they claim, is tendentious. Instead of an Orientalist bias against Islam, which permeates so much of western scholarship over the past century, the opposite holds true here. By conveniently removing the more sensitive Qur'anic passages – those that would surely offend and alarm a typical western, non-Muslim reader – Michael Sells has misrepresented Islam, critics say, not by focusing on its more controversial elements, but by meretriciously suppressing them. This is tantamount to a kind of "spin" – a public relations ploy that critics allege neatly packages Islam as something it is not. By giving a partial view of the Qur'an, the positive verses effectively hide the negative. This may be thought of as a kind of reverse stereotyping that idealizes, whitewashes, and romanticizes the Qur'an. This "spin doctoring" is problematic, yet is the author's prerogative. Apologetic literature does this characteristically by lionizing the "true" religion and demonizing the "false" religion. Such criticisms as these tend not to come from Professor Sells's peers, but rather from Christian conservatives and evangelicals.

While any scholar or other author is perfectly at liberty to do this, a public university becomes complicit in the process once such a book itself is adopted as part of a curriculum. That means state action, and that action, critics charge, is tantamount to establishment of religion. The UNC Qur'an controversy raises precisely this kind of allegation. While Michael Sells, a respected Islamicist (a scholar of Islam, although presumably not a Muslim himself), has affirmatively disavowed and repudiated all such charges, when the debate moved into the legal arena, it was for the courts to decide.

Facts and Case Analysis

In 2002 and again in 2004, the University of North Carolina at Chapel Hill was sued over its 2002 freshman orientation program. This program had been initiated relatively recently, two years before 9/11. In 1999, UNC established its "Carolina Summer Reading Program" as part of its "First Year Initiative." This orientation program for incoming freshmen had been recommended by the "Report of the Chancellor's Task Force on Intellectual Climate" in August 1997. The goal of this three-year pilot project was to provide "an intellectual uplift of the freshman orientation experience" so that Carolina students would "value an active intellectual life."[15]

Prior to the fall orientation experience, incoming students were required to participate in a summer reading program. This special summer reading assignment happens annually. Each year, a book is chosen according to an adopted theme. 9/11 prompted the theme for 2002 – unquestionably topical and highly relevant subject matter. However, *Approaching the Qur'an* drew widespread criticism from the religious right as intellectual propaganda by presenting a beautified picture of Islam that was fundamentally skewed and that failed to really explain to students the background and genesis of Muslim extremism, as represented by Osama bin Laden and his ilk. While the latter criticism is well-founded, it is misplaced, precisely because explaining the roots of 9/11 was simply not a stated objective of the reading program. The subject falls quite outside the purview of the book itself, which was published before the national tragedy of 9/11.

The terrorist events of 9/11 sparked a huge public interest to know more about Islam. Chain bookstores across the nation responded to and profited from that interest. The sudden attacks immediately riveted national attention on the security threat, and executing appropriate (or inappropriate) responses to that threat has dominated U.S. foreign policy from then (beginning with the "regime change" in Afghanistan, when American forces ousted the ruling Taliban) until now. Thus, it was not surprising that UNC adopted a book about Islam to help incoming students familiarize themselves with the religious underpinnings of Islamic radicalism, although somewhat remotely. Of course, the choice of Michael Sells's *Approaching the Qur'an*, while providing an introduction to the core religious text of Islam, did little to illuminate current events.

Having taught Islam at the university level over the years has given me some firsthand experience in approaching Islam. In one course, I adopted Michael Sells's *Approaching the Qur'an* to help explain Islamic origins rather than present-day Islam. While modern Islam may be explained by showing how various Muslims today may interpret the Qur'an, a reading of the Qur'an itself will simply and utterly fail to accomplish such a task. In approaching modern Islam, I have found it useful to present students with a typology that accounts for the wide-ranging, often disparate and even conflicting attitudes towards the West that find ideological and political expression throughout the Muslim world today.

Thus, I have taught students (including my Muslim students) to clearly differentiate among seven Islamic "responses to modernity." From "right to left," so to speak, they are: 1. radical Islamism; 2. traditionalism; 3. neo-traditionalism; 4. modernism; 5. secularism; 6. postmodernism; and 7. post-Islamism. Michael Sells's *Approaching the Qur'an*, and even a complete study of the Qur'an in its entirety, would not prepare students to understand radical Islamism in its present-day manifestations. For this, a history of various works of *tafsīr* (Qur'an commentary) would provide some necessary connections, purely as a point of departure. The overall context would then have to be supplemented by a history of the modern Muslim Middle East, beginning from the intrusion and subsequent hegemony of European colonialism (from Napoleon's invasion of Egypt in 1798 onward) and its reconstructive yet destabilizing aftermath.

Much writing of the history of the modern Muslim Middle East has been tainted by what has come to be known as Orientalism, a term that is brilliantly illuminated by the work of Professor Edward Said. Then, there is the ubiquitous presence of globalism, in all of it economic, cultural, and ideological intersections with traditional and developing societies, that must be considered as tinting the spectacles of western scrutiny of all things "Oriental" in general, and Muslim in particular. Thus, in light of western caricatures of the so-called "Green Threat" (green being a sacred color in Islam), an enlightened position would take pedagogical note of the tendency towards cultural bias in representations of Islam in both the media and in university curricula.

Therefore, UNC's adoption of a text that is quite sensitive to (and sympathetic with) Islam provides students with a necessary counterbalance to the infrared vision with which the West has tended to view Islam: conveniently forgetful of the fact that Islamic civilization stands as a largely unacknowledged root of pre- and post-Enlightenment western civilization, especially when Islam was the world's superpower for around 800 years. Carl W. Ernst, UNC's resident Islamicist, made the following statement on August 28, 2002 as to UNC's selection of *Approaching the Qur'an* as required reading for incoming Carolina freshmen: "The Koran assignment at the University of North Carolina, where I am a professor of religious studies, is a belated attempt to catch up with the one-way flow of globalizing culture."[16] Yet this "one-way flow" precipitated a two-way collision on campus and in court. The actual reading assignment is still on UNC's "Carolina Summer Reading Program" official site:

> The Carolina Summer Reading Program is designed to introduce you to the intellectual life of Carolina. Required of all new undergraduate students (first year and transfer), it involves reading an assigned book over the summer, writing a one-page response to a particular subject, participating in a two-hour discussion, and sharing your written response with others. The goals of the program are to stimulate discussion and critical thinking around a current topic, to introduce you to academic life at Carolina, to

enhance a sense of community between students, faculty and staff, and to provide a common experience for incoming students. Some find they enjoy sharing the reading with members of their family during the summer.

This year's reading is *Approaching the Qur'án: The Early Revelations*, translated and introduced by Michael Sells. Although the summer reading is required, if any students or their families are opposed to reading parts of the Qur'an because to do so is offensive to their own faith, they may choose not to read the book. These students should instead complete their one-page response on why they chose not to read the book.

...all students are expected to...bring their one-page response to their small group discussions led by selected faculty and staff. This is an opportunity for you to connect with members of Carolina's learning community and to share a common academic experience with your new peers.[17]

Note that provision was made for students who took umbrage at the reading to opt out of it and to simply explain the rationale behind their decision in a short essay. Originally, UNC required all its students to do the reading, without exception. However, when exception was taken (by critics), UNC backtracked to make an exception. Disaffected students could opt to write an essay as to why they elected not to read *Approaching the Qur'an*. The actual number of students who exercised this option is not available, and so assessing the level of controversy that the summer reading program had generated in the student population is quite impossible to tell.

While the internal situation was relatively protected from the glare of public scrutiny, the controversy did make the national press.[18] It hit a raw nerve and tapped into public interest in Islam – a piqued desire to learn more about Islam that predated the UNC controversy itself. One instance of the highly visible (and audible) press coverage was a segment of National Public Radio's *Talk of the Nation*, "Studying Islam," broadcast on August 15, 2002,[19] the day of the first court challenge and ensuing decision when a court injunction was sought to suspend the UNC program (see below).

Guests included eminent Islamicist John Esposito, Professor of Religion and International Affairs, Georgetown University, and author of *Unholy War: Terror in the Name of Islam*,[20] and Michael Sells, Professor of Comparative Religion, Haverford College (Haverford, PA), and author of *Approaching the Qur'an: The Early Revelations*.[21] Also interviewed was former Sunni Muslim, Emir Caner (whose surname is misspelled as "Canner" on the NPR web site), Assistant Professor of Church History, Southeastern Baptist Theological Seminary, (Wake Forest, N.C., where he is now Associate Dean[22]), and co-author of *Unveiling Islam*.[23] At that time, Caner was erstwhile advisor to the Family Policy Network, the conservative Christian advocacy group that brought suit against UNC. Caner complained that "reading a portion of the Qur'an" that selectively beautifies the more universal features of Qur'anic discourse and expurgates by omission some of the more controversial passages effectively "becomes a propaganda tool." While not aimed at actually converted students to Islam, the nature of the propaganda tool presents Islam as an inherently peaceful religion. For this and other reasons, Professor Caner objected to the fact that some 4,200 incoming freshmen would be "forced" to read a text that promotes a positive view of the Qur'an that distorts the real picture by presenting the early Makkan surahs (the first revelations of the Qur'an, which, as a whole, were revealed to the Prophet Muhammad over a period of twenty-three lunar years). The required reading did little to shed light on an event that shed such blood and tears as 9/11.

When host Neal Conan asked Professor Sells for his views as author of the controverted text, Sells disclaimed his book of having any propagandistic purpose whatsoever. *Approaching the Qur'an* is purely an introductory text on the Qur'an and offers insights as to how the text is read and appreciated by Muslims. It simply does not deal with why Islamic extremists commit terrorism in the name of Islam (and based on an extremist reading of key passages of the Qur'an that are not part of the early Makkan surahs and are therefore not found in the text of *Approaching the Qur'an*). Sells disavowed such an ulterior motive or agenda for the book, and advocated what he called a "non–conflictual view of religion" that allows for a dispassionate inquiry into religions. In Sells's defense, Professor John Esposito, the other Islamicist guest on NPR, pointed out that Sells's book was written before 9/11 and therefore could not be expected to address its implications for a nuanced understanding of the mentality that animated the terrorists themselves.

Altogether, four actions were brought against UNC that dealt directly with the Qur'an controversy: two lawsuits in 2002 and two more in 2004. (There was an additional suit over UNC's Islamic awareness week, mentioned below.) Ironically, the 2002 suits attracted widespread publicity, both nationally and internationally, while the 2004 actions registered scarcely any notice in the press. The UNC itself became the target of criticism and court action in 2002, but was off the media's radar screen in 2004. The first round of challenges proved newsworthy, while the latter was not. This resulted in an inverse pattern of publication: while the 2002 suits were widely reported by the press, they were judicially unreported, which is to say that the court decisions themselves remain unpublished.

Quite the reverse occurred with respect to the 2004 cases. Although the press virtually ignored the story, the two 2004 cases were judicially reported, widely available, and readily accessible to law students and legal professionals through both the Lexis–Nexis and Westlaw proprietary databases. This situation is easy enough to explain in terms of proximity and distance from the 9/11 terrorist attacks. The national press reported the 2002 court cases when they were still within in the psychosocial wake of 9/11, whereas the 2004 cases were considerably removed from the immediate aftermath of 9/11. Yet they were judicially reported (and published), whereas the 2002 cases were not. By means of the reportage available, the 2002 court battles may be reconstructed as follows.

Yacovelli v. Moeser (University of North Carolina, Chapel Hill), Case No. 02-CV-596 (U.S. Dist. Ct., Middle District of N.C., Aug. 15, 2002) (Unreported)
On Thursday, August 15, 2002, two taxpayer members of the Family Policy Network (a conservative Christian advocacy group), James Yacovelli (North Carolina State Director of FPN) and fellow activist Terry Moffitt (FPN Chairman of the Board and UNC-CH alumnus), along with three anonymous UNC students, sought a court-ordered

emergency injunction in an attempt to stop some 180 Qur'an discussion groups from meeting on Monday, August 20 to discuss their reading of Michael Sells's *Approaching the Qur'an*. Although this initial action was widely reported by the national and internal press, the case was judicially unreported (unpublished), and its details would perforce have to be gleaned from media accounts of it. However, the present writer has now obtained a transcript of this proceeding.[24]

The case was heard by the Hon. N. Carlton Tilley, Jr., Chief District Judge, U.S. District Court, Middle District of North Carolina, in Greensboro. Two of the three student plaintiffs were aged 18, and the third was a 17-year-old minor, represented by the parents. The first student, bearing the pseudonym John Doe No. 1, was an evangelical Christian. John Doe No. 2 (the minor, represented by "John and Jane Doe, Sr.") was a Roman Catholic, and Jane Doe was Jewish. The action was originally filed on July 22 in the Federal District Court.[25] The plaintiffs were represented by Stephen M. Crampton and Michael J. DePrimo of the American Family Association/Center for Law and Policy. The two attorneys have publicly stated their personal convictions ("What We Believe") as it relates to the law:

> The principles that inform the Center for Law and Policy's jurisprudence and policy positions derive from the Bible, for as Sir William Blackstone wrote over two centuries ago, the law of the Creator is "the true law." Blackstone's understanding of "true law" has resonated throughout the corridors of history from voices as diverse as Moses, Plato, Cicero, Jefferson, and countless other theologians, philosophers, jurists, and statesmen. Liberty stems only from the true law and the principles drawn therefrom. It is these principles, embodied in the Declaration of Independence, upon which the Center for Law & Policy premises its actions.[26]

Presumably, in a further effort not to reveal their identities, none of these students were present in Tilley's Greensboro court. Over UNC's objections to the contrary, Judge Tilley allowed the three students to remain unknown due to their age, even though there was no indication that these students stood in any danger or faced any reprisal for their legal actions. "I think it could be disruptive to the education and the mental health of those three students to be identified," Tilley stated.[27]

UNC Chapel Hill was represented by Assistant Attorney General Celia Grasty Lata and Joyce S. Rutledge, and Susan H. Ehringhaus and David Parker, General Counsel, University of North Carolina. Counsels for the Defendant argued that the case was not about religious freedom, but censorship of ideas. Lata argued that to halt the reading program would have a chilling effect on freedom of speech in the University, causing professors to be wary of choosing other books that might spark controversy. "It might have done that already," Tilley remarked in court.[28]

As plaintiffs' advocate, Stephen M. Crampton, chief counsel for the Mississippi-based American Family Association Center for Law and Policy, played the Muslim call to prayer, in Arabic, from the audio CD that accompanies *Approaching the Qur'an*. "We would like to ask how this stimulates critical thinking?" Crampton asked, as the recording played in the background. "I would submit that's a quintessential religious exercise." Judge Tilley later responded to this contention in his holding: "The two-hour discussion session is not a religious activity, just as playing the CD in this courtroom did not convert it into a religious activity."[29]

Playing a CD in Arabic has educational value in creating an impression as to what the Qur'an actually sounds like when recited. Whether the playing of the CD also has a religious effect "certainly goes to the question of how academically that might be considered and discussed instead of promoting or endorsing Islam or a possible view of Islam, whether it is palliated or not."[30] Recital of the Qur'an is a religious activity, but listening to a recitation is not, unless one happens to be a Muslim, understands Arabic, and is a participant in the liturgical experience. As Tilley further observed: "Presumably, very few people entering Chapel Hill would speak Arabic and be able to understand the words."[31] The role of the listener is thus that of an interested observer. It is the "music appreciation" akin to listening to a Gregorian chant.

After hearing the merits of the controversy, Judge Tilley held that there was simply no evidence that the University chose *Approaching the Qur'an* in an effort to convert students to Islam: "I do not believe an objective person reading the book would believe the University is suggesting a preference for Islam, a particular interpretation of Islam or religion itself."[32] In reading the book for himself, Judge Tilley remarked:

> Now, with regard to the book, Mr. Crampton read certain small portions of the book which he contends support his position that the book does not fairly teach the Qur'an and, therefore, would instill in persons who are participating in the program an unduly positive view of the Qur'an. My own review of the book was not to that effect. My own review was that the book did present Dr. Sells' opinion that he was not endorsing as truth any of the revelations. He does point out in there that Muhammad claimed he had those revelations. Dr. Sells is not saying he did have those revelations.[33]

Judge Tilley then reviewed *Approaching the Qur'an* in general terms, highlighting specific passages he found particularly relevant.[34] His overall conclusion was that the book was strictly academic, not religious in nature, and therefore did not amount to a religious activity. He ended his analysis with an application of the *Lemon* test – a test for Establishment Clause violations deriving from *Lemon v. Kurtzman*, 403 U.S. 602.[35] In closing, Judge Tilley complimented attorneys on both sides, in saying:

> I think the case has been very well-handled by all the lawyers. You've done an excellent job on your briefs. You've done an excellent job on your arguments, and if every case that came into court were as well-represented as the persons in this particular case had been, I think the state of our jurisprudence would be elevated several levels.[36]

As expected, the plaintiffs appealed, still seeking an injunction, primarily on anti-establishment grounds, for a halt to the Qur'an discussion sessions scheduled for August 20.

Yacovelli v. Moeser, Aff'd, Case No. 02-1889
(4th Cir., Aug. 19, 2002)

As expected, the plaintiffs appealed, still seeking an injunction for a halt to the Qur'an discussion sessions. The appeal was filed on August 16 in the 4th U.S. Circuit Court of Appeals in Richmond. In the meantime, the UNC Qur'an controversy was debated in the halls of the Virginia state legislature. On August 7, the House Appropriations Committee voted to bar public funds for use in UNC's 2002 summer reading program, in what amounted to a legislative reaction to the University's selection of *Approaching the Qur'an*.[37] In the Associated Press report, "The committee voted 64-10 to bar UNC-Chapel Hill from using public funds for its plan to teach new students about a book on the Qur'an unless it gives equal time to 'all known religions.'"[38] No committee imaginable would have the proportions indicated by this vote! The vote was surely a House of Representatives vote, based on its committee's recommendation that it was the North Carolina General Assembly and that the bill passed by a vote of 64–12.[39] But this information has to be wrong. UNC-CH Chancellor James Moeser himself (one of the two named defendants in *Yacovelli v. Moeser*), commented on this proposed legislation in a speech:

> The House of Representatives of the North Carolina General Assembly attached a proviso to the budget to disallow the use of state funds for any program or course that deals with a single religion unless all known religions are given equal treatment. (This proviso, which also would affect many offerings in the Department of Religious Studies, was quietly removed when the state budget finally [passed] in mid-September.)
>
> And in response to this clear threat to academic freedom, the Board of Governors of the 16-campus University of North Carolina system failed in an initial vote to endorse a resolution in support of academic freedom. (Later, after our program was over, the Board of Governors approved a resolution reaffirming academic freedom.)
>
> Finally, on August 19, after the Family Policy Network's legal efforts to shut us down had failed, we went on with our discussion groups. Nothing terrible happened; our students read a book, talked about it and learned.

> But the combination of the lawsuit, the legislative threat and the
> governing board debate – all occurring within a short period of time –
> made this a very hot story.[40]

Thus the legislation failed, but its passage by the North Carolina House of Representatives rightly alarmed academics by directly threatening their academic freedom. While this equal time requirement raises some interesting curricular issues, the House Appropriations Committee was clearly more interested in barring Islamic awareness than in promoting awareness of all world religions. If this is a fair and accurate reading of the committee's proposal and the House's overwhelming vote in support of it, then the real legislative intent did not really match the stated curricular condition precedent. Legislators were simply responding to a number of complaints from their constituents. Because it was such a threat, the vote immediately drew criticism from the university community. Joseph Farrell, UNC Professor of Public Law and Policy, characterized the House vote as "nothing more than political theater."[41] Even had the bill passed North Carolina General Assembly, the measure would still have required the governor's signature before it became law, and even then would probably have not withstood constitutional scrutiny once challenged in court.

One academic's protest over the House's vote deserves to be cited at some length, because it so eloquently represents the views of the vast majority of academics. In 2002, Dr. Richard Veit, Professor of English at the University of North Carolina at Wilmington since 1977, was chair of the elected Faculty Assembly, representing the faculty of the sixteen University of North Carolina campuses. In his "Statement to the Educational Planning, Policies and Programs Committee of the Board of Governors" on August 22, 2002, Professor Veit took a stand for academic freedom against the House's threatened budgetary sanctions for promoting the study of Islam by means of the Qur'an. Speaking on behalf of some 13,000 UNC professors, Dr. Veit stated:

> Inseparable from the search for truth is the search for understanding. It is
> the obligation of scholars, faculty, and students to examine the world as it

is, in all its aspects. In a diverse, complex, dangerous, and increasingly interconnected world, we must gain the fullest possible understanding of others and of ourselves.

As faculty we have the obligation to teach students, not to indoctrinate them, not to provide them with a store of facts, but to expose students to diverse thought, to teach them to analyze, compare, and evaluate ideas. In short, we must train students to think for themselves.

It was in the spirit of open inquiry and the quest for understanding that the faculty at Chapel Hill assigned the reading and discussion of a scholarly book, *Approaching the Qur'an: The Early Revelations*. If legislators impose what would be, in effect, a ban on the study of a particular book, they would limit academic freedom in a way no different or less destructive than the shackles placed on academic inquiry by the Taliban in pre-9/11 Afghanistan.

Academic freedom entails that academic and curricular decisions in a university must be made, through orderly academic processes, by the faculty. When the faculty's considered professional judgments are limited or overturned by others, academic freedom ceases to exist and the university ceases to function as a university.

Academic freedom is a powerful idea, but it is constantly under attack, and it exists only when it is vigilantly and vigorously defended. As faculty we urge the North Carolina General Assembly to reject the proposal in the House budget that would curtail academic inquiry.[42]

The appeal itself was timely, but not persuasive. Speaking from the Louis F. Powell, Jr. U.S. Courthouse in Richmond, Virginia, the Court handed down a unanimous decision, rendered by Judge Robert B. King, and joined by Judges Roger L. Gregory and William B. Traxler Jr., in which the three-judge panel upheld the federal district court's decision by ruling that "the appellants have failed to satisfy the requirements for such relief."[43] According to the Associated Press, "No further explanation was contained in the brief ruling."[44] A copy of the actual order bears this out.[45] The FPN's effort to get an injunction having failed, UNC's Qur'an discussion groups proceeded as planned the very next day.

The story was far from over - the Family Policy Network did not give up. Another event provided the pretext for a new action: an Islamic awareness week. In early October 2002, the American Family

Association's Center for Law and Policy, which had represented the FPN in its previous actions, amended its federal court complaint in an effort to block UNC from hosting the round-table discussions and seminars on Islam, scheduled for November 11-15. According to Michael DePrimo, an attorney for the Center for Law and Policy: "There's a lot more going on than we thought there was when we first filed our complaint."[46] The amended complaint was filed on Oct. 4, giving UNC 20 days to respond. "The issue" DePrimo stated, "is whether or not the University is advancing the religion of Islam." To which he hastened to add: "And clearly they are." The issue would again be decided in the Federal District Court in Greensboro.[47] Reports of the outcome of this action, as of this date, are unavailable. However, the FPN continued to mount challenges to UNC policies promoting Islamic awareness. The eventual federal responses, published in 2004, would prove to be as articulate as they were definitive.

Yacovelli v. Moeser, 2004 U.S. Dist. LEXIS 9152
(M.D.N.C. May 20, 2004)
There were seven "players" in this lawsuit. Alleging that UNC's orientation program violated both the Establishment Clause and the Free Exercise Clause, this action was brought by three anonymous students (named by the pseudonyms of "John Doe No. 1" and "John No. 2," along with a seventeen-year-old minor represented "by and through his parents, John and Jane Doe, Sr."), together with two taxpayers, James Yacovelli and Terry Moffitt, against the University of North Carolina at Chapel Hill, represented by two leading UNC officials, these being captioned as "James Moeser, individually and in his official capacity as Chancellor of the University of North Carolina at Chapel Hill, and Cynthia Wolf Johnson, in her official capacity as Associate Vice Chancellor for Student Learning for the University of North Carolina at Chapel Hill." The Plaintiffs alleged, in part, the following:

> ...*Approaching the Qur'an* presents a biased view of Islam as a peaceful religion and that it leaves out less flattering stories about Muhammad. Plaintiffs conclude that this positive portrayal of both Muhammad and Islam constitutes an endorsement of Islam. Furthermore, Plaintiffs

contend that the inclusion of surahs and a compact disk ("CD") containing a reading of these surahs in Arabic is impermissible. While Sells explains that listening to a reading of the text in Arabic creates a different experience than simply reading a translation, Plaintiffs argue that listening to the CD exposes students to "the spell cast by a holy man of Islam."[48]

The last sentence is surprising and might have added a refreshing touch of levity, were it not for the fact that the Plaintiffs were quite serious in this allegation. The notion that a recital of the Qur'an is an act of sympathetic magic probably derives from a demonic view of Islam from within a conservative Christian perspective. Both religions, in a sense, not only require a belief in a Supreme Being and in prophetic figures (Jesus and Muhammad in Christianity and Islam, respectively, although the Qur'an recognizes the divine mission of Jesus as well) who are commissioned by that Being to convey a message of salvation to the world, but entail a belief in Satan (Islam: Iblīs) as well. More liberal interpretations of each religion have tended to treat Satan as the personification of human evil, a development that can be seen in the youngest independent world religion, known in the West as the Bahai Faith, which has disenchanted the universe of demonic principalities altogether and shifted the burden of responsibility for evil back onto the shoulders of its effective agents, human beings.

Since, from an evangelical Christian perspective, Satan may assume angelic qualities in order to trick the spiritually susceptible into believing a false religion, it makes perfect sense that a recital of the Qur'an would be construed as a satanic impulse with the power to cast a spell over the audience. This particular allegation should have been edited out, because it betrays the clearly religious bias that informs the complaint itself. This is not the ACLU lodging a protest here. Had UNC required the Gospel of Luke for its summer reading program, it is highly unlikely that the Family Policy Network and the three anonymous student plaintiffs would have found a cause of action. Quite the contrary, they might well have endorsed it. If so, this would point to an obvious contradiction at the level of principle.

The reader may well wonder why, some two years later, the plaintiffs persisted in their cause of action against UNC. The Court notes their rationale: "Although the program has now been completed, Plaintiffs urge this Court to enjoin UNC from organizing such a program in the future. Plaintiffs also seek nominal damages and attorneys' fees."[49] This case was pursued on juridical (and religious) principle and for its largely symbolic value. For "their alleged lack of standing to challenge the reading assignment," the Court granted UNC's motion to dismiss the Taxpayer Plaintiffs, James Yacovelli and Terry Moffitt.[50] Although there is no requirement of economic injury, the Yacovelli and Moffitt failed to show a constitutionally mandated "case or controversy." Their "intangible injury" simply did not rise to the threshold of a legally cognizable harm for which relief (here, injunctive relief) might be sought.

Although absent from their amended complaint, the Court still addressed the Taxpayer Plaintiffs' contention that "UNC's display of the assignment and study questions on the University's website is, in effect, an offensive state sponsored religious display."[51] Plaintiffs' procedural error notwithstanding, the Court explained that mere observation of religiously offensive conduct did not constitute a real injury for purposes of standing. Furthermore, UNC's website, while state-sponsored, was hardly religious and therefore "could not properly be deemed a religious display."[52] The Court observed that UNC's website simply "provided a brief synopsis of *Approaching the Qur'an* without including any portions of either the book or the Qur'an" and that, at most, the site gave straightforward information "about an orientation session that may or may not be constitutional."[53] The Taxpayer Plaintiffs' complaint failed because they could not "present a direct injury sufficient to confer standing."[54] Beyond their argument that they had suffered a direct injury, the Court also rejected their allegation of having been "injured as taxpayers."[55]

Flast v. Cohen[56] carves out an exception to the general rule that taxpayers have standing purely by virtue of their taxpayer status. The Court recited the rule that "[p]laintiffs asserting taxpayer status must allege more than a violation of the Establishment Clause. They must contend that, by use of the taxing and spending power, the government has exceeded its constitutional authority under the Establishment Clause."[57] In the instant case, the Court found that plaintiffs' complaint over UNC's expenditure of operating funds in support of its orientation program did not amount to a challenge of "congressional or state legislative exercise of the power to tax and spend" nor "any specific appropriations measure."[58] The Court clearly distinguished the UNC fact scenario from situations adumbrated by *Flast* that involve permissible "challenges to legislation governing the appropriation of tax moneys."[59] Having shown no personal injury, and having failed to demonstrate a relevant challenge to state spending under *Flast*, the Court dismissed James Yacovelli's and Terry Moffitt's taxpayer claims.[60]

Yet the Court preserved the complaint of the three UNC students, who did have standing. First, the Court "granted the 'rare dispensation' of proceeding anonymously,"[61] balancing the public's right of access to open court proceedings versus citizens' right to privacy. The Court enumerated the five factors outlined in James[62] that courts must weight in deciding whether to conceal the true identities of plaintiffs: 1. to protect a "specific sensitive and personal privacy interest;"[63] 2. to seriously contemplate any "threatened consequences of the identification of plaintiffs;"[64] 3. to give due regard to the "ages of the plaintiffs" who seek to safeguard their privacy interests;[65] 4. to explore "whether the plaintiff is pursuing legal action against a governmental or private party;"[66] 5. to weigh any "risk of unfairness and prejudice to the other party."[67]

Without recapitulating its close application of the five James factors, which tipped in favor of the student plaintiffs,[68] the Court considered an additional factor, that of possible adverse publicity: "[T]his Court may also consider the fact that the case has received intense media coverage. The threat of harassment and public hostility is therefore potentially more severe and harmful than that in a less publicized case."[69] Based on the five *James* factors plus the additional sixth, the Court allowed the three student plaintiffs to proceed anonymously.

By 2004, these students' allegations were mooted once the orientation program had run its course (having been announced in May and finished in August 2002). Normally, there would be no constitutionally required "case or controversy to adjudicate. But an exception obtains in any allegedly aggrievous situation that is "capable of repetition, yet evading review."[70] As to the plaintiffs themselves, the situation they faced and the harms they feared simply had no chance of recurring. Had such an action been permissible if brought on behalf of other students, the outcome might have been different. In other words, if the student plaintiffs' could have brought a "future class action" suit (as distinguished from a class action suit) where future harm may be legally prevented that might affect a class of prospective victims (even though that may be too strong a term), then the Court could have contemplated an injunction against UNC from ever again selecting a religious text for its summer orientation program. The Court recognized Justice Scalia's dissent "for the proposition that a risk of harm to persons other than the complaining party may suffice under extraordinary circumstances," but, as the Court was quick to add, "the current state of the law is otherwise."[71] Thus, the plaintiffs' injunctive demands were dismissed.[72]

The Court next granted defendant's motion to "dismiss the nominal damages claim against Chancellor Moeser in his individual capacity as to the Establishment Clause claims based on qualified immunity."[73] Qualified immunity shields state officials performing discretionary duties where the official's conduct "does not violate clearly established statutory or constitutional rights of which a reasonable person would have known."[74] Of course, the student plaintiffs alleged UNC's violation of the Establishment Clause, which bars federal and state governments from endorsing, financing, or coercing any religious claims, initiatives, or beliefs, respectively. The Court applied the standard, three-pronged *Lemon* test, requiring that state action 1. evinces a secular purpose; 2. has the primary effect of neither advancing nor inhibiting religion; and 3. without causing excessive government entanglement in religion.[75] UNC's actions would violate the Establishment Clause if any one of the three Lemon factors were not met. As for the first, the Court held: "Because UNC's stated secular purpose does not appear to be a sham, this Court will give deference to this stated secular purpose."[76] Can a religious text, such as the Qur'an (and especially the Qur'an), be studied for a secular purpose? The Court applied to following rationale to find that UNC's purpose was indeed secular:

The study of religious texts can be secular in purpose. If the religious text is presented as part of an objective secular program in which the school intends to explore the history, civilization, ethics, literary, or historical aspects of the text, or if the text is used in the study of comparative religions, the use of the religious text is secular.77

The Court found that UNC had satisfied Lemon's second inquiry in that *"Approaching the Qur'an* simply cannot be compared to religious practices which have been deemed violative of the *Establishment Clause*, such as posting the Ten Commandments, reading the Lord's Prayer or reciting prayers in school."78 The excessive entanglement prong involves both "kind and degree."79 The Court points out that the only institution to benefit from the reading program was UNC itself, and that there simply was no institutional affiliation with any Islamic organizations. Moreover, no Muslim clerics were present at any of the two-hour discussion sessions. In favor of the legal status of the academic study of religion, the Court pressed this decisive distinction:

The Supreme Court has made a distinction between "the discourse of the scholar's study or the seminar room" or the "merely descriptive examination of religious doctrine" and "the evangelist's mission station." *Rosenberger v. Rector & Visitors of the Univ. of Va., 515 U.S. 819, 868, 132 L. Ed. 2d 700, 115 S. Ct. 2510 (1995)* (noting that an article discussing how Christ alone provides spiritual fulfilment [sic] fell in the latter category). UNC's orientation program involved the examination of both period writing, comparisons to earlier Arabic thought, and imagery as they relate to religious doctrine. It was scholarly discourse, not a proselytizing mission.80

The Court here makes a crucial distinction that has been absolutely vital to the legal, political, and fiscal survival of departments and programs of comparative religions across the U.S., Canada, and Europe. What used to be called "religious studies" is more properly termed the "academic study of religion." During my doctoral studies at the University of Toronto, what was called the Centre for Religious Studies at entrance in 1991 was later changed to the Centre for the

Study of Religion, in order to disambiguate the term "religious" from "religious" orientation and exercise in the traditional, faith-based sense of the word. While the academic study of religion is necessarily "religious" as to its subject matter, it is decided secular as to its methodology. Of course, there are a number of "engaged" (religiously committed) scholars in the profession. However, they endeavor to make their work intersubjectively available by adhering to the canons of free inquiry and academic rigor.

After giving a ringing endorsement of academic freedom, the Court concluded the issue by saying: "In short, UNC's orientation program passes the *Lemon* test. Because there has been no violation of the Establishment Clause, Defendant Moeser is entitled to qualified immunity as to the Establishment Clause claims."[81] There remained the issue of the plaintiffs' Free Exercise claim: "The Plaintiffs' Motion for Leave to File a Second Amended Complaint will be GRANTED as it relates to the Pseudonymous Plaintiffs' Free Exercise claims."[82] Beyond some minor procedural issues, this decision paved the way for the final stage of the litigation, which took place several weeks later.

Motion granted by, dismissed by Yacovelli v. Moeser, 324 F. Supp. 2d 760, 2004 U.S. Dist. LEXIS 12815 (M.D.N.C., July 7, 2004)
The subsequent ruling had narrowed to a single issue, and the published opinion was correspondingly shorter. In *Yacovelli v. Moeser*,[83] decided on July 7, 2004, the very same U.S. district judge, Judge N. Carlton Tilley, granted UNC's (D) motion to dismiss the plaintiffs' Free Exercise claim and issued a memorandum opinion summarizing the facts and setting forth the reasons for his holding. In relating the instant case back to the 2002 actions, the Court encapsulated the procedural history in this nutshell summary:

> A preliminary injunction was denied both by this Court and by the Fourth Circuit, and the orientation program took place as scheduled. Thereafter, this Court dismissed the Taxpayer Plaintiffs for lack of standing, dismissed any further claims for injunctive relief as moot, and dismissed any claims that the defendants violated the Establishment Clause. Plaintiffs were permitted to add new factual allegations as they

related to the sole remaining claim, the Free Exercise Claim. The defendants have now moved to dismiss the Free Exercise claim.[84]

At this final stage of the litigation, the "sole remaining claim" was "the Free Exercise Claim."[85] It did not rise to an actionable claim because the complaint failed to allege facts sufficient to state a claim for a Free Exercise violation. In other words, the plaintiffs failed to make their case. Judge Tilley enumerated four reasons for this:

> The complaint does not allege a factual basis for the conclusion that UNC either 1. compelled affirmation of any particular religious belief, 2. lent its power to a particular side in a controversy over religious dogma, 3. imposed special disabilities on the basis of religious views or religious status, or 4. punished the expression of any particular religious doctrines.
>
> There is not a sufficient factual or legal basis for the conclusion that UNC either compelled affirmation of Islam, or lent its power in favor of Islamic dogma.[86]

The Court had previously "found that UNC's assignment was academic, and not religious, in nature" and that "UNC, instead of endorsing a particular religious viewpoint, merely undertook to engage students in a scholarly debate about a religious topic." The ensuing discussion groups, moreover, "were likewise intended to encourage scholarly debate about the Islamic religion," where "[s]tudents were free to share their opinions on the topic whether their opinions be positive, negative or neutral."[87] The offending of some students' religious sensitivities notwithstanding, nothing in the required reading assignment nor in the discussion sessions that followed amount to religious indoctrination or exercise. UNC's original objective of helping students gain a more informed perspective on Islam in response to the tragic events of 9/11, and in sharpening their analytical and critical thinking skills in the process, has entirely to do with program design and not with any subterranean religious motives. Any positive portrayal of Islam was an incidental effect that, if nothing else, served as a counterpoint to already existing stereotypes of Islam in general and the deservedly negative public perceptions of Radical Islamism in particular.

The whole issue of coercion was sidestepped when UNC revised its original requirement that all incoming students read *Approaching the Qur'an* and each write a reflective essay based on it. In accommodating those students who might find this assignment religiously offensive, UNC officials adopted an opting out policy. The Court recognized the positive value of this policy in saying: "Allowing students to express their own religious views, or to choose not to do so, did not punish student expression of religious beliefs. Instead, this type of assignment specifically encouraged students to address any and all views they may have had on either the Qur'an [sic] or on the Islamic faith."[88] The fact that there was no grade attached to the assignment was also important, in that a charge of religious coercion might have been possible had there been any negative academic consequences for opting out of the assignment, or even for boycotting the assignment altogether.[89] The Court concluded:

> UNC implemented a freshman orientation program which did not infringe upon the rights of its students under the Free Exercise Clause. The Second Amended Complaint fails to provide sufficient allegations to show that UNC compelled students to perform acts which burdened their religious beliefs, or otherwise punished students on the basis of their religion. To the contrary, UNC implemented a program asking students to discuss a religion thrust into recent controversy, and to do so from an academic perspective. Part of the purpose of this program was to introduce students to the type of higher-level thinking that is required in a university setting. Students who were not members of the Islamic faith, probably the great majority of students, were neither asked nor forced to give up their own beliefs or to compromise their own beliefs in order to discuss the patterns, language, history, and cultural significance of the Qur'an [sic].[90]

Conclusion

This is really a test case of religious pluralism and of its possibilities and limitations within the university context. The study of the Qur'an focalizes all these issues and intensifies them. The terrorist events of 11 September 2001 provided the catalyst. That dark day was the decisive factor in the University of North Carolina at Chapel Hill's selection of *Approaching the Qur'an* as the required text for its 2002 summer reading program. The Family Policy Network's challenge of that choice was a judicial protest that took on national proportions. The following section restates the pedagogical case for the Qur'an and then reflects on the constitutional question (and the answer) provided by *Yacovelli v. Moeser*.

Muslims (including American Muslims, of course) have a coherent worldview, one that originates from the Qur'an itself. (This is not to obscure the contours of serious internal rifts within the Muslim community itself, and significant variances within Muslim self-understanding.) To appreciate the Qur'an is to develop a keener sensitivity to the operation of the divine in a culture once far removed from the Euro-American world but now increasingly an integral part of it. The Qur'an is a world unto itself, a palatial architecture of meaning that is multidimensional and comprehends the totality of the human experience. On the moral and spiritual foundation of the Qur'an, an entire history and civilization has been built. One can only gain from such an appreciation of the Qur'an's role in world history and in contemporary world affairs. Indeed, one may be enriched by a study of the Qur'an (as with the Bible as well), but only if one's prejudices are first abandoned.

Yes, the Qur'an is a text of monumental historical importance. Yet it may have an even greater contemporary relevance, for in an increasing number of western nations, the population of Muslims is beginning to surpass the number of Jews. Islam is rapidly entrenching itself as a French religion, as part of British society, as a feature of the Canadian mosaic, and as an essential element of the spiritual landscape of America. To acknowledge the beauty and depth of the Qur'an is not to convert to Islam, but to converse with it and with Muslims who are enlivened by it. Therefore, to know the Qur'an is to better prepare oneself for inevitable encounters with Muslims both in America and abroad – not as the exotic "other" somewhere in the distant Orient, but as the religion and way of life of our fellow compatriots at home – friends, neighbors, and, through increasing religious intermarriage, that of our immediate and extended families.

The Qur'an can and should be taught in the University, not to convert students into pious Muslims, but to convert pious Muslim beliefs into something students can understand, so that they can appreciate the power of the book to influence those who believe in it. However, beyond the question of *why* the Qur'an should it be taught, there is the problem of *how* it should be taught within constitutional bounds. In whatever course and context it may be taught, the real challenge is how to engage students in the study of this text, and to assist them in discovering the Qur'an for themselves.

The Qur'an is a text of world-historical proportions that institutions of higher learning can scarcely afford to ignore, because our domestic life, as well as international affairs, will be increasingly informed by it. Discovering the Qur'an on a personal basis can be rewarding for its own sake. Studying the Qur'an will equip university students with a competence they are sure to find useful in an increasingly multicultural world, one-fifth of which is already under Islam's spiritual, political, and cultural authority, with an even greater part of the world affected by it. The Qur'an is the constitution of Islamic society in far more profound way than the Constitution is to American society.

The constitutionality of religious studies in university settings has generated a vigorous debate,[91] and the instant case was no exception. One original thesis, sure to spark a lively debate, is Leslie Griffin's distinction between the academic standard and the constitutional standard as to justifying the integration of religious studies in university curricula.[92] In the case of *Yacovelli v. Moeser*, the FPN's persistence preserved the issue, yet constitutional consistency prevailed. Constitutionally, the UNC's adoption of *Approaching the Qur'an* rested on solid ground, over and above FPN's bedrock faith in the merits of its challenge. The FPN's advocacy ultimately resulted in the UNC's vindication. While the subject matter (the Qur'an) was religious, the University of North Carolina's approach was not. Judge Tilley's rationale, although it did not set precedent, faithfully followed it.

The UNC Qur'an controversy should be viewed within a broad spectrum of cases that form the body of educational law as regards the teaching of religion in public schools and institutions of higher learning. The Courts have already weighed in on the University of North Carolina Qur'an controversy. While reading the Qur'an cannot be required, it is required reading for religious, political, cultural and global literacy. In its own way, it is a democratic as well as academic enterprise. It strengthens our Constitution by testing its limits and expanding the juridical horizons of this quintessentially American counterpart of the Qur'an.

NOTES

1   I would like to thank Maurice E.R. Munroe, LL.M., Professor of constitutional law at the Thomas M. Cooley Law School, and Todd Lawson, Professor of Islamic studies at the University of Toronto, for their valuable comments on this paper prior to submission for publication.

2   William E. Shepard, "Islam and Ideology: Towards a Typology," *International Journal of Middle East Studies* (1987), vol.19, no.3, pp.307-336.

3   Michael Sells, *Approaching the Qur'an: The Early Revelations* (Ashland, OR: White Cloud Press, 1999).

4   Michael Burdei, "Approaching the Controversy: How UNC chose *Approaching the Qur'an* and the lessons liberals *and* conservatives can learn from the Summer Reading Program," *Carolina Review* (September, 2002), vol.10, no.1, pp.5-7, at http://www.ibiblio.org/cr/wp-content/uploads/2009/12/2002_09.pdf.

5   Donna R. Euben, "Curriculum Matters," *Academe: Bulletin of the American Association of University Professors* (November-December, 2002), vol.88, no.6, at http://www.aaup.org/AAUP/pubsres/academe/2002/ND/Col/LW.htm.

6   Michael Sells, "Suing the Qur'an," *The American Muslim* (September-October, 2002), at http://www.theamericanmuslim.org/tam.php/features/articles/ suing_the_quran/.

7   *Yacovelli v. Moeser*, 2004 U.S. Dist. LEXIS 9152 (M.D.N.C. May 20, 2004), *aff'd Yacovelli v. Moeser* (University of North Carolina, Chapel Hill), 324 F.Supp.2d 760 (2004).

8   *Abington v. Schempp*, 374 U.S. 203, 224, n. 9 (1963).

9   Ibid.

10 *Edwards v. Aguillard*, 482 U.S. 578, 607 (1987) (Powell and O'Connor, JJ., concurring).

11 On teaching religion in state universities and public schools generally, see the following: Leslie Griffin, "We do not preach. We teach: Religion Professors and the First Amendment," *Quinnipiac Law Review* (2000), vol.19, no.1; Jay D. Wexler, "Preparing for the Clothed Public Square: Teaching about Religion, Civic Education, and the Constitution," *William and Mary Law Review* (2002), vol. 43, no.1159,; Kent Greenawalt, "Symposium,Beyond Separatism: Church and State: Teaching About Religion in the Public Schools," *Journal of Law & Politics* (2002), vol.18, no.329; Philip C. Kissam, "Let's Bring Religion into the Public Schools and Respect the Religion Clauses," University of *Kansas Law Review* (2001), vol.49, no. 593; James L. Underwood, "The Proper Role of Religion in the Public

Schools: Equal Access Instead of Official Indoctrination," *Villanova Law Review* (2001), vol. 46, no. 487; Matthew D. Donovan, "Religion, Neutrality, and the Public School Curriculum: Equal Treatment or Separation?" *Catholic Law* (2004), vol. 3, no.187.

12   Unless otherwise noted, the following remarks on the academic study of the Qur'an are based on my textbook chapter: Christopher Buck, "Discovering the Qur'an in the Modern University," *The Blackwell Companion to the Qur'an*, ed. Andrew Rippin (Oxford: Blackwell, 2005).

13   Sayyid Ali-Muhammad Shirazi (known as "the Bāb"), *Dala'il-i Sab'ih* (The Seven Proofs) (Tehran: 1950, reprinted, Lansing, MI: H-Net, 1998), at http://www.h-net.org/ṭbahai/areprint/bab/A-F/dalail/dalail.htm. See also Todd Lawson, "Interpretation as Revelation: The Qur'an Commentary of Sayyid 'Alí-Muhammad Shírází, the Báb," *Approaches to the History of the Interpretation of the Qur'an*, ed. Andrew Rippin (Oxford: Oxford University Press, 1988), pp.223-53.

14   Michael Sells, *Approaching the Qur'an*, p.5.

15   University of North Carolina at Chapel Hill, "The Carolina Summer Reading Program," at http://www.unc.edu/srp/.

16   "Does the Koran Belong in Class?" *The New York Times* (September 3, 2002), at http://www.nytimes.com/2002/09/03/opinion/L03KORA.html.

17   UNC, "Summer Reading Program."

18   Alan Cooperman, "A Timely Subject, and a Sore One: UNC Draws Fire, Lawsuit for Assigning Book on Islam," (Wednesday, August 7, 2002), A01; Michael Sells, "Understanding, Not Indoctrination," (Thursday, August 8, 2002), A17, at http://www.washingtonpost.com/ac2/wp-dyn?pagename=article&contentId=A57379-2002Aug7&notFound=true; Michael Sells, "Interview," *Religion & Ethics Newsweekly*, (August 23, 2002), episode no.551, Public Broadcasting System (PBS), accessed at http://www.pbs.org/wnet/religionandethics/week551/sells.html.

19   "Studying Islam," *Talk of the Nation*, National Public Radio (August 15, 2002), at http://www.npr.org/templates/story/story.php?storyId=1148332.

20   John Esposito, *Unholy War: Terror in the Name of Islam* (New York: Oxford University Press, 2002).

21   Ashland, OR: White Cloud Press, 1999.

22   See Dr. Caner's home page at http://www.emircaner.com/.

23   Ergun Mehmet Caner and Emir Fethi Caner, *Unveiling Islam: An Insider's Look at Muslim Life and Beliefs* (Grand Rapids: Kregel, 2002).

24   "Partial Transcript of Proceedings Before the Honorable N. Carlton Tilley, Jr., U.S. District Judge," Civil Action No. 1:02CV596 (31pp.). Obtained from the Office of the Attorney General, State of North Carolina, Education Section (January 11, 2005), whose faxed copy was originally obtained from the UNC Chancellor's Office. Copy provided courtesy of John C. Michaud, Reference and Faculty

Services Librarian, Thomas M. Cooley Law School Library.

25 The Associated Press, "Freshmen sue university over required reading of Islamic book," at http://www.freedomforum.org/templates/ document.asp? documentID =16580.

26 American Family Association Divisions, Center for Law and Policy, "What We Believe," at http://www.afa.net/clp/believe.asp.

27 Jane Stancill, "UNC Qur'an Reading Is Upheld," *The News and Observer* (Raleigh, Durham, Cary, Chapel Hill, August 16, 2002), at http://www.naspa.org/netre-sults/PrinterFriendly.cfm?ID=719, transcript, p.18. (At the time of going to the press, the referenced webpage was no longer available).

28 Ibid.

29 Ibid., p.15, where the punctuation differs: "The two-hour discussion session is not a religious activity. Just as playing the CD in this courtroom did not convert it into a religious activity…"

30 Transcript, pp.14-15.

31 Ibid., p.14.

32 Jane Stancill, "UNC Qur'an Reading Is Upheld," *The News and Observer* (Raleigh, Durham, Cary, Chapel Hill, Aug. 16, 2002) at http://www.naspa.org/netre-sults/PrinterFriendly.cfm?ID=719. (At the time of going to the press, the referenced webpage was no longer available).

33 Transcript, pp.10-14.

34 Ibid., pp.28-29.

35 Ibid., pp.24-28.

36 Ibid., pp.28-29.

37 The Associated Press, "N.C. lawmakers Condemn University Reading Assignment," at http://www.freedomforum.org/templates/document.asp? docu-ment ID=16705.

38 Ibid.

39 Michael J. McManus, "Approaching the Qur'an," (August 24, 2002), at http:// www.marriagesavers.org/Columns/C1095.htm. (At the time of going to the press, the referenced webpage was no longer available).

40 Chancellor James Moeser, "NASULGC Panel: Free Speech and Its Implications Post 9/11," (Monday, November 11, 2002), at http://www.nasulgc.org/AM 2002/presentations/AM2002_Moeser_remarks.pdf. (At the time of going to the press, the referenced webpage was no longer available).

41 The Associated Press, "Critics: N.C. Lawmakers Threatening University's Academic Freedom," (August 9, 2002), at http://www.freedomforum.org/tem-plates/document.asp?documentID=16708.

42 Richard Veit, "Statement to the Educational Planning, Policies and Programs Committee of the Board of Governors," *The Seahawk* (September 5, 2002), at http://www.theseahawk.com/news/2002/09/05/Oped.

43 The Associated Press, "Court Won't Halt Student Discussions of Book about Qur'an," at http://www.freedomforum.org/templates/document.asp? document ID=16769.

44 Ibid.

45 Two-page document obtained from the Office of the Attorney General, State of North Carolina, Education Section (January 11, 2005), whose faxed copy was originally obtained from the UNC Chancellor's Office. Copy provided courtesy of John C. Michaud, Reference and Faculty Services Librarian, Thomas M. Cooley Law School Library.

46 The Associated Press, "Group Tries to Derail Campus Islamic Awareness Week," (October 14, 2002), at http://www.freedomforum.org/templates/document.asp? documentID=17106.

47 Ibid.

48 *Yacovelli v. Moeser*, 2004 U.S. Dist. LEXIS 9152, pp.8-9 (only pagination provided).

49 *Yacovelli v. Moeser*, 2004 U.S. Dist. LEXIS 9152, p.10.

50 Ibid.

51 *Yacovelli v. Moeser*, 2004 U.S. Dist. LEXIS 9152, p.14.

52 Ibid., p.15.

53 Ibid.

54 Ibid.

55 Ibid.

56 Flast v. Cohen, 392 U.S. 83, 20 L. Ed. 2d 947, 88 S. Ct. 1942 (1968).

57 *Yacovelli v. Moeser*, 2004 U.S. Dist. LEXIS 9152, 17 (citing *Flast*, 392 U.S. at pp.102-103).

58 Ibid.

59 Ibid.

60 Ibid., p.18.

61 Ibid., p.19.

62 James v. Jacobson, 6 F.3d 233, 238-39 (4th Cir. 1993) (enumerating factors that courts must weigh for a party to proceed pseudonymously).

63 *Yacovelli v. Moeser*, 2004 U.S. Dist. LEXIS 9152, 20.

64 Ibid., p.21.

65 Ibid., p.23.

66 Ibid., p.24.

67 Ibid., p.25.

68 Ibid., p.26.

69 Ibid., p.26.

70 Ibid., p.30 (citation omitted).

71 *Yacovelli v. Moeser*, 2004 U.S. Dist. LEXIS 9152, 31 (citing Honig v. Doe, 484 U.S. 305, 335-36, 98 L. Ed. 2d 686, 108 S. Ct. 592 (1988)).

72   *Yacovelli v. Moeser,* 2004 U.S. Dist. LEXIS 9152, 31.

73   Ibid., p.32.

74   Ibid., p.32 (citation omitted).

75   *Yacovelli v. Moeser,* 2004 U.S. Dist. LEXIS 9152, p.32 (citing *Lemon v. Kurtzman,* 403 U.S. 602 at 612-13, 29 L. Ed. 2d 745, 91 S. Ct. 2105 (1971)).

76   *Yacovelli v. Moeser,* 2004 U.S. Dist. LEXIS 9152, p.37.

77   Ibid. (citations omitted).

78   Ibid., p.43.

79   Ibid., p.44 (citation omitted).

80   Ibid., p.45.

81   Ibid., p.46.

82   Ibid., p.50.

83   Yacovelli v. Moeser, 324 F. Supp. 2d 760, 2004 U.S. Dist. LEXIS 12815 (M.D.N.C., July 7, 2004).

84   Yacovelli v. Moeser, 324 F. Supp. 2d 760 at 762.

85   Ibid.

86   Ibid. at 763-764.

87   Yacovelli v. Moeser, 324 F. Supp. 2d 760 at 764.

88   Ibid.

89   Ibid.

90   Ibid.

91   See Jay D. Wexler, "Preparing for the Clothed Public Square."

92   See Leslie Griffin, "We do not preach."

Islam 101: A Survey of "Introduction to Islam" Courses in American Colleges and Universities

FAISAL ISLAM & ZAHID H. BUKHARI

Context

ISLAM is one of the fastest-growing religions in the U.S. and yet it is one of the most misunderstood religions. The unfortunate events of 9/11 and its aftermath have sparked the interest of learning and knowing Islam. The intrigue to know Islam more is not limited to the public level but also reflects in academic life, especially in the universities and colleges where Islam or its related courses have been offered since 9/11.

Many American courses related to Islam or the Islamic world have observed a dramatic increase in enrollment. At Columbia University, during 2003 fall registration, a number of students wishing to take Arabic language courses were refused. They were told they could not be accommodated, even after that year's addition of two sections and the hiring of a new adjunct professor. A decade ago, this level of interest would have been nearly unthinkable. Similarly, an existing course at Harvard Law School, "Islamic Legal Systems" observed an increase in enrollment up to 50 percent more when it was offered after 9/11. The instructor for the course is quick to point out that students are not specifically citing 9/11 as their reason for taking the courses, but the event has certainly sparked interest in Islam both as a religion and a legal system. Despite the growing interest to know Islam more in American universities and colleges, we lack information about the state of Islamic studies in the U.S. and its history and development.

Islamic studies in North America is believed to have emerged from Orientalism. The early American scholars of Islam were mostly missionaries with typically vocal opposition to Islam. Islamic studies on American campuses occupied some place through the Middle Eastern and/or Near Eastern Studies centers after the World War II. During this period, much attention was given to different subjects related to the area studies rather than to Islam itself. Islam as a religion was so diminished that there was only one person who presented a paper on Islam in the annual conferences of the American Academy of Religion in 1973. The situation is different nowadays. We are now in the beginning of a new phase where Islamic studies has started to occupy its place in American universities and colleges. Still, more information is needed about the status of Islamic studies, which is fairly new in the U.S.

The role of academic courses on Islam in vital. Unlike other religious studies, Islamic studies faces a challenge to addressing many stereotypes and misconceptions such as violence, terrorism, and gender inequality that are usually associated with Islam and Muslims. Teaching Islam in an appropriate way can dispel those stereotypes and misconceptions and can help in understanding this religion correctly. It is important to analyze and understand the state of Islamic studies in the U.S. universities and colleges and to find responses to some pertinent questions such as who is teaching Islam: What are the characteristics of those who are teaching Islam? What course goals and required text have been selected to teach Islam in America?

In this context, this study attempts to respond to the above questions by analyzing the current state of Islamic studies in the U.S. campuses through an empirical survey of fundamental courses on Islam. We hope the study will fill an important gap in understanding the state of Islamic studies in America.

The report is divided into the following sections: survey design, sample size, and methodology; demographic characteristics of the instructors who are teaching introductory courses on Islam; discussion on course goals and approaches in teaching Islam; commentary on required texts and authors of the required texts; enrollment and grading method; and conclusion and some key recommendations.

Survey Design, Sample Size, and Methodology

The survey was conducted by collecting 105 course syllabi of basic courses on Islam from mainstream American universities and colleges. The courses introduce Islam either as a religion, civilization, culture, or legal and political system, historically and in the contemporary world. Through syllabi, information related to course goals, required text and authors, and methods to evaluate the students were collected. In addition, the characteristics of the instructors teaching these courses were collected, such as instructor qualification, course enrollment or class size, and the frequency the course was offered over the past few semesters or years. Only one course from each instructor is included in this study. If any instructor is found teaching more than one courses on different aspects of Islam, the course closer to Islam 101 was taken for this survey. No department was represented more than once in the sample size of 105.

The first draft of our recently initiated database of American graduate and undergraduate programs offering at least one course on Islam is used to identify the courses. Using this initial database, all 200 departments in undergraduate and graduate programs that have offered a full basic course on Islam during 2000 and 2005 were identified and contacted through emails to gather information regarding course syllabi, instructor characteristics, course enrollment, and frequency of the course offerings over the past years. In addition, web search and departmental websites were also used to download the required information. Out of 200 potential courses, we received responses and information regarding 105 courses (a sample of a course syllabus is attached at Appendix 1) which served as our sample size for this study. These 105 cases represent 35 states across the U.S. (Appendix 2) and were from America's mainstream institution with 17 colleges and remaining universities. The data related to course outlines and other characteristics were collected during August 2004 and May 2005.

Using the available information related to instructor characteristics, course goals, required text, and evaluation method, a code book was developed for data entry and data analysis. The data was entered and maintained in the Microsoft ACCESS 2003 but was analyzed in a specialized statistical package, STATA version 7.

Instructor Demographic Characteristics

Gender, Highest Education, and Religion

In our survey study, a large number of instructors were male and non–Muslim. Approximately 79 percent of the instructors were male and about 21 percent were female. Most of the instructors teaching Islam were non–Muslims and only 21 percent were Muslims. Almost all scholars (99 percent) had a Ph.D. as their highest education. (Table 1).

Table 1: Gender, Highest Qualifications, and Religion of the Instructors

Gender		
	N	%
Male	83	79.05
Female	22	20.95
Total	*105*	*100*
Highest Qualifications		
	N	%
Ph.D.	102	99.03
Masters	1	0.97
Total	*103*	*100*
Religion		
	N	%
Muslims	22	21.12
Non–Muslims	72	69.23
Total	*94*	*100*

Institutions

Instructors teaching Islam in our analysis graduated from 40 different institutions worldwide (Appendix 3), mainly from the U.S. institutions. The largest number of instructors graduated from the University of Chicago (17 percent) followed by Harvard University (10.89 percent), McGill University (6.93 percent), Yale University (5.94 percent), University of California (4.95 percent), Princeton University

(4.95 percent), and University of Toronto (4.95 percent) as shown in Table 2.

Table 2: Top 5 Institutions where Instructors Graduated
(in terms of their highest qualification)

Institution	N	%
University of Chicago	17	16.83
Harvard University	11	10.89
McGill University	7	6.93
Yale University	6	5.94
University of California at Los Angeles	5	4.95
Princeton University	5	4.95
University of Toronto	5	4.95
Others	56	55.45
Total	101	100

Year of Graduation

There is clear evidence that a majority of the instructors teaching Islam are relatively young or recently graduated. In our analysis, we found most of the instructors were graduated during the last decade (44 percent) compared to the preceding decades since 1974. Only 8 out of 105 instructors graduated before 1974 (Table 3).

Table 3: Instructor Year of Graduation
(in terms of the highest qualification)

Time Period	N	%
1995 or after	35	44.30
Between 1985 and 1994	18	22.78
Between 1975 and 1984	18	22.78
Before 1974	8	10.14
Total	79	100

Though instructors of Islamic studies were fairly diverse in terms of areas of expertise, they lacked a genuine expertise in Islamic studies (Table 4). The instructors of Islamic studies had their specialization in 8 different disciplines with as much as 48 percent in religious studies (excluding Islam), followed by Near Eastern/ Middle Eastern languages and civilization (15 percent), history (12.63 percent) and Islamic studies (12.63 percent).

Table 4: Primary Areas of Expertise of Instructors
(based upon the area in which they received their highest qualification)

Area of Expertise	N	%
Religious studies (other than Islam)	46	48.42
Near Eastern/Middle Eastern languages and civilizations/literature	14	14.73
History	12	12.63
Islamic studies	12	12.63
Philosophy	4	4.21
Political science	3	3.16
Law	2	2.11
Anthropology	2	2.11
Total	95	100

The finding that approximately 13 percent of the instructors had their primary expertise in Islam is important and merits discussion. It endorses the contention that majority of the courses that focus on Islam are taught by scholars whose primary expertise is in another field, such as Biblical and Jewish studies or Indian religions. The trend to borrow scholars to teach Islam from other areas of expertise that was observed in 1980s seems to continue even after 20 years, though the number of professors whose primary expertise is in Islam has risen. Although it does not mean scholars who are teaching Islam with expertise on other religions are not competitive enough or capable to teach Islam, it is against the conventional wisdom.

The role of academic institutions, and especially their hiring procedures to hire a scholar of Islamic Studies is also critical. Unfortunately, it lacks consistency in hiring a scholar for Islamic studies and other religions. Most of the institutions do not follow the same rigorous criterion to hire a scholar of Islamic studies and a scholar of other religions. McAulifee observed:

> No American university would hire a research scholar of "Biblical studies." It would recruit a specialist in John or Luke-Acts or Christian origins. Or it would advertise for a biblical archaeologist, an authority in Israelite and Canaanite religion, or a scholar of northwest Semitic languages. That same university, however, would feel no hesitancy in advertising for a specialist in 'Qur'anic Studies,' if it were even willing to diversify its faculty beyond a single, all-purpose Islamicist.

Almost 78 percent of the scholars had published at least one book related to their areas of expertise. Almost 39 percent had published two to five published books and 16 percent of the instructors had published more than five books. 22 percent of the total scholars had several published articles and book chapters but have not published any books (Table 5).

Table 5: Number of Publications by Instructors

Published Books and Articles	N	%
More than 5 books	16	16.33
2 – 5 books	38	38.78
1 book	22	22.45
Published articles (no book)	22	22.45
Total	*98*	*100*

Trends in Teaching Islam: Analysis of Course Goals and Required Text

Islam is a very broad subject and teaching Islamic studies is rather complex. Many scholars on Islam have deliberated with this issue of what should be included in an introductory course on Islamic studies. The state of teaching Islam becomes more complex as there is no measure of unity in teaching Islam, such as race in Jewish studies or geography in area centers. Realizing the breadth of Islamic studies, clear boundaries of what has been taught in Islamic studies were framed after carefully reviewing the received course syllabi. The course goals received from the survey were divided into following 12 major themes or course topics: 1. Islamic faith/belief and practice; 2. Islamic sources; 3. Islamic institutions; 4. Islamic history; 5. Islamic culture and civilization; 6. Islamic theology and intellectual currents; 7. Law and Shariʿah; 8. Islam in the modern world; 9. Islamic revival and reform movements; 10. Gender and human rights; 11. Islam in the West/America; and 12. Islam and the other religions. With this categorization, the data were analyzed as follows.

Course Topics
A growing consensus among the instructors was observed related to what should be taught or included in an introductory course on Islam. Almost 69 percent of the instructors were teaching "Islamic theology and intellectual currents," 62 percent of the instructors are teaching "Islamic history," 60 percent of the instructors are teaching "Islamic sources," 52 percent of the scholars are teaching "Islam and the modern world," 43 percent are teaching "Law and Shariʿah," 42 percent are teaching "Islamic faith/belief and practice," 38 percent are teaching "Gender and human rights," and 37 percent are teaching "Islamic culture and civilization" in their introductory classes (Table 6).

Table 6: Themes or Course Goals Selected by Instructors

Name of Theme/Course Goal	N	%
Islamic theology and intellectual currents	73	69.52
Islamic history	65	61.90
Islamic sources	63	60.00
Islam in the modern world	55	52.38
Islamic faith/belief and practice	45	42.86
Law and Shariʿah	44	41.90
Gender and human rights in Islam	40	38.10
Islamic culture and civilization	39	37.14
Islamic revival and reform movements	33	31.43
Islam in the West/America	22	20.95
Islamic institutions	18	17.14
Islam and other religions	10	9.52
N=105		

A changing trend in teaching Islam that was rare some decades ago was also noticed. Topics such as "Islamic theology and intellectual currents," "Islamic sources," and "Islam in the modern world" were receiving more emphasis than topics such as "Islamic history" and "Islamic culture and civilization." Previously, it was only "Islamic history" and "Islamic culture and civilization" that were the most-emphasized areas in teaching Islam across the U.S. Yet all courses on Islam are not comprehensive and some areas such as Islam in America, Islamic institutions, Islamic contributions to science, and relationship with other religions were found least covered.

In view of the sensitiveness of teaching Islam in American and the West due to existing negative perceptions, it is essential to cover all important aspects of Islam as a religion to portray its true and accurate picture in any introductory course. Any attempt to cover some aspects and ignore others could be misleading. Therefore, after a careful analysis of the received syllabi, a comprehensive sample syllabus was derived for teaching an introductory course on Islam (Figure 1). The syllabus covers all important aspects related to Islam that could be covered in a full semester (3 credit hours) course, possibly with a title "An Introduction to Islam."

Figure 1: Comprehensive Sample Syllabus of Course
"An Introduction to Islam"

Goals	Topics Could be Discussed	Timeline
Islamic faith/belief and practice	*Tawḥīd*, Prophets, Angels, Holy Books, Day of Return, and the five pillars	1 week
Islamic sources	Qur'an, Hadith, and the life of the Prophet	1–2 weeks
Islamic institutions	Role of Mosque, judiciary, and the state	1 week
Islamic history	Origin and emergence, spread of Islam, and the golden era	1–2 weeks
Islamic culture and civilization	Contributions to art, architecture, music, literature, poetry, and science	1–2 weeks
Islamic theology and intellectual currents	Sufism, sects, and philosophy	1–2 weeks
Law and Shariʿah	Source and principles of Islamic jurisprudence, major schools of thoughts, family law, Islamic economics, etc	1–2 weeks
Islam in the modern world	Media stereotypes, politics, and geography	1 week
Islamic revival and reform movements	Orientalism, fundamentalism, major movements in the Muslim world, and jihad	1 week
Gender and human rights	Myths and reality, Islamic teachings, current feminist and human rights movements in the Islamic world	1 week
Islam in the West/America	The origin, current profile, issues and challenges, and prominent Muslim individuals' work in western/American society	1 week
Islam and other religions	Relationship with other religions, similarities, tolerance, and co-existence	1 week

The selection of course goals by instructors according to their gender and the year of graduation were also analyzed in this study. Male instructors were found focusing more on "Islamic history," "Islam in the modern world," and "Islamic institutions" compared to their female counterparts. Female instructors were found relatively more focused on "Gender and human rights in Islam" and "Law and Shariʿah" (Table 7).

Table 7: Selection of Themes or Course Goals by Instructor Gender

Theme Name	Male		Female	
	N	%	N	%
Islamic theology and intellectual currents	57	68.67	16	72.73
Islamic history	56	67.47	9	40.91
Islamic sources	51	61.45	12	54.55
Islam in the modern world	46	55.42	9	40.91
Islamic faith/belief and practice	36	43.37	9	40.91
Law and Shariʿah	34	40.96	10	45.45
Islamic culture and civilization	32	38.55	7	31.82
Gender and human rights in Islam	30	36.14	10	45.45
Islamic revival and reform movements	28	33.73	5	22.73
Islamic institutions	17	20.48	1	4.55
Islam in the West/America	17	20.48	5	22.73
Islam and other religions	7	8.43	3	13.64
Total N (male=83, female=22)				

Selection of course topics by the instructors across the year of their graduation is interesting. Instructors who received their doctorates after 1985 were focusing more on topics such as "Islam in the modern world," "Islamic faith/belief and practices," "Gender and human rights in Islam," and "Islam in the West/America" (Table 8). This clearly indicates that instructors who graduated during the past two decades are more likely to cover issues related to modern era in their introductory courses compared to those instructors who graduated before 1985. The only course that appeared to be more emphasized by the instructors who graduated before 1985 is "Islamic culture and civilization" than by the instructors who received their doctorate degrees after 1985.

Table 8: Selection of Themes or Course Goals by Year of Graduation of Instructors (in terms of highest qualification)

Theme Name	After 1985		On or Before 1985	
	N	%	N	%
Islamic theology and intellectual currents	41	77.36	21	80.77
Islamic sources	33	62.26	18	69.23
Islam in the modern world	33	62.26	10	38.46
Islamic history	31	58.49	16	61.54
Islamic faith/belief and practice	28	52.83	8	30.77
Law and Shari'ah	23	43.40	14	53.85
Gender and human rights in Islam	22	41.51	5	19.23
Islamic revival and reform movements	18	33.96	7	26.92
Islamic culture and civilization	15	28.30	11	42.31
Islam in the West/America	14	26.42	3	11.54
Islamic institutions	6	11.32	4	15.38
Islam and other religions	6	11.32	1	3.85
Total N (>1985=53, <=1985=26)				

Required Texts and Authors

Required Text from Course Syllabus

No general consensus was observed in selecting the required text in teaching the above topics or themes, making the required text selection very diverse. More than 200 books (Appendix 4) were used by the instructors as required text in teaching the different topics related to Islam. The optional text and course pack provided by the instructors to students were in addition to the required text. Availability of such a large number of text books for teaching Islam shows a wide range of choices. On the other hand, it signifies that a quality primer to teach Islam that has a general agreement among the instructors who teach Islam in the U.S. is missing.

Among the texts that had some agreement, *Introduction to Islam* by Frederick Mathewson Denny (Prentice Hall, 1993) was the most widely-used book for teaching fundamental Islam. Almost 27 percent of instructors were teaching this book. Professor of Religious Studies at the University of Colorado at Boulder, Dr. Denny provides students a thorough introduction of Islam in this book. The book places Islam within a cultural, political, social, and religious context and examines its connections with Judeo-Christian morals. The text's integration of the doctrinal and devotional elements of Islam enables students to see how Muslims think and live – engendering understanding and breaking down stereotypes. *An Introduction to Islam, Second Edition* also reviews pre-Islamic history so students can see how Islam developed historically.

Islam: The Straight Path by John L. Esposito (Oxford University Press, 1997) and *Approaching the Qur'an: The Early Revelations* by Michael Sells (White Cloud Press, 1999, and CD) emerged as the second most widely-used books. 12 percent of the instructors were using these books as required texts for teaching introductory Islam.

John L. Esposito is Professor of Religious Studies and International Affairs and Director of the Prince Alwaleed Center for Muslim-Christian Understanding at Georgetown University. He is a famous author and has written several books on Islam. *Islam: The Straight Path* is a widely-acclaimed guide to Islamic history, faith, culture, and politics. It gives readers an understanding of the faith, belief, and practice of Islam from its origins to the present. The book traces the emergence of this dynamic faith and its impact on world history and discusses the formation of Islamic belief and practice in such areas as law, theology, philosophy, and mysticism. The third edition has been updated throughout and is enhanced by new material that reflects the diversity of Muslim cultures. In particular, Esposito broadens the study of Islam beyond the Middle East with a new study of Pakistan as well as a new section on the Muslim presence in the U.S. and the impact of prominent figures such as Malcolm X, Warith Uddin Muhammad, and Louis Farrakhan. In the final chapter, Esposito discusses modern Muslim thinking on religious pluralism, democracy, and human rights.

Michael Sells is Professor of Comparative Religion at Haverford College and Chairperson of the Haverford Department of Religion. Author of many books on Islam, Sells provides a general introduction to the Qur'an and its role in Islamic culture in *Approaching the Qur'an: The Early Revelations*. The goal of the book is to make the early Makkan period of the Qur'an, in its literary and oral qualities, approachable and accessible to those not conversant in Arabic.[1] The book translates early Makkan surahs with facing commentaries and discusses the sound nature and gender aspects of the Arabic text. An accompanying CD with Qur'anic reciters from around the world reciting the *adhān* and six surahs in various styles provides readers an opportunity to feel the Qur'an.

Unfortunately, the book came under legal controversy when a Christian activist group sued the University of North Carolina at Chapel Hill's selection to teach this book as the required reading for its 2002 summer reading program. Although there were no sanctions on students who declined to participate, the plaintiffs of this case were of the view that the assignment (making the book assigned reading for incoming students) is unconstitutional and it promotes Islam. The group after losing the case in the U.S. District Court, Middle District of North Carolina, immediately appealed to the 4th Circuit Court of Appeals, but lost it again.

The fourth widely-used text in our analysis appeared to be *Koran*, translated by N.J. Dawood (Penguin Series, U.K.) As many as 9.5 percent of the instructors were using this translation. A Jewish-Arab scholar, N.J. Dawood is best-known for this translation of the Qur'an, the first in contemporary English idiom. The translation was first published in 1956 and has since sold over one million copies. The translation is simple and easy. In the early editions of the translation, it is noted that the sequence of the surahs in this translation was changed, beginning with "the more Biblical and poetic revelation" and ending with the "more topical chapters." However, in the present edition, the arrangement of the surah follows the traditional sequence (Penguin Books Limited, 2005). The critics of this translation also doubt the quality and accuracy of translation and believed that at some places the verses were "mistranslated."

Other widely-used texts observed in this analysis were *The Venture of Islam* by Marshall G.S. Hodgson (6.7 percent) and *The Vision of Islam* by William Chittick and Sachiko Murata (6.7 percent). The top five books that were used by the instructors in teaching the courses are listed in Table 9.

Table 9: Top Five Books Used by Instructors as a Required Text

Name of Book (with Author)	N	%
An Introduction to Islam (Frederick Mathewson Denny)	27	25.71
Islam: The Straight Path (John L. Esposito)	13	12.38
Approaching the Qur'an: The Early Revelations (Michael Sells)	13	12.38
Koran (translated by N.J. Dawood)	10	9.52
The Venture of Islam (Marshall G. S. Hodgson)	7	6.67
The Vision of Islam (Visions of Reality. Understanding Religions) (Sachiko Murata, William C. Chittick)	7	6.67
The Wedding of Zein and Other Stories (Tayeb Saleh)	6	5.71
The Glorious Qur'an (Muhammad M. Pickthall)	6	5.71
Islam (Fazlur Rahman)	6	5.71
The Word of Islam (John Alden Williams)	6	5.71
N= 105		

Authors of the Required Text from the Course Syllabus

A lack of general consensus in selecting books is already reported and the trend is consistent when it comes to selecting authors. Published work of more than 150 authors (Appendix 4) was found referred as compulsory requirements by the instructors of the received course syllabi. The number of authors is less than the number of books reported above, because some authors have written more than one book, and instructors were teaching different books of the same author.

Frederick Matthews Denny, because of his book *An Introduction to Islam*, was still on the top of the list and as many as 26 percent of the instructors were using his book. John L. Esposito (20 percent) followed Professor Denny and his seven books: *Islam: The Straight Path*, *Unholy War: Terror in the Name of Islam*, *The Oxford History of Islam*, and *What Everyone Needs to Know About Islam*, *The Islamic Myth: Threat or Reality*, *Contemporary Islam: Reformation and Revolution*, and *Voices of Resurgent Islam* were used as required texts. Michael Sells (13 percent) was noted as the third most-widely referred author. Fazlur Rahman (11 percent), John Renard (9.9 percent), and Carl Ernst (9.9 percent) were the other top authors observed in this analysis (Table 10).

Table 10: Top Five Authors whose Books are Used as a Required Text

Name of Authors	N	%
Frederick Mathewson Denny	27	25.71
John L. Esposito	21	20.00
Michael Sells	14	13.33
Fazlur Rahman	12	11.43
Carl W. Ernst	10	9.52
John Renard	10	9.52
N.J. Dawood	10	9.52
N= 105		

Course Frequency, Class Enrollments, and Methods of Evaluation

The frequency by which the courses were offered over the years, class size, and different methods used to evaluate the students were also examined. Approximately 63 percent of the courses were offered either every year or in every semester. Of them, 44 percent of the course offerings were once every year and 19 percent were in every semester (Table 11). Mostly, the course was offered in the fall or spring semester.

Table 11: Frequency of Course Offerings

Frequency	N	%
Once a year	35	44.30
Once every two years	23	29.11
Every semester	15	18.99
Once every 3 years	3	3.80
One time only	3	3.80
Total	79	*100*

Under class size, a minimum class size of 12 students and a maximum of 145 students was observed. The average class size seemed to be 40.2 students per course (Table 12). Further, this average class size was even higher to 42 students per course if we drop those 13 cases who reported capping their class size between 30-35 students. In any case, the average class size of the courses on Islam is on the higher side than the average class size of any other courses in many universities.

For example, the average class size in Arts and Science at the University of Chicago was 22 students, and in the Divinity School the average class size was 12 students during 2000-2001.[2] Similarly, the California State University at Los Angeles has reported average class sizes of about 30.4 for lower division courses, 25.5 for upper division courses, 13.6 for graduate courses, and 26.5 overall. The higher average class size in our analysis demonstrates the high demand of learning an introductory course on Islam from the perspective of students.

Table 12: Course Enrollment or Class Size

N	Mean	Std. Deviation	Min	Max
80	40.2	26.50	12	145

A large majority (65 percent) of the instructors were evaluating students by using all the three standard approaches, i.e., class participation, writing assignments (term/research papers), and midterm/final exams. 9 percent of the instructors were using only class participation and writing assignment as methods to evaluate registered students for the course (Table 13).

Table 13: Methods of Course Evaluation

Methods of Evaluation	N	%
Papers, exams, and class participation	64	66.67
Class participation and exams (no paper)	9	9.38
Papers and exam (no class participation)	8	8.33
Class participations and paper (no exam)	6	6.25
Only exam/quizzes (no papers and class participation)	5	5.22
Only papers (no exam and class participation)	4	4.17
Total	*96*	*100*

Conclusion and Recommendations

The state of Islamic studies in the U.S. was analyzed by conducting a survey of 105 fundamental courses on Islam. The survey included an analysis of the course goals, characteristics of the instructors, required texts and authors, class size for each of the course, the methods of students' evaluation, and the frequency with which the course was offered over the period of semesters or years.

Under instructor demographic characteristics, 79 percent of the instructors were male and 21 percent were female. Almost all instructors had a doctoral degree in their areas of specialization and 17 percent of the instructors received their doctoral degrees from the University of Chicago. Other prominent universities observed were Harvard University (10.89 percent) and McGill University (6.93 percent). Less than one-fourth of the instructors were Muslims and remaining were non-Muslims.

All instructors teaching introductory Islam were found well-qualified from reputable institutions but lacked genuine expertise and background in Islam. Only 12.6 percent of the instructors had primary expertise in Islamic studies. The trend to borrow instructors to teach

Islam with their primary areas of expertise or disciplines other than Islam is still observed. Other areas of expertise observed were in religious studies (other than Islam) (48.4 percent), Near Eastern/Middle Eastern languages and civilizations/ literature (14.7 percent), and history (12.6 percent).

It is encouraging that a general agreement was observed in what should be included in an introductory course on Islam. Topics such as "Islamic theology and intellectual currents" (69.5 percent), "Islamic history" (61.9 percent), "Islamic sources" (60 percent), and "Islam in the modern world" (52.4 percent) were found the most widely-used course goals in the introductory classes. Yet there is a need to teach an introductory but comprehensive course on Islam that captures all its important aspects and major themes. Based upon the received course outlines, a comprehensive sample outline was derived for teaching an introductory course on Islam (Figure 1).

Male instructors were found focusing more on the course topics "Islamic history," "Islam in the modern world," and "Islamic institutions" than female instructors. While analyzing the themes or course topics selection by gender, it is found that the male instructors were more likely to cover topics such as "Islamic history" (27 percentage point difference), "Islam in the modern world" (15 percentage point difference), and "Islamic institutions" (16 percentage point difference) than the female instructors. Similarly, those instructors who graduated after 1985 were emphasizing more on course topics "Islam in the modern world" (24 percentage point difference), "Gender and human rights in Islam" (22 percentage point difference), "Islam in the West/America" (15 percentage point difference), and "Islamic faith/belief and practices" (12 percentage point difference) than the instructors who graduated before 1985.

Unlike a general agreement on what should go into an introductory course on Islam, there was a little consensus on the selection of required textbooks for teaching Islam. More than 200 books (Appendix 4) were used as a required text to cover different parts of the course syllabus. The top four books noticed in our analysis were: *An Introduction to Islam* by Fredrick Mathews Denny (25.7 percent), *Islam: The Straight Path* by John L. Esposito (12.4 percent), *Approaching the*

Qur'an: The Early Revelations by Michael Sells (12.38 percent), and *Koran* translated by N.J. Dawood (9.5 percent). Among authors, Frederick Matthews Denny (25.7 percent), John L. Esposito (20 percent), Michael Sells (13.3 percent), and Fazlur Rahman (11.4 percent) were found as the top four scholars whose books were used as a required text by the instructors.

There is certainly a strong demand to learn Islam through academic courses as the average class size in our analysis was 40-42 students per course. It is further observed that 65 percent of these courses were offered either every semester or once in every year. This shows that every year there were approximately 2500-3000 students who took these introductory courses on Islam. The methods of evaluating students of these courses seemed comprehensive as 60 percent of the instructors asked students for class participation, writing assignments, and mid-term/final examinations.

Based upon the above findings, we would like to make the following recommendations:

1) It is encouraging to note that Islamic studies has started to find its place on American campuses. The demand is certainly there but the challenge is how to match the demand with quality supply. Expansion of Islamic studies across colleges and universities is certainly the best way to meet the demand. Besides expansion, it is equally important to consolidate and improve the existing efforts, and ask: Who is teaching Islam? What is being taught as Islam? What is the impact of Islamic studies on society, and what kind of scholarship is emerging from the Islamic studies programs? These are some of the questions that will be asked more and more often. Developing a new quality primer or having a general agreement on a list of quality books as required texts to teach introductory courses on Islam could be an important step.

2) More important, Islamic studies should be treated as a specialized discipline within its own framework or within the broader framework of the department of religions studies. The practice to borrow scholars from other disciplines to teach Islam should be changed

and a focus should be placed on hiring a specialized faculty on Islam. Following the same extensive criteria to recruit Islamic scholars as is the practice for recruiting a faculty member for other prominent religions or disciplines could be a first step in the right direction.

3) The U.S. is a diverse, pluralist, and free society. It has the advantage that its academic institutions as well as its society represent all the three Abrahamic religions: Judaic, Christianity, and Islam. Islamic studies in the U.S. universities and colleges is relatively new and still developing. Attention must be focused on developing Islamic studies in America in a way that reflects a true picture of this great religion. Teaching Islam correctly and comprehensively will not only help America to understand Islam accurately but also help the Islamic world to understand America correctly. Placing quality programs on Islamic studies with nationwide coverage will certainly help in building a generation that could help in creating a so-called threat of "clash of civilizations" into a "co-existence of civilizations."

APPENDIX 1

A Sample from 105 Received Course Syllabi

Religion 155
An Introduction to Islam
xxx³
Spring 2004

Instructor: xxx
Office: xxx
Office Hours: xxx
Phone ext.: xxx
Course URL: xxx

Course Description:
This course is an introduction to Islam as a prophetic religious tradition. It explores the different ways Muslims have interpreted and put
into practice the prophetic message of Muhammad through historical
and phenomenological analyses of varying theological, philosophical,
legal, political, mystical, and literary writings. These analyses aim for
course participants to develop a framework for explaining the sources
and symbols through which historically specific experiences and
understandings have been signified as Islamic. The course focuses in
particular on the classical and modern periods of Islamic history.

Required Texts:
Available on reserve and at the bookstore:

Ahmed, Leila. *Women and Gender in Islam: Historical Roots of a Modern
    Debate*. New Haven: Yale University Press, 1992.
Attar, Farid ud-Din. *The Conference of the Birds*, trans. Afkham
    Darbandi and Dick Davis. New York: Penguin Books, 1984.

Calder, Norman, Jawid Mojaddedi, and Andrew Rippin. *Classical Islam: A Sourcebook of Religious Literature*. London: Routledge, 2003.

Eickelman, Dale and James Piscatori. *Muslim Politics*. Princeton: Princeton University Press, 1996.

Hodgson, Marshall. *The Venture of Islam: Conscience and History in a World Civilization*, vol. 1, *The Classical Age of Islam*. Chicago: The University of Chicago Press, 1974.

Kourouma, Ahmadou. *The Suns of Independence*, trans. Adrian Adams. New York: Africana Publishing Company, 1981.

Mottahedeh, Roy. *Mantle of the Prophet: Religion and Politics in Iran*. New York: Pantheon Books, 1985, (repr. Oxford: Oneworld Publications 2000).

Qutb, Sayyid. *Milestones*. Salimiah, Kuwait: International Islamic Federation of Student Organizations, n.d.

Other texts assigned are available on reserve at the library and/or at the student lounge on the second floor of the ETC building. Look for the bookshelf marked REL 155.

Recommended Books:
Koran, trans. N.J. Dawood, rev. ed. New York: Penguin Books, 1990.

Course Requirements:
Active participation in conference. This requires you to read all assigned texts carefully so as to be an informed and thoughtful participant in conferences. It also requires you to attend lectures and conferences regularly.

Participation in a debate on the status of drinking alcohol in Islamic law. In preparation for the debate, you are required to write a fatwa and post it on the course website. After the debate, you are required to post a reflection paper on the course website on the nature of religious law.

Site-visit paper. Six-to ten-page paper (double spaced) analyzing a visit to an Islamic center or a mosque. **Due by April 25**. List of Portland mosques and guidelines for the paper will be handed out on February 12. This requirement could be fulfilled anytime between February 12 and April 25.

Short paper. Four-to five-page paper (double spaced) on *The Suns of Independence*, using this novel to explore issues of local practice and diversity within Islam and the challenges these issues pose to defining or representing Islam. **Due by noon on Monday, February 16.**

Take-home midterm exam. This exam will test your knowledge of key concepts, events, and persons in Islamic history and will require you to analyze their significance for understanding Islam and Muslim societies. **Due by noon on Monday, March 29**.

Take-home final exam. You will be asked to synthesize the content of the course by forming a thoughtful explanation of Islam and its role in the social and personal lives of Muslims. Part of the final exam will include a critical review of Eickelman and Piscatori's *Muslim Politics*. The final exam will be handed out on the last day of class and it will be **due in my office by 9 a.m. on Monday, May 10.**

Policy on Extensions and Late Assignments. Deadlines for course assignments have been carefully selected because the assignments directly complement the teaching content of the course. A *fatwa* turned in after our debate, for example, will not serve its teaching purpose and thus will receive no credit. For this reason you must fulfill each course requirement by its respective deadline in order to receive credit. Extensions will *only* be granted in case of serious illness or extreme emergency that is verified in writing by the Student Health Services (in case of illness) or the Dean of Students (in case of extreme emergency). Having too many papers due at the same time does not constitute an emergency.

Course Schedule

Jan. 27 (Tu)—Dilemmas in Representing Islam

Carl Ernst, "Islam in the Eyes of the West" and "Approaching Islam in
    Terms of Religion" in *Following Muhammad*, 2-69. (A thoughtful
    response to popular and media misrepresentations of Islam in the
    U.S., aimed at the general public).
Edward Said, *Orientalism*, 1-28 and 314-321.
Bernard Lewis, "The Question of Orientalism" in *Islam and the West*,
    99-118.
Hodgson, *Venture of Islam*, vol. 1, 3-99.

Foundations of Islam

Jan. 29 (Th)—Islamic Revelation and Scripture: The Qur'an and Its
Exegesis

Classical Islam, 3-15, 59-82, and 97-133.
Feb. 3 (Tu)—Divine and Prophetic Sayings: Muhammad as Exemplar
    Classical Islam, 16-26 and 36-58.
"Mohammed's Nocturnal Journey to Jerusalem and His Visit to the
    Seven Heavens and to Hell" in Jan Knappert, *Swahili Islamic Poetry*,
    vol. 3, 227-275.
Süleyman Celebi, "The Mevlidi Sherif," 17-39.

Feb. 5 (Th)—Individual Worship and Personal Piety

Vincent Cornell, "Fruit of the Tree of Knowledge: The Relationship
    between Faith and Practice in Islam" in *The Oxford History of Islam*,
    63-105.

Feb. 10 (Tu)—Communal Worship and Religious Public Space

Malcolm X (or Malik el-Shabazz), "Mecca," chapter 17 of *The
    Autobiography of Malcolm X*.

Farid Esack, "Pepsi Shows the Way" in *On Being a Muslim*, 12-17.
Paper topics for *The Suns of Independence* to be handed out.

Feb. 12 (Th)—Lived Islam: Problematizing the Foundations

Ahmadou Kourouma, *The Suns of Independence*, in entirety.

Short paper on *The Suns of Independence* are due in my office by **noon on Monday, February 16.**

Formative Experiences in Faith and Community

Feb. 17 (Tu)—Fruits of Labor: Conquests and Salvation

Hodgson, *Venture of Islam*, vol. 1, 103-186.
Ahmed, *Women and Gender in Islam*, 11-78.
Classical Islam, 27-35 and 88-93.

Feb. 19 (Th)—Labor Pangs: Factionalism and Religious Legitimacy I

Hodgson, *Venture of Islam*, vol. 1, 187-314.
Ahmed, *Women and Gender in Islam*, 79-101.

Feb. 24 (Tu)—Labor Pangs: Factionalism and Religious Legitimacy II

Hodgson, *Venture of Islam*, vol. 1, 354-358.
Classical Islam, 83-87.
Muhammad b. Jarrir al-Tabari, "The Account of the Murder [of 'Uthman]" in *The History of al-Tabari*, vol. 15, 181-223.
Lewis Pelly, *The Miracle Play of Hasan and Husain*, vol. 2, 81-103.

Intellectual Traditions and Islamic Praxis

Feb. 26 (Th)—Islamic Philosophy and Theology: *Falsafa* and *Kalam*

Hodgson, *Venture of Islam,* vol. 1, 410-443.
Classical Islam, 134-177.

Recommended: Majid Fakhry, "Philosophy and Theology: From the Eighth Century C.E. to the Present" in *The Oxford History of Islam*, 269-303.

Mar. 2 (Tu)— Islamic Law: *shar'a, usul al-fiqh*, and *fiqh*

Mohammad Hashim Kamali, "Law and Society: The Interplay of Revelation and Reason in the Shariah" in *The Oxford History of Islam*, 107-153.
Classical Islam, 178-227
Recommended: Hodgson, *Venture of Islam*, vol. 1, 315-358.
Readings for debate on drinking alcohol to be handed out.

Mar. 4 (Th)— Debating Epistemology: Reason, Revelation, and Religious Experience

Abu Hamid al-Ghazzali, selections from *Deliverance from Error*.
Averröes (Ibn Rushd), *The Decisive Treatise* and "Epistle Dedicatory" in their entirety.

* * *

Post your *fatwa* on the drinking case on the course website and turn in a hard copy at my office by **NOON on Monday, March 8**.

* * *

Mar. 9 (Tu)— Religious Law in Practice: Is Drinking Divinely Forbidden? The Debate

* * *

Reflection papers on the debate should be posted on the course website before class on **Thursday, March 11**.

* * *

Mar. 11 (Th)—An Overview of Sufism: A Reality without a Name or a Name Devoid of Reality?

Qur'an 18:59-82. (You could find three translations of the Qur'an presented alongside one another at http://www.usc.edu/dept/MSA/Qur'an/).
Hodgson, *Venture of Islam*, vol. 1, 359-409.
Classical Islam, 228-252.

Mar. 15-Mar. 19—SPRING BREAK

Mar. 23 (Tu)—A Journey through the Stations and States of the Sufi Path

Farid ud-Din Attar, *The Conference of the Birds*, 29-153.

Mar. 25 (Th)—Edifying the Masses and Disciplining Initiates through Aesthetic and Devotional Practices: Signs and Symbols on the Path

Farid ud-Din Attar, *The Conference of the Birds*, 153-229.
Classical Islam, 253-268.

* * *

Take-home midterm handed out. Due in my office by **noon on Monday, March 29**.

* * *

Tradition, Colonialism, and Modernity

Mar. 30 (Tu)— Colonialism and the Emergence of Modern Muslim Societies

S.V.R. Nasr, "European Colonialism and the Emergence of Modern Muslim States" in *The Oxford History of Islam*, 549-599.
Tayeb Salih, "The Doum Tree of Wad Hamid" in *The Wedding of Zein*, 1-20.

Apr. 1 (Th)—Transmission of Knowledge as Religious Work: A

View of Islamic Education, Past and Present I

Mottahedeh, *Mantle of the Prophet*, 7-133.

Apr. 6 (Tu)—Transmission of Knowledge as Religious Work: A View of Islamic Education, Past and Present II

Mottahedeh, *Mantle of the Prophet*, 134-247.

Apr. 8 (Th)—Reforming Muslims and Renewing Islam for the Modern Era

Andrew Rippin, "Describing Modernity" in *Muslims: Their Religious Beliefs and Practices*, 167-188.
Selections from the writings of al-Tahtawi, al-Afghani, Abduh, Gökalp, Ahmad Khan, and Iqbal in *Modernist Islam, 1840-1940: A Sourcebook*, ed. Charles Kurzman, 31-39, 103-110, 50-60, 192-197, and 291-313.

Apr. 13 (Tu)—Participating in Modernity through Islam: A View from the Iranian Revolution

Mottahedeh, *Mantle of the Prophet*, 248-end.

Apr. 15 (Th)—Participating in Modernity through Islam: A View from African America

Kambiz Ghanea Bassiri, "African-American Muslims" in *Competing Visions of Islam in the U.S.*, 135-166.

Apr. 20 (Tu)—Participating in Modernity through Islam: Sayyid Qutb's View
"Qutb" in *The Oxford Encyclopedia of the Modern Islamic World*, ed. John Esposito.
Qutb, *Milestones*, in entirety.

Appendix 1

Post-Modernity, Feminism, and Islam

Apr. 22 (Th)—Postmodern Approaches to Islam: Progressive Islamic Identity and Practice

Farid Esack, "In Search of Progressive Islam beyond 9/11" in *Progressive Muslims*, 78-97.
Ebrahim Moosa, "The Debts and Burdens of Critical Islam" in *Progressive Muslims*, 111-127.

* * *

Friday, April 23—Last day site-visit papers will be accepted.

* * *

Apr. 27 (Tu)—Modern and Postmodern Issues in Feminism, Colonialism, and Islam

Ahmed, *Women and Gender in Islam*, 127-248.
Sayyida Shaikh, "Transforming Feminism: Islam, Women and Gender Justice" in *Progressive Muslims*, 147-162.

Conclusion

Apr. 29 (Th)—Revisiting the Dilemma of Representing Islam: A Roundtable Discussion based on Site Visits

Talal Asad, *The Idea of an Anthropology of Islam*, 1-17.

APPENDIX 2

Location / States of Institutes Represented in Survey

State	No. of Institutions Represented in Survey
AZ	2
CA	8
CO	8
CT	4
DC	2
FL	1
GA	2
HI	1
IL	5
IN	3
KY	1
LO	1
MA	6
MD	3
MI	3
MN	3
MO	1
MS	1
NC	7
NH	1
NJ	3
NY	9
OH	6
OK	2
OR	2

Appendix 2

State	No. of Institutions Represented in Survey
PA	6
SC	3
SD	1
TN	1
TX	4
UT	1
VA	5
VT	1
WA	2
WI	2

APPENDIX 3

List of Institutions where Instructors Received Highest Degrees

Claremont Graduate University
Columbia University
Duke University
Emory University
George Washington University
Georgian University, Rome
Harvard University
McGill University, Montreal
Miami University
New York University
Princeton University
Syracuse University
Temple University
The Catholic University of America
Tulane University
University of British Columbia, Vancouver.
University of California at Los Angeles
University of California, Santa Barbara
University of Cape Town, South Africa
University of Chicago
University of Cincinnati
University of Edinburgh, Scotland
University of Minnesota
University of Pennsylvania
University of Texas at Austin
University of Toronto
University of Virginia
Vanderbilt University
Washington University, St. Louis
Yale University

APPENDIX 4

List of Required Texts Used by Instructors

"A Text of the 1979 Constitution of the Islamic Republic of Iran."

Abdo, Geneive, *No God But God: Egypt and the Triumph of Islam*. Oxford University Press, 2000.

Ahmad, Khurshid, *Islam: Its Meaning and Message*. The Islamic Foundation, 1980.

Ahmed, Akbar S., *Discovering Islam: Making Sense of Muslim History and Society*. Routledge, 2002.

Algar, Hamid, *Surat Al-Fatiha: Foundation of the Qur'an*. Islamic Publications International, 1998.

Ali, A. Yusuf, trans., *The Holy Qur'an*. Kindle, 2009.

Ali, Ahmed, trans., *Al-Qur'an*. Princeton University Press, 1984.

Ali, Tariq, *Shadows of the Pomegranate Tree*. Verso, 1993.

———, *The Clash of Fundamentalisms: Crusades, Jihads and Modernity*. Verso, 2003.

Anonymous, *Guidance from the Messenger*.

Anonymous, *The Miraculous Journey of Mohomet: Miraj Nameh*.

Arberry, A.J., trans., *The Koran Interpreted: A Translation*. Touchstone, 1996.

Arkoun, Mohammed, *Rethinking Islam*. Westview Press, 1994.

Armstrong, Karen, *Islam: A Short History*. Modern Library, 2002.

———, *Muhammad: A Biography of the Prophet*. HarperCollins, 1992.

———, *The Battle for God*. Ballantine Books, 2001.

Asad, Muhammad, *The Road to Mecca*. The Book Company, 1993.

Asma, Barlas, *Believing Women in Islam: Unreading Patriarchal Interpretations of the Qur'an*. University of Texas Press, 2002.

Attar, Farid ud-Din, *The Conference of the Birds,* trans., Afkham Darbandi and Dick Davis. Penguin Classics, 1984.

Baderin, Mashood, *International Human Rights and Islamic Law*. Oxford University Press, 2003.

Barboza, Steven, *American Jihad: Islam After Malcom X*. Doubleday, 1994.

Barks, Coleman, trans., *Rumi: We Are Three*. Maypop Books, 1988.

Barraclough, Geoffrey, *The Times Concise Atlas of World History*, 6th edn. Time Books, 1997.

Berkey, Jonathan, *The Formation of Islam: Religion and Society in the Near East, 600-1800*. Cambridge University Press, 2002.

Bernard, Cheryl, *Civil Democratic Islam: Partners, Resources, and Strategies*. RAND Corporation, 2004.

Bloom, Jonathan, and Blair, Sheila, *Islam: A Thousand Years of Faith and Power*. Yale University Press, 2002.

Bowen, Donna Lee, and Early, Evelyn, *Everyday Life in the Muslim Middle East*. Indiana University Press, 2002.

Brown, Daniel, *A New Introduction to Islam*. Blackwell Publishing, 2004.

Calder, Norman, et al, *Classical Islam: A Sourcebook of Religious Literature*. Routledge, 2003.

Chick, Jack, *The Prophet*: Alberto, Part Six. Chick Publications (comic book).

Chittick, William, *Vision of Islam*. Paragon House Publishers, 1995.

Chishti, Hamim M., *The Book of Sufi Healing*. Inner Traditions International, 1985.

Cleary, Thomas, *The Essential Koran: The Heart of Islam*. HarperOne, 1994.

_____, *The Qur'an: A New Translation*. Starlatch Press, 2004.

_____, *The Wisdom of the Prophet: Sayings of Muhammad: Selections from the Hadith*. Shambhala Classics, 2001.

Cook, Michael, *Forbidding Wrong in Islam*. Cambridge University Press, 2003.

_____, *Muhammad*. Oxford University Press, 1990.

_____, *The Koran: A Very Short Introduction*. Oxford University Press, 2000.

Cooke, Miriam, *Women Claim Islam: Creating Islamic Feminism through Literature*. Routledge, 2000.

Cornell, Vincent, *The Way of Abu Madyan: The Works of Abu Madyan Shu'ayb*. Islamic Texts Society, 1996.

Cragg, Kenneth and Speight, Marston, eds., *Islam From Within: Anthology of a Religion*. Wadsworth, 1979.

Crime or Custom? Violence Against Women in Pakistan. Human Rights Watch, 1999.

Darbandi and Davis, Dick, *The Conference of the Birds*. Penguin Books, 1984.

Dawood, N. J., *Tales from the Thousand and One Nights*. Penguin Classics, 2004.

Denny, Frederick Matthews, *An Introduction to Islam*. Prentice Hall, 2005.

Djebar, Assia, *Fantasia: An Algerian Cavalcade*. Heinemann, 1993.

Egger, Vernon, *A History of the Muslim World to 1405: The Making of a Civilization*. Prentice Hall, 2004.

Eickelman, Dale, and Piscatori, James, *Muslim Politics*. Princeton University Press, 1996.

El Fadl, Khaled, *Islam and the Challenge of Democracy*. Princeton University Press, 2004.

_____, *Speaking in God's Name: Islamic Law, Authority and Women*. Oneworld Publications, 2001.

_____, *The Place of Tolerance in Islam*. Beacon Press, 2002.

El Kouloub, Out, *Ramza*. Syracuse University Press, 1994.

Ernst, Carl, *Following Muhammad: Rethinking Islam in the Contemporary World*. University of North Carolina Press, 2004.

———, and Lawrence, Bruce, *Sufi Martyrs of Love: The Chishti Order in South Asia and Beyond*. Palgrave Macmillan, 2002.

———, *Teachings of Sufism*. Shambhala, 1999.

———, *The Shambhala Guide to Sufism*. Shambhala, 1997.

Esack, Farid, *Qur'an, Liberation and Pluralism: An Islamic Perspective of Interreligious Solidarity Against Oppression*. Oneworld Publications, 1997.

———, *The Qur'an: A Short Introduction*. Oneworld Publications, 2001.

Esposito, John, *Contemporary Islam: Reformation and Revolution?* In Esposito (ed.) *The Oxford History of Islam*. N.Y.: Oxford University Press, 1999.

———, *Islam: the Straight Path*, 3rd edn. Oxford University Press, 2004.

———, and Voll, John, *Makers of Contemporary Islam*. Oxford University Press, 2001.

———, *The Islamic Threat: Myth or Reality?* Oxford University Press, 1999.

———, ed., *The Oxford History of Islam*. Oxford University Press, 2000.

———, *Unholy War: Terror in the Name of Islam*. Oxford University Press, 2003.

———, and Voll, John, *Voices of Resurgent Islam*. Oxford University Press, 1983.

———, *What Everyone Needs to Know About Islam*. Oxford University Press, 2002.

Euben, Roxanne L., *Enemy in the Mirror*. Princeton University Press, 1999.

Fadiman, James, et al, *Essential Sufism*. HarperOne, 1991.

Federspiel, Howard, *The Usage of Traditions of the Prophet in Contemporary Indonesia*. Arizona State University, 1993.

Fernea, Elizabeth, *Guests of the Sheikh: An Ethnography of an Iraqi Village*. Anchor, 1995.

Fisher, Sydney Nettleton, *The Middle East: A History*. McGraw-Hill, 1996.

Freud, Sigmund, *Moses and Monotheism*.

Friedl, Erika, *Women of Deh Koh: Lives in an Iranian Village*. Penguin, 1991.

Forward, Martin, *Muhammad: A Short Biography*. Oneworld Publications, 1997.

Gerges, Fawaz, *America and Political Islam: Clash of Cultures or Clash of Interests*. Cambridge University Press, 1999.

Ghali, Waguih, *Beer in the Snooker Club*. Ivan R. Dee Publishers, 1989.

Al-Ghazali, Abu Hamid, *Deliverance from Error: Five Key Texts Including his Autobiography*. Fons Vitae, 2004.

Gibb, H.A.R., *Muhammadanism*. Oxford University Press, 1969.

Goldziher, Ignaz, *Introduction to Islamic Theology and Law*. Princeton University Press, 1991.

Haddad, Yvonne Yazbeck, *The Globalization of Islam: The Return of Muslims to the West*. In Esposito (ed.) *The Oxford History of Islam*. N.Y.: Oxford University Press, 1999.

Hallaq, Wael, *A History of Islamic Legal Theory: An Introduction to Sunni usul al-Fiqh*. Cambridge University Press, 1997.

Halm, Heinz, *Shi'a Islam: From Religion to Revolution*. Princeton University Press, 1997.

Hamid, Mohsin, *Moth Smoke*. Picador USA, 2001.

Hasan, Amsa Gull, *American Muslims*. Continuum International Publishing Group, 2002.

Hashmi, Sohail and Miles, Jack, *Islamic Political Ethics: Civil Society, Pluralism, and Conflict* (selected essays). Princeton University Press, 2002.

Heyneman, Stephen, *Islam and Social Policy*. Vanderbilt University Press, 2004.

Hodgson, Marshall, *The Venture of Islam*. University of Chicago Press, 1977.

Holt, P.M., ed., *The Cambridge History of Islam*. Cambridge University Press, 1971.

Hosain, Attia, *Sunlight on a Broken Column*. Penguin Books, 1992.

Hourani, Albert, *A History of the Arab Peoples*. Harvard University Press, 2003.

Humphreys, Stephen, *Islamic History*. Princeton University Press, 1991.

Ibrahim, Ezzeddin, trans. and Johnson-Davies, Denys, *An-Nawawi's Forty Hadith: An Anthology of the Sayings of the Prophet Muhammad*. Islamic Texts Society, 1997.

Itzkowitz, Norman, *The Ottoman Empire and Islamic Tradition*. University of Chicago Press, 1980.

Jayyusi, Salma Khadra, ed., *The Legacy of Muslim Spain*. Brill, 1994.

Kanafani, Ghassan, *Men in the Sun*. Lynne Rienner Publishers, 1998.

Kane, Cheikh Hamidou, *Ambiguous Adventure*. Heinemann, 1972.

Kane, H., *The Ambiguous Adventure*, Rene Julliard, trans. Heinemann, 1963

Kepel, Gilles, *Jihad: The Trail of Political Islam*. Harvard University Press, 2002.

Kourouma, Ahmadou, *The Suns of Independence*, Adrian Adams, trans. Africana Publishing Company, 1981.

Kurzman, Charles, *Liberal Islam: A Sourcebook*. New York: Oxford University Press, 1998.

Lalani, Arzina, *Early Shi'i Thought: The Teachings of Imam Muhammed al-Baqir*. Institute for Ismaili Studies, 2004.

Lawrence, Bruce, *Shattering the Myth: Islam Beyond Violence*. Princeton University Press, 1998.

———, *The Eastward Journey of Muslim Kingship: Islam in South and Southeast Asia*. In Esposito (ed.) *The Oxford History of Islam*. N.Y.: Oxford University Press, 1999.

Laye, Camara, *The Dark Child: The Autobiography of an African Boy*. Farrar, Straus and Giroux, 1954.

Leaman, Oliver, *A Brief Introduction to Islamic Philosophy*. Polity Press, 1999.

Lewis, Bernard, *The Crisis of Islam: Holy War and Unholy Terror*. Random House, 2003.

———, *The Middle East: A Brief History Of The Last 2000 Years*. Scribner, 1996.

———, *What Went Wrong? Western Impact and Middle Eastern Response*. Oxford University Press, 2001.

Lings, Martin, *Muhammad: His Life Based on the Earliest Sources*. Inner Traditions, 2006.

———, *What is Sufism?* Islamic Text Society, 1999.

Lombardi, Clark Benner, *Islamic Law as a Source of Constitutional Law in Egypt: The Constitutionalization of Shari'a in a Modern Arab State*, 37 Column. J. Transnational L. 81, 1998.

Maalouf, Amin, *Leo Africanus*. New Amsterdam Books, 1998.

——, *Samarkand*. Interlink Publishing Group, 1998.

Makiya, Kenan, *The Rock: A Tale of Seventh-Century Jerusalem*. Vintage, 2002.

Al-Maqasid, *Nawawi's Manual of Islam*. Amana Publications, 2003.

Martin, Richard, *Islamic Studies: A History of Religions Approach*, 2nd edn. Prentice Hall, 1996.

Maudoodi, Seyyed, *Towards Understanding Islam*. New Era, 1994.

McCloud, Aminah Beverly, *African American Islam*. Routledge, 1995.

McNeill, William and Waldman, Marilyn, *The Islamic World*. University of Chicago Press, 1984.

Menocal, Maria Rosa, *The Ornament of the World: How Muslims, Jews, and Christians Created a Culture of Tolerance in Medieval Spain*. Little, Brown, and Co., 2002.

Mernissi, Fatima, *Beyond the Veil: Male-Female Dynamics in Modern Muslim Society*. Indiana University Press, 1987.

——, *Dreams of Trespass: Tales of a Harem Girlhood*. Basic Books, 1995.

——, *The Veil and the Male Elite: A Feminist Interpretation of Women's Rights in Islam*. Addison-Wesley, 1996.

Michell, George, *Architecture of the Islamic World: Its History and Social Meaning*. Thames & Hudson, 1984.

Moaddel, Mansoor and Talattof, Kamran, *Modernist and Fundamentalist Debates in Islam: A Reader*. Palgrave Macmillan, 2002.

Moghadam, Valentine, *Modernizing Women: Gender and Social Change in the Middle East*. L. Rienner, 2003.

Moghissi, Haideh, *Feminism and Islamic Fundamentalism: The Limits of Postmodern Analysis*. Zed Books, 1999.

Morewedge, Parviz, *Essays in Islamic Philosophy, Theology and Mysticism*. Global Scholarly Publications, 2004.

Mottahedeh, Roy, *Mantle of the Prophet: Religion and Politics in Iran*. Oxford: Oneworld Publications, 2000.

Murata, Sachiko and Chittick, William C., *The Vision of Islam*. Paragon, 1995.

Nasr, Seyyed Hossein, *Islamic Life and Thought*. ABC International, 2001.

——, *Muhammad: Man of God*. Kazi Publications, 1995.

——, *Three Muslim Sages*. Caravan Books, 1964.

Nyang, Sulayman, *Islam in the U.S.* ABC International Group Inc., 1999.

Peters, F. E., *A Reader on Classical Islam*. Princeton University Press, 1993.

Pickthall, Mohammed Marmaduke, trans., *The Meaning of the Glorious Koran*. Tahrike Tarsile Qur'an, 2001.

Postman, Neil and Powers, Steve, *How to Watch TV News*. Penguin, 1992.

Qasim, Abd al-Hakim *Rites of Assent*. Temple University Press, 1995.

Rahman, Fazlur, *Islam*. University of Chicago Press, 1979.

———, *Major Themes of the Qur'an*. University of Chicago Press, 2009.

Rashid, Ahmed, *Taliban: Militant Islam, Oil and Fundamentalism in Central Asia*. Yale University Press, 2001

Renard, John, *Seven Doors to Islam: Spirituality and the Religious Life of Muslims*. University of California Press, 1996.

———, *Windows on the House of Islam: Muslim Sources on Spirituality and Religious Life*. University of California Press, 1998.

Rifaat, Alifa, *Distant View of a Minaret and Other Stories*. Heineman, 1987.

Rippin, Andrew, *Muslims: Their Religious Beliefs and Practices*, 2nd edn. Routledge, 2005.

———, and Knappert, Jan, *Textual Sources for the Study of Islam*. University of Chicago Press, 1990.

Robinson, Neal, *Islam: A Concise Introduction*. Georgetown University Press, 1999.

———, *The Islamic World*. Cambridge University Press, 1999.

Rosen, Lawrence, *The Justice of Islam: Comparative Perspectives on Islamic Law and Society*. Oxford University Press, 2000.

Ruthven, Malise, *Islam: A Very Short Introduction*. Oxford University Press, 2000.

Safi, Omid, ed. *Progressive Muslims: On Justice, Gender, and Pluralism*. Oneworld, 2003.

Saleh, Tayeb, *Season of Migration to the North*. New York Review of Books Classics, 2009.

———, *The Wedding of Zein and Other Sudanese Stories*. Heinemann, 1991.

Sanders, Paula, *Ritual, Politics, and the City in Fatimid Cairo*. SUNY, 1994.

Schimmel, AnneMarie, *Islam: An Introduction*. State University of New York Press, 1992.

———, *Mystical Dimensions of Islam*. Chapel Hill: University of North Carolina, 1975.

Schuon, Frithjof, and Schimmel, Annemarie, *Understanding Islam*. World Wisdom Books, 1998.

Sells, Michael, *Approaching the Qur'an: The Early Revelations*. White Cloud Press, 2007.

———, *Early Islamic Mysticism*. Paulist Press, 1995.

Shadid, Anthony, *Legacy of the Prophet: Despots, Democrats, and the New Politics of Islam*. Westview Press, 2002.

Shakir, M.H., trans., *The Qur'an*. Kindle, 2009.

Shalabi, Abdul Wadod, ed., *Islam: Religion of Life*. Chicago: Starlatch Press, 2001.

Smith, Jane, *Islam in America*. Columbia University Press, 2000.

Stowasser, Barbara, *Women in the Qur'an, Traditions, and Interpretation*. Oxford University Press, 1996.

Tayob, Abdulkader, *Islam, a Short Introduction: Signs, Symbols and Values*. Oneworld, 1999.

The Classical Age of Islam. Chicago: The University of Chicago Press, 1974.

Tibi, Bassam, *The Challenge of Fundamentalism: Political Islam and the New World Disorder*. University of Calif. Press, 2002.

Toledano, Ehud, *Slavery and Abolition in the Ottoman Middle East*. University of Washington Press, 1998.

Appendix 4

Tusi, Nasir ad-Din, *The Metaphysics of Tusi*. New York, 1970.

Von Denffer, Ahmad, *'Ulum al-Qur'an: An Introduction to the Sciences of the Qur'an*. The Islamic Foundation, 2009.

Wadud, Amina, *Qur'an and Woman: Rereading the Sacred Text from a Woman's Perspective*. Oxford University Press, 1999.

Waines, David, *An Introduction to Islam*. Cambridge University Press.

Watt, W. Montgomery, *Introduction to the Qur'an*. Edinburgh University Press, 2001.

———, *Islamic Philosophy and Theology*. Aldine Transaction, 2008.

———, *Muhammad: Prophet and Statesman*. Galaxy Books, 1974.

Weiss, Bernard, *The Spirit of Islamic Law*. University of Georgia Press, 2006.

Wickham, Carrie, *Mobilizing Islam: Religion, Activism and Political Change in Egypt*. Columbia University Press, 2002.

Williams, John, *The Word of Islam*. University of Texas Press, 1994.

Zebiri, Kate, *Muslims and Christians Face to Face*. Oneworld Publications, 1997.

NOTES

1   Accessed at http://www.haverford.edu/relg/sells/home.html. (At the time of going to the press, the referenced webpage was no longer available).
2   Council on Teaching, 2002.
3   The information is hidden for the sake of instructor's privacy.

ESSAY X

Islamic Studies in American Universities: Conversations, Discourses, & Dialogue with Scholars

MUMTAZ AHMAD

ONE of the important parts of the Islamic Studies Project was to assemble a group of prominent scholars in the field and provide them with a forum to discuss the questions raised in the questionnaire already circulated among them. We organized two formal focus group discussion sessions, one at the Georgetown University in Washington, D.C., and the other at the Temple University in Philadelphia. Besides these two formal brainstorming sessions, some scholars were also contacted individually to respond to these questions and share their thoughts, experiences, and observations on the state of the Islamic studies in American academia. What follows is a report of these conversations and dialogues.

On April 29, 2005 the Islamic Studies group met a panel of experts at Georgetown University to examine the state of the arts in Islamic Studies in American universities. The chairman for the event was Dr. Sulayman S. Nyang, a professor of African and Islamic Studies at Howard University. He opened the meeting and asked the participants to introduce themselves before the meeting could move on to the substance of the discussion. Following this protocol, the conference members engaged in a series of conversations on the history, nature and impact of the field of Islamic Studies in the U.S.

Professor John Voll, Deputy Director at the Center for Muslim-Christian Understanding at Georgetown University, began the discussion on the historical development of the field. In his presentation, he identified a number of relevant issues. First of all, he reminded the panelists that there is a contemporary crisis which is clearly embodied in the impact of 9/11 on the American academy through the personal saga of Dr. Tariq Ramadan, a Swiss Muslim academic who was appointed to serve as a professor of Islamic Studies at Notre Dame University but was denied entry in the U.S. The controversy, according to Professor Voll, was occasioned by his pedigree, scholarship, and activism. With respect to his pedigree as a grandson of the late Hassan al–Banna, the Egyptian leader who founded the Muslim Brotherhood that presently affects the intellectual understanding of many Muslims in the Arab World and beyond, Voll saw him as a symbol of the new relationship between traditionality and modernity among young Muslims living in western Europe. Not only is Dr. Ramadan an important broker between Islam and the West, but he could become an effective bridge through his writings, speeches and activism on behalf of the young Muslims.

According to Professor Voll, Dr. Ramadan's case symbolized one other instance of the negative consequences of 9/11 and the ongoing Middle Eastern crisis festering between pro–Palestinian and pro–Zionist groups. The controversy surrounding Dr. Ramadan's appointment at Notre Dame is the result of the activism of elements such as Daniel Pipes. Through their campaign against academics believed to be pro–Palestinians and pro–Islamists, Pipes and activists like him seized upon the Tariq Ramadan case to secure his exclusion from the American academy. Voll noted that although the academic administrators of Notre Dame made their presentation to the U.S. government asking for reasons for his visa denial, the issue has continued to be unresolved. Through this careful and serious examination of the Tariq Ramadan issue, Dr. Voll set the stage for the historical development of the subject matter.

On the question of the historical origins of the study of Islam in the U.S., Voll identified several stages in his narrative. The first period goes back to the importation of Islamic studies ideas from the European academy and from the activities of the American missionary studies of Islam and Christianity in the Middle East. The first phase was largely driven by the nature and contents of Islamic studies from Europe. The writings of American missionaries such as Samuel Zwemer and others linked to several Christian seminaries, have served as useful entry points for the American Christian opinions on and attitudes toward Islam and Prophet Muhammad.

Most of these scholarly enterprises were limited both by the seminarian agendas of the writers but also by their anti-Islamic considerations. Related to, but radically different from, these writings on Islam and the Middle East were the works of American political and diplomatic agents serving in various capacities in the Mediterranean. Those who were engaged in the early epochs of American encounter with peoples of the Barbary Coast were not necessarily interested in Islamic studies as such. Concerned about the safety and welfare of American merchants in this part of the world and determined to guarantee the rising image of a new nation, this American cadre of writers and interpreters of the Muslim encounter with America, saw Muslims more as potential sources of violence through the Barbary Coast assaults and less as agents and advocates of Islam.

This is particularly evident in the early writings of the generation of leaders after the founding fathers. Certainly, a careful study of the writings on the foreign policies of the Adams and Monroe, a period when America gradually established itself at home and abroad, provided evidence on how America encountered Muslims. There were occasional reports of violence between Muslims and the Americans living in the region. One of the famous instances is the song on Tripoli, a song that still resonates in American military music. Focusing on the activism of a group of American military officers who felt wounded by what they believed to be atrocities of the peoples of the Barbary Coast, this episode is one of many examples of the negative perceptions of and misunderstandings between Americans and Muslims in the Mediterranean areas.

The second body of knowledge, according to Voll, is now part and parcel of the American historiography on Islamic studies in the U.S., and consists of the writings associated with the business activism of American corporations. Aramco in Saudi Arabia and the other oil industries gradually developed a growing body of knowledge about the exploration and geography of oil products from the Arabian Peninsula. Much of this body of knowledge, however, was based on economic and technical data and did not help us understand the larger socio-cultural aspects of the region. Rather than enhance our knowledge of Muslims and their religion, these technically-oriented writings limited our view of the Arab world that was good only as a source of oil.

According to Voll, this body of knowledge was soon connected to another source of information and knowledge about the region and its religion. This was the work of scholars writing within the Cold War framework. Talking about this period in the development of the study of Islam, Voll raised a number of issues. There was the ongoing competition between the West and the East. Divided on a wide range of issues, and determined to win the hearts and minds of Muslims from around the world, the American academy initiated a number of programs to study the Muslim world, starting with the Middle East. This discourse has to be examined in the light of the development of area studies in American universities with extensive financial support from government agencies. This period also is marked by the scholarly writings of men such as H.A.R. Gibb, Von Grunebaum, Leonard Binder, Bernard Lewis, Albert Hourani, and a host of other scholars. Though their view of Islam as seen through the writings of these scholars was basically driven by Orientalism, their more modern and Cold War-driven colleagues were less classical in their orientation.

In his recounting of the narrative, Voll mentioned the contributions of scholars like Edward Said and the challenges from the postmodern school of thought. While acknowledging the contributions of Said, Bryan Turner, and others, there developed in the course of our conversations a series of issues relating to the motivations of the authors now identified with Orientalism. At this juncture, Voll and several other participants discussed the writings of different authors identified with post-Orientalism. Several participants distinguished between writers on the Islamic past and those who wrote primarily from the point of view of the modern Muslim world. Within the framework of classicists and medievalists, studies focused on the Qur'an, hadith literature, and the developments of Islamic legal systems and Sufi *ṭarīqahs*. Those who wrote in this vein primarily worked on the intellectual efforts of their counterparts in Europe.

Professor Louis Cantori of the Department of Political Science at the University of Maryland agreed with Voll that the controversy about the believer versus non-believer scholar is not confined to the field of Islamic studies. Yet he wondered how a curriculum sensitive to the concerns of Islamic or religious studies in general can be constructed with a secular leadership on campuses. Cantori believed that in the pre-modern period the study of Islam and the belief system of the scholar were integrally related. Only in the era of the ascendancy of social sciences did religion became a variable. Now, the phase known as postmodern has created its own problems and confusions.

Marcia Hermansen, Professor in the Department of Theology at Loyola University in Chicago, discussed the role of the government in the study of Islam. Viewed in historical context, increased government support for the study of the Muslim world and Islamic languages began in the U.S. during the postwar period in an era of Cold War contestations over developing nations in Asia and Africa. Government programs such as Title VI provided scholarships at major research institutions for students pursuing advanced study related to these security and defense interests. Scholars trained during this period were the first cohort to have the possibility of government subsidies for research that not directly tied to military objectives. However, the Cold War was definitely part of the background that sustained the need to promote American expertise in critical defense languages such as Arabic, Persian, and Urdu. Additional resources were provided through Public Law (PL) 480, a program in which from 1966-1980, U.S. foreign aid in food and agricultural assistance was reciprocated by having recipient nations provide copies of all books published locally to the library of Congress and selected research universities. In 1980, libraries had to begin paying for this material.

Language training programs on site such as the Center for Arabic Studies Abroad in Cairo, the Berkeley Urdu program in Pakistan, and Bogazici University in Turkey were established for American students. Consequently, American scholarship on the Muslim world became increasingly vigorous. According to Hermansen, the recipients of these scholarships for the study of "critical defense languages" were the most capable students and did not have to repay the government through any particular service or internship. Ironically, many of the students attracted to Islam and religious studies during the 1970s could be characterized as part of the "generation of seekers" who sought personal edification as well as professional depth in graduate programs. For the first time, large numbers of students from non-privileged backgrounds were provided the resources to study abroad for extended periods and were subsidized in mastering the classical Islamic languages requisite for serious study.

Dr. Sumaiya Hamdani of George Mason University observed that the very concept and discipline of Islamic Studies is of relatively recent origin. "I have an areas studies background and disciplinary background (history)," Hamdani said. "I am happy to see a thing called Islamic studies. I thought it was a work in progress." For her, the real issue was "what does Islam mean in the context of our discussion on Islamic studies? The desire is urgent to figure it out. The current events and atmosphere have created a greater need for it. They have tended to expand the perimeters of the field to include more and new concerns," Hamdani said. "For me the question is what do we mean by Islam when we talk about the academic programs: religion, culture, politics, history, civilization? A little bit of Islamic hate? When we set up Islamic Studies at George Mason, we wanted to decenter the study of Islam, decenter the current geographical focus, and broaden the perimeters and look at Islam in depth, and not just a global political phenomenon. The idea is to broaden the extent of Islam and help students take other classes in dance, music, art, architecture, and politics of Islam and more."

Dr. Ahmed Dallal of Georgetown University agreed that Islam is back on the map as a vital subject to study. "The question is how do we go about to teach it? There are many variables there…Many of us see different components of Islam. But the larger issue is that despite what Louis [Cantori] described as "postmodern" phase, I think we are not yet beyond the orientalism phase when it comes back to the basic body of knowledge about Islam," Dallal observed. He said that a good way to think about Islamic studies is to start discussing the basic ingredients for the curriculum. The body of knowledge in the mainstream of Islamic studies should also include contemporary concerns, such as Muslims in the modern period to the rise of the Muslims in the West. "There aren't many scholars of Islamic studies, and Georgetown has half of them," Dallal observed.

Professor Osman Bakr, Visiting Professor at the Center for Muslim-Christian Relations, Georgetown University, agreed that the current study of Islam in the U.S. "does not represent the rich diversity of Islamic intellectual traditions and experiences." The other issue, according to Bakr, was that the dominant trend "remains the study and critique of Islam from without" and a total lack of appreciation of categories derived from within Islam. "We will not be able to do full justice to Islamic scholarship if we don't bring into play both perspectives – from within and without," he said. Bakr believed that the body of knowledge developed from within the Islamic traditions is the only source to understand Muslims' own perspectives on theology, law, ethics, and spirituality.

Hamdani asked how the perspectives developed from within the tradition were less critical than the ones developed from without. Voll intervened that the distinctions he made earlier were based on the controversies in the AAR [American Academy of Religion] between the believing and non-believing scholars of religion. He said that working from within the tradition "doesn't mean that one cannot bring critical perspectives on the subject." Bakr agreed that those who study religion from within can be as critical as those who study it from without. But the problem arises when one religious tradition is looked at from the perspective of another religion, that is, when Islam is examined from the perspective of Christianity. Bakr believed each religion has its own structure and that "the structure of Islam isn't the same as that of other religions." He said that we have people who study Sufism but do not share the Sufi method. "We can benefit from their work in some way but they cannot represent Sufism as an important religious tradition in Islam," he said. Hamdani wanted to revisit the question of the difference between pre-modern and modern periods in the study of Islam. Cantori said that the pre-modern period was characterized by the view of Islam as a complete system of knowledge, while in the modern period we seem to have fragmented Islam and "reduced it to an ideology."

Dr. Mumtaz Ahmad, Professor of Political Science at Hampton University, agreed with Bakr that it would be inappropriate to study Islam from the perspective of religious and intellectual categories derived from Christianity, or for that matter, other religions. "We are frequently asked, for example: 'Where is your clergy? Where is your Luther? Where is your Pope? Where is your excommunication authority?' Islam, in other words, is supposed to produce the same structural features that are used in the study of Christianity. Is this a legitimate intellectual and academic exercise to look for the same features in Islam that we find in Christianity?"

The issue is not only confined to imposing extraneous religious categories on Islam, Ahmad said, "it is also prevalent in academic discourses and research methodologies." He recalled a conference of the "Fundamentalism Project" of the American Academy of Arts and Sciences at the University of Chicago in 1989 where Professor Abdulaziz Sachedina [University of Virginia] gave a paper on Islamic fundamentalism in Iran and Lebanon where he tried to understand the ideas and worldview of Ayatollah Khomeini. Professor Marvin Zonis of the University of Chicago opposed Sachedina's sympathetic understanding of Khomeini's ideas. Zonis admonished Sachedina for not strictly observing the rules of the game established by the western social science research methods and, in effect, told Sachedina to abide by the rules of western academic discourse or stay out of it. One cannot engage in "our" discourse without employing the methods and rules that "we" have established. In other words, Ahmad continued, the idea was that if you are a Muslim scholar, you cannot be objective. Being a Muslim automatically disqualifies you from engaging in critical and objective analysis: you can be a preacher but not a scholar.

Ahmad also highlighted another development that, according to him, was likely to have important consequences for the field of Islamic studies: the recent interventions in the field by a group of Muslim scholars who are not mainstream Islamic studies scholars. Ahmad mentioned the names of such scholars as Ali Mazrui, Talal Asad, Anour Madjid, Mamoud Mamdani, and Boby Sayeed, who are raising important and fresh questions from the perspectives of political sociology, anthropology, post-colonial studies, and cultural and literary theory. The question is where to place them in the broader scheme of Islamic studies, Ahmad said. Ahmad was also interested in further exploring the evolution of certain intellectual trends in Islam. A significant line of inquiry, for example, would be "to identify certain important socio-economic and political developments in Islamic history and then see how the dominant intellectual trends of a particular period correspond with these developments. The idea is to situate intellectual history in its material context and see how what we call as purely intellectual trends were, in fact, responses to certain concrete, material factors and developments."

This brought the discussion to the fundamental question of methodology in the study of religion. Marcia Hermansen, Professor in the Department of Theology at Loyola University in Chicago, observed that the prevailing methodological orientation of western scholars of religion during most of the twentieth century has been "phenomenology," a term used within the study of religion with less than technical philosophical rigor. One definition holds that the phenomenology of religion is that method of religious studies characterized by a search for the structures underlying comparable religious data that does not violate the self-understanding of the believers.

In addition, the search for similarity is premised on an assumption of similar underlying structures rather than on the dynamics of any historical interaction. Such an approach, according to Hermansen, privileges Sufism among the sub-fields of Islamic studies. In fact, the role of Islam in the academic study of religion dramatically shifted over the twentieth century. In the late nineteenth century, the project of developing a scientific study of religion was framed in a quest for origins. As a latecomer on the religious scene, Islam was much less germane to the quest than primal religion or even Hinduism and the Sanskrit corpus of texts.

The phenomenological approach to religion, flowering after the carnage of World War I in Europe, derived from a philosophical endeavor to shift from neo-Kantian abstractions to religious things and religious subjects. Here again, Islam was at the periphery rather than at the center of concern. According to Hermansen, among the dominant approaches to comparative religion during the 1960s and 1970s was the patternist school, inspired by the works of Mircea Eliade. This was characterized by the assumption that there were universal patterns underlying human religiosity, somewhat analogous to Jungian archetypes. Eliade's work posited a homo religiosos; i.e., that humans were by nature religious although the disenchantment of the modern world resulted in a rupture from the sense of connecting to an eternal present as primal religious traditions preserved. All this made Islam less interesting for patternists, some of whom espoused the view that Islam was born in "the full light of history" and thus had minimal space for myth and other real "religious" elements of interest to the phenomenologist of religion.

Still, among elements of Islam, Sufism was one of the more interesting topics. Hamdani wanted to go back to the "insider-outsider" question raised earlier by Voll, Bakr, and Ahmad. She said that looking at Islam from the outside also means to compare Islamic religious developments to what other religions have undergone. "At the end of the day, we are teaching a non–Muslim group of students and we need to inform them of other logics and other traditions in Islam," Hamdani said. "It would be too simplistic to say that they separate church and the state and we don't. That would be another essentialism that we would impose on Islam," she said. The fundamental question, according to Hamdani was, "who represents Islam?" Bakr responded that while it is difficult to determine "who speaks for Islam," it is possible to identify a group of Muslim scholars who can, and are willing, to show us the entire theological, philosophical, intellectual, and legal spectrum of Islam.

Hamdani said, "I have a problem with who speaks for Islam. Which Islam is being taught? I teach a course on Islamic Studies and I teach about all different types of sects in it from Sunni to Shiite. I show that all of them are Islam. Most of the [Muslim] students get upset and I am seen as anti–Islam…I have to remind my students that this isn't a class where you get *da'wa*. But the way they respond is, in effect, ask me to reaffirm my commitment to Islam."

Professor Charles Butterworth of the University of Maryland wondered if he came into a wrong room. "I am not a Muslim," he said, "and don't plan on becoming a Muslim and if you want me to leave I will leave." He felt that the discussion on "who speaks for Islam" was drifting to an internal dialogue between Muslim scholars. Butterworth thought that "If we are talking about universities, we aren't talking only about the religious departments. We are also talking about social sciences. What is it that we are trying to do in Islamic Studies? Yes, there are Jewish Studies programs in the universities but very seldom do we find in these programs something about Judaism. Maybe you don't want to pattern Islamic Studies after Judaism Studies but trying to shape Islamic Studies into faith studies won't fly."

"For example, I am interested in Islamic culture, the highest aspect, in my view, of Islam Studies. It is only then that we can have some meaningful discussion." Butterworth also wanted to know whether we were looking at the graduate or undergraduate levels of teaching. A number of things can be done at the graduate level that we cannot do at the undergraduate level courses that, by definition, have to be more general and survey type. At the undergraduate level the idea may be to make the students more aware of the Islamic world, Butterworth observed. He said he was teaching a course on government and politics in Islam and asking his students to read the Qur'an in order to understand the political philosophy of the Qur'an. Now, "it is both from within because the students are reading the Qur'an and from without because a non-Muslim is teaching." He wondered if the goal of this meeting and the project was to have more of this in our universities and also to move from Judeo-Christian perspective to a more inclusive Abrahamic perspective.

Nyang said Judeo-Christian is a construct that should now be abandoned in favor of an all-encompassing Abrahamic tradition. "As John [Voll] points out, the current narrative has changed the way we look at ourselves as human beings. Nationalism, both in politics and religion, has no place in the emerging global village." Nyang was of the view that "you don't have to be a Muslim in order to be an expert on Islam; I knew perhaps more about the American society than many Americans long before I became an American," Nyang said. Similarly, an American can know better Mandarin than many Chinese.

Voll was of the view that the categories such as *taqlīd* and *bidᶜah* are not only confined to religion but are also creeping into modern social sciences. Referring to the Zonis-Sachedina incident narrated by Ahmad, Voll said that since Sachedina was not a true *muqallid* of the standard social science research methodology according to Zonis, he accused him of *bidᶜah*, and did not see that Sachedina was exercising ijtihad. "We all seem to have become *taqlidi* as far as social science methodology is concerned, and anyone who goes against the standard academic structures is accused of committing *bid'ah*," Voll remarked. Voll recalled that when Professor Khurshid Ahmad [of the *Jamaat-e-Islami* Pakistan] gave his presentation on Islamic economics in Florida, the *taqlidi* economists thought that he was transgressing the boundaries of traditional economics as they knew it. While disciplinary methods were developed as a part of the modernity package, the challenge now is how to work out interpersonal and interfaith methods.

Voll talked about his own experience of working with Professor Osman Bakr over the past five years and said, "When we talk about Islamic history, it never occurs to me that he is 'within' and I am 'without.' We never saw any boundaries between us in our discussions. Similarly, when Mumtaz [Ahmad] mentioned Anour Madjid's name, I remembered that I had reviewed his latest book. It didn't occur to me that I am a non- Muslim reviewing a book written by a Muslim. But it did occur to me that I like history and I am reviewing a book about history…I was going to tease Ahmed [Dallal] about essentialism by saying that the only way to not be an essentialist is not to use the word Islam. One can say that art history is very essentialist as its talks about art as opposed to what is not art."

Hamdani thought that the model of area studies with its interdisciplinary approach was relevant to our discussion. "We operate from our different disciplinary perspectives and have these boundaries and still try to work around them, even if in patchwork."

Butterworth once again raised the question about the objectives of the conversation and the project. Professor Yvonne Haddad of the Center for Muslim-Christian Understanding, Georgetown University quipped; "Are we re-baptizing the Islamic knowledge"? Mumtaz Ahmad responded by saying that the project was intended to take stock of the present state of a particular discipline – Islamic studies – with critical examination of its current trends and future directions. It is also concerned with looking at various theoretical and methodological approaches employed in the field. Further, we are also interested in looking at how the discipline evolved and where it is heading. The purpose of this conversation is to see "whether we can come up with a coherent picture of the scene; we are not here to draw boundaries between 'insiders' and 'outsiders' and to make judgments as to whose understanding and interpretations are more authentic. Genuine scholarship knows no boundaries."

Haddad informed that she had written a piece for Pew on the development of Islamic Studies and that she had information on "every course in Islamic Studies at every university in my office but it is a mess." Mumtaz Ahmad asked, "The office or the course"? Said Haddad, "Both."

One question that came up often during the discussion was why, compared to the educational institutions in the traditional "Muslim world," Sufi studies has played a larger role within the western academic study of Islam. Marcia Hermansen, Professor, Department of Theology, Loyola University, Chicago, whose own work on Sufism is regarded as seminal, believes the location of the study of Islam in American universities shifted during the 1970s from being centered in departments or institutes of Oriental or Near Eastern Studies to becoming a component of courses offered in religious studies programs. Within the American academy, Near Eastern Studies departments are relatively rare today, for generally only major research institutions can offer the range of languages and specialties to support serious work in this area.

Religious studies, on the other hand, has during the last forty years become recognized as a central discipline within a liberal arts curriculum and is therefore offered at a greater number and broader range of universities. For these reasons institutionally, and therefore ultimately economically, there is a broader scope for offering courses on Sufism, a topic that engages student interest within the undergraduate curriculum. Consequently, training in such an area would seem more likely to lead to employment for the prospective graduate. At the same time, Hermansen believes it would be a distortion to attribute the crest of interest in the academic study of Sufism to economic pragmatism alone for the study of Islamic mysticism has proven particularly appealing to western academics attracted to the study of Islam as well as to the western general public.

Yet developments outside the academy engendered an interest in the study of Sufism in America, said Mumtaz Ahmad. Hermansen replied:

> Yes. This was also an era of liberalism and cultural protest in America. It was likewise a period in which Sufi movements and Muslim immigration began to increase in the U.S. in the aftermath of the 1965 relaxation of immigration quotas from non-European nations. At this time (the 1970s) graduate students interested in the study of Islam in American graduate programs were overwhelmingly from white middle class and upper middle class backgrounds. There were few foreign students, students from Muslim societies or backgrounds, or African Americans. A good number of these American students eventually converted to Islam and pursued Sufism as a personal commitment in addition to being a subject for academic research. Therefore, currently in terms of personal attitude, most scholars of Sufism in American universities are themselves Sufis, crypto-Sufis, or religious persons from other traditions who are sympathetic to Sufism. This would be in contrast, for example, to the case of American scholars of Islamic law or Qur'anic studies.

Hermansen continued that at universities in the Muslim world, Sufism is generally considered marginal to Islamic studies, and issues of the Qur'an and law are so sensitive that serious academic work and critical studies are more difficult to undertake. Therefore, Sufi studies in North America may be characterized as the sub-field of Islamic studies most engaged in bridge-building and dialogue, whereas some other sub-fields tend to be perceived by Muslims as the home of those who wish to "chip" away at confidence in Islam.

An interesting question that has attracted the attention of many observers of the state of Islamic studies in the U.S. relates to the role played by Muslim academics. Hermansen reviewed the approaches to the study of Islam within American academia through the works of three expatriate academics from the Muslim world as emblematic of ideological and methodological diversity: Fazlur Rahman (d.1988), Ismail al-Faruqi (d.1986), and Seyyed Hossein Nasr (b.1933). Of the three, Nasr definitely represented the Sufi tendency. Each of these three individuals could be characterized as an engaged Muslim scholar in his own way. Rahman was committed to Islamic modernism, Faruqi to Muslim intellectual nativism (Islamization of knowledge) and political Islam, and Nasr to a specific interpretation of Sufism known as perennialism or traditionalism. This gives Nasr's work on Islam coherence and at the same time an advocacy of a particular interpretation of Islam that has proven sympathetic and acceptable to a broader American public, although it has achieved less centrality and even garnered some suspicion in the academic study of Islam.

Traditionalists, according to Hermansen, are influenced by the interpretations of Rene Guenon (d.1951) and Fritjhof Schuon (d. 1998), both independent scholar/practitioners of Sufism whose interpretations stressed a transcendent unity of religions, esotericism, and a condemnation of the modern desacralization of the world. Through Nasr and his students and academic disciples this interpretation has come to play an important, if not a dominant role, in certain sub-fields of Sufi studies, for example, the interpretation of the works of Ibn al-ʿArabī and the Akbarian school by scholars such as James Morris, William Chittick, and Sachiko Murata. Nasr's co-followers of Schuon include Martin Lings (d.2005), Victor Danner (d.1990), and Huston Smith who popularized Sufism through his work in religious studies.

Perennialism may play a continuing role through the next generation of students of Nasr who seem inclined to approach Islamic studies from a philosophical perspective, and engage in theological reflection on topics such as Islam and environmentalism or peace studies. This new cohort includes many young scholars from the Muslim world and the new cohort of born or raised in America as children of Muslim immigrant families.

Hermansen also talked about Mircea Eliade, scholar of religion who taught at the University of Chicago Divinity School and whose "patternist" approach to comparative or history of religion dominated the study of religion in the U.S. in the 1970s. While Eliade was not particularly interested in Islam, his favoring of the search for the sacred as displayed in archetypal symbols had a certain affinity for approaches to Sufism. The perennialist school influences publishing through Nasr's editing of a series from SUNY Press and the work of the Islamic Texts Society/Fons Vitae that concentrates on translations of Sufi classics and Islamic and other spiritualities in a Traditionalist mode.

However, said Hermansen, in the American (immigrant) Muslim community outside of the academic world, the most sympathy would have been felt for Ismail al-Faruqi's approach to Islamic thought, which, like that of the modern Islamist movements such as the Muslim brotherhood (*Ikhwān al-Muslimīn*) and *Jamaat-e-Islami*, would have seen Sufism as decadent, deviant, and superstitious. Contemporary Islamist discourse tends to view cultural adaptations with suspicion, such as the use of music in some Sufi traditions, and the general sense that western or academic interest in Sufism is largely irrelevant to the concerns of Muslims.

Interestingly, current academic approaches to Sufism and some of its more recent inroads into Muslim discourse in North America share certain intellectual roots. These would be the teachings of the Algerian *Shādhily* Sufi, Shaykh al-Alawi (d. 1934) and his interpreters, popularized among academics and non-Muslims through Schuon and Nasr in one line, but also through contemporary *Shādhily* Sufi groups such as the *Murābiṭūn*, the Zaytuna Institute (Hamza Yusuf), and Nuh Keller among diaspora Muslims.

Pakistani-American scholar Fazlur Rahman's relationship to Sufism was quite complex. He seems to have been heir to the rationalism of modernists such as Muhammad Abduh (d. 1905) and Muhammad Iqbal (d. 1938) in finding the superstitious and fantastic claims of Sufism and its popular manifestations in folk practices distasteful. In his comprehensive overview of the tradition from a Modernist perspective, *Islam*, Rahman coined the expression "neo-Sufism." Rahman's erudition in Islamic philosophy provided readings of Sufis such as Aḥmed Sirhindī (d. 1625) and Ibn al-ʿArabī (d. 1240) that inspired interest in Sufism among his students. One may even speak of a "Chicago" school of literary readings of Sufism by scholars such as Michael Sells, Tom Emil Homerin, and later Franklin Lewis, influenced by other Chicago faculty such as Jaroslav Stetkeyvich and Heshmat Moayyad.

Other of Fazlur Rahman's students who worked on aspects of Sufism ironically were interested in popular forms and the role of local cultures, although with reference to classical texts and teachings. These include students by one of the earliest figures trained in both religious studies and Islam at the University of Chicago Divinity School, Earle Waugh, and Fazlur Rahman's later students in Near Eastern languages and civilizations, for example, Valerie Hoffman. Mumtaz Ahmad pointed out that Professor Marcia Hermansen also falls in the latter category.

On the question of the current state of Islamic studies in American universities, Carl W. Ernst of the Department of Religious Studies at the University of North Carolina at Chapel Hill notes that out of over 2,500 members listed in the directory of the Middle East Studies Association (MESA), fewer than 100 listed their specialty as Islam or religious studies. Graduate students and European scholars claimed this specialization. The number of academics who represent the study of Islam in religious studies today is therefore quite small, especially when one realizes that there are over 900 academic departments of religious studies in North America (according to the *Directory of Departments of Religious Studies in North America*).[1]

This is not the first time that anyone has pointed to the short supply of expertise in Islamic studies. Charles Adams drew attention to this situation in an informative article in 1973, when he discovered he was the only person to present a paper on Islam at the annual conference of the American Academy of Religion. The scope of that paper, written a quarter-century ago, "was limited, but it presented a portrait of the institutional and disciplinary constraints that still result in conflicts and tensions between religious studies generally and the study of Islam as carried out by Orientalists and area studies specialists."

Revisiting Adams' paper "as a kind of snapshot of that time" and "with a view to understanding what has happened to the study of Islamic religion over the past twenty-five years," Ernst believes that the "study of Islam has been in effect uneasily poised between Orientalism and area studies on the one hand and religious studies, on the other." For Ernst, it is "important to examine the implications of both area studies and religious studies if the academy is to deal with issues relating to Islam in the global public culture that is being formed today."

Commenting on the origins of the study of Islam in Europe and America, Ernst says that "what we today can call Islamic studies emerged from Orientalism, the erudite study of texts and ideas that became a highly developed field in the nineteenth and twentieth centuries in Europe and America." As Edward Said noted, Europe's Orient then corresponds to today's Islamic Middle East. It is not necessary to subscribe to Said's Foucaldian analysis to acknowledge there were issues of power associated with the institutional aspect of Orientalist study. The term "Near East," the primary designator for Orientalist departments today, was coined by a British naval historian in the period before World War I. Likewise, "Middle East" is a term invented by the OSS (precursor to the CIA) during World War II, and it had its main applicability during the Cold War.

Both departments of Near Eastern Studies and Middle Eastern Studies can be conveniently listed under the category of area studies rather than any particular discipline. Near Eastern Studies typically include a large array of languages from Akkadian to Arabic, with an enormous temporal range covering several discrete religions and civilizations. Departments of Middle East studies, which focus on the modern period, are supported in America by about 16 federally funded National Resource Centers for Middle Eastern studies (supported by the Title VI program in the U.S. Department of Education). These were created on the justification of the relevance of the Middle East to policy end users. Most Middle East specialists are social scientists (historians, anthropologists, political scientists, sociologists) or experts in language and literature.

The academic study of religion in Euro-America emerged over the last century, first from Protestant seminaries, then Catholic and eventually Jewish institutions. While academic departments of religious studies are frequently found in private universities with religious affiliations (some of which have divinity schools), the period since World War II has seen the establishment of departments of religious studies in public universities as well. Religious studies has struggled to gain recognition as a humanities discipline, in the face of opposition from both secularists and sectarians.

Adams described the study of religion in his day mainly under the heading of History of Religions, and he used the German term *Religionswissenschaft* to present its genealogy. In his view, the field was primarily the phenomenology of religion as defined by Mircea Eliade and other scholars at the University of Chicago. His critique of it began with the observation that departments of religion, when attempting to overcome their parochialism, generally preferred to concentrate on Asian traditions such as Hinduism, Buddhism, or Far Eastern religions. He observed that there were hardly any graduate programs in religious studies that included Islamic studies as a field. Area studies centers and departments, he maintained, generally considered religion to be a secondary subject of no major importance. In addition, the publishing industry offered very few books on Islam, in comparison with eastern religions. Finally, the bias toward archaic religions in the History of Religions excluded historical and rational religions like Islam. The result was a situation of impoverishment, in which the History of Religions had failed seriously to engage with a major world-historical civilization. His observations still in part hold true.

To counter this situation, Adams proposed a stern remedy: what was needed was "old-fashioned historical, literary, and philological studies directed to the Islamic tradition, the mastery of linguistic tools, and the study of an enormous textual tradition." This immersion was unavoidable, because highlighting the general and the comparative will necessarily make the study of Islam superficial.

Are Adams' prescriptions, formulated a quarter-century ago, still valid and relevant? According to Ernst:

> There are a number of items missing from his [Adams'] description of religious studies which would definitely be needed today. He makes no mention of the reactions of Muslims to Euro-American scholarship, or to their participation in it. His discussion of Islamic studies does not consider

the impact of having Muslim students in the classroom. He does not discuss the massive stereotypes of Islam relating to terrorism, violence, oppression of women, etc. He makes no mention of recent history, particularly European colonialism, modernity, or the 'F' word (fundamentalism). Furthermore, he does not refer at all to the role of the media and journalistic presentations in establishing the image of Islam today. And of course, the more recent phenomena of post-structuralism, deconstructive literary criticism, feminist and gender studies, post-colonial discourse, and the critique of Orientalism itself, were all to enter scholarship over the next two decades.

Contemporary political events on the world scene have had a powerful influence on how Islam is perceived in Europe and America, though it should also be pointed out that attitudes toward religion in the academy have also been profoundly shaped by these trends. While Harvey Cox in his 1965 *The Secular City* could proclaim the demise of religion as a public force, the Iranian revolution of 1979 and the rise of the religious right in America have provided a decisive refutation of that position. In any case, the use of religious Islamic slogans by violent factions, whether in conflict with the state of Israel or in struggles against repressive secular governments, has firmly fixed in place the media image of the Muslim as terrorist. This actually creates a unique problem for educators. There is no other religion that is so uniformly identified with hateful characteristics as Islam. Over a billion people, and over a millennium of history, are collapsed by stereotypes into a banal set of shocking film clips and sound bites. Because of the default Eurocentrism of our curricula, this is all that most people ever know about Muslim countries. Most Islamicists that I know, and quite a few Middle East historians, find themselves beginning their introductory classes with explorations of these stereotypes, which they highlight through quick media analysis in order to get their students to begin historicizing and humanizing their subject.

Regarding how the field of Islamic studies has changed over the past 25 years in America, Ernst notes:

…increasing attention to the presence of religious pluralism in American life, so that academics necessarily take account of the current actuality of domestic versions of religions once considered foreign. It is also increasingly the case that Muslims, Hindus, and Buddhists are joining the ranks of the professoriate alongside Protestants, Catholics, and Jews. While textbooks of world religions used to have a largely classical and scriptural bias, they now frequently attempt to include at least some reference to contemporary religious practices and views. And all fields of religious studies have been affected to some extent by the various discourses of post-modernity, if only through defensive reaction.

How has the field of Islamic studies actually changed over the past 25 years in America? Who are the major figures and scholars? Who has had the biggest public impact on the understanding of Islam? Without making the slightest claim to being comprehensive, I have done a little subjective checking with other scholars to come up with some lists.

Ernst lists Leonard Binder, G.E. von Grunebaum, Marshall G.S. Hodgson, Fazlur Rahman, Bernard Lewis, Dale Eickelman, Richard Eaton, Barbara Metcalf, Hamid Algar, Richard Bulliett, Michael Gilsenan, S. D. Goitein, Gilles Kepel, Nikki Keddie, Ali Mazrui, Clifford Geertz, and Talal Asad on the area studies/Orientalism side who have "contributed greatly to the study of various aspects of Islamic religion and culture."

Yet, as Ernst notes, "none of these scholars has had an appointment in a department of religious studies." The list tends to be far smaller when we try to think of religious studies specialists on Islam: Wilfred C. Smith, Marilyn Waldman, Annemarie Schimmel, Mohammad Arkoun, Josef Van Ess, Seyyed Hossein Nasr, Bruce Lawrence, and Richard Martin. As for the impact of these scholars on the wider field of religious studies, Ernst notes, "hardly any names will get much recognition. And very few of the area studies scholars are read outside their own fields, with the exception of Clifford Geertz (ironically, most Islamicists find his *Islam Observed* to be highly problematic in spite of its widespread popularity, while most non–Islamicists are unaware of the devastating critique of Geertz by Mark Woodward in *Islam in Java*)."

As an example of what constitutes the source of the popular understanding of Islam in the West, Ernst asks "an embarrassing question: what is the single most widely distributed book relating to Islam over the past 25 years, possibly over the past century? Although I do not have precise data at hand to prove the case, in my mind there is no doubt that this book must be Salman Rushdie's *The Satanic Verses*. Now, whether one likes Rushdie as a novelist or not, the fact remains that this book would be a very odd source from which to draw a picture of the Islamic religion or any of its history. Yet the 1989 media explosion over this book, which focused on the negative reaction of Muslims (particularly the Iranian death threat), did not result in any greater interest in Islam or in providing a more accurate picture of it. As Shabbir Akhtar (*But be Careful With Muhammad*) pointed out, "while nearly every major periodical in the U.K., America, and most European countries carried front-page stories on *The Satanic Verses*, their analysis of Islam almost without exception remained on the most superficial and hostile level. This seems to be a clear sign that the academic study of Islam has had a fairly limited impact."

As for the American scholar of Islamic Studies who has had the most public recognition, the answer, according to Ernst, "is easy, but also depressing. Several years ago Bernard Lewis was asked to give the Jefferson Lectures, one of the most prestigious national academic recognitions, but the burden of his presentation is one that most Islamicists shrink from. Like Samuel Huntington, who paints a paranoid post-Cold War picture of "the West against the rest," Lewis speaks of Islam as the eternal other to western civilization. Despite his considerable erudition, Lewis is content to view Muslims as eternally driven by an unchanging scripture; somehow they alone among all humanity are not subject to the influences of class, gender, ethnicity, nationality, politics, or economics." This, in the final analysis, is unfortunately an anti-humanist thesis. Ernst believes there is a problem here:

> Part of the difficulty lies in the way that academics in all fields have sometimes been content to write for a small circle of specialists, leaving the popular sphere for others to stake out. Statistics from *Publishers Weekly* indicate that publishing on religious studies is by far the largest growth area in publishing, outstripping all other subjects over the past few years. This growth has not been based on academic publishing, however. As with other areas of the academic study of religion, there is a real need (and a demand) for good popular writing by experts; we know what the alternative is. It also appears that religious studies has not had a very big impact

on the study of Islamic religion and culture, which has been dominated by area studies concerns.

As for the future development of Islamic studies in the U.S., Ernst believes that the problem of funding will be critical for the academy:

> Area studies, despite its theoretical flaws, is an extraordinarily successful method of training people in the languages and histories of particular regions. It is not clear how the different federally funded area studies programs will fare, however, in the changed political climate of the new world order. Private patronage is perhaps an option, but here too there are potential problems. Recently immigrant communities have not yet become socialized to the private support of higher education. On the other hand, one positive sign for Islamic studies is the noticeable number of institutions that have made first appointments in this field; last year, the number of academic positions in Islamic studies was actually larger than the number of viable candidates. While it is still true that the older established American universities with Ph.D. programs in religious studies (Harvard, Yale, Princeton, Chicago) do not really include Islam, newer configurations (e.g., the Carolina-Duke-Emory Institute for the Study of Islam) are forming to undertake the task of successfully integrating Islamic studies into religious studies. The key to recovering Islamic studies for religious studies is summarized by two words: comparative and critical. The comparative dimension is important not only to reveal the existence of differences within and among Islamic societies, but also to explore Islamic themes in relation to other traditions in multiple contexts. The critical approach takes account of the most stringent recent theoretical tests and methodologies, to elevate this study out of the unselfconscious attitudes of nineteenth-century positivism that too often characterized Orientalism. With these provisos, I think it will be possible to articulate a way for religious studies to have an impact on the study of Islam. But the problem of explaining religion to the public is a task that needs to be taken up by scholars in all fields.

One question we wanted our participants and respondents to address was the comparison of the study of Islam with the study of other religions in American campuses from the perspective of comparative religious studies. Do the scholars of comparative religion apply the same intellectual standards and same theoretical and methodological tools in the study of Islam as they do in the study of Christianity, Judaism, or Hinduism? And what about the tradition of textual criticism applied to the Islamic scriptural and canonical texts?

Marcia Hermansen responded by saying that, in the interest of fairness, it must be pointed out that the role of the critical historical textual scholar is not necessarily politically motivated. In the approach to the study of religious texts established by nineteenth-century Biblical criticism, the quest for textual and redactive anomalies and the investigations of authorship, multiple sources, and the identification of their polemic or other motivations became recognized as the primary methodology for studying scripture. It is therefore only natural that scholars shaped by this tradition would find it necessary and appropriate to subject the Qur'an and hadith to the same scrutiny. The fact that such historical critical methodologies are taboo in much of the Muslim world reflects negatively on the intellectual integrity and objectivity of scholarship there and ultimately ensures that the leading academic work in Muslim primary sources will be done elsewhere and later filter back to Muslim societies. This will ultimately have an even more deleterious impact than had this project been undertaken by Muslims themselves since in this case Muslims will be relegated to the roles of editors and compilers of the past rather than interpreters and molders of the present.

Dr. Khaleel Mohammed, Associate Professor, Department of Religious Studies at San Diego State University, believes that presently "there seems to be an obsession with presenting, even covertly, Judaism and Christianity as "vera religio" and Islam as "falsa religio" or at best, the other religion. Students come expecting to hear a negative presentation, and unfortunately, there is no scarcity of professors who give them what they want. There is a vast plethora of books, supposedly objective, that presents Islam in the most negative of lights, and professors in many cases rely on this. Typical examples of such works are Mordecai Nisan's *Identity and Civilization* or Karsh's *Islamic Imperialism*.

In studying Shiite eschatology, the twelfth imam is viewed as something generally nonsensical. While when one discusses the second advent of Jesus, it is done without the same smirking and focus on it as an irrational expectation. The terminologies applied to Islam are pejorative. One hears of moderate Muslim, dhimmitude, jihad. The methodology of putting things into historical and political context is all but lost. One hears of wars of Islam without reference to the reason why the Muslims were fighting. One hears of Wahhabism and "the Sudani Mahdist Movement" without any study of why these movements became accepted.

On the question of the main focus of the study of Islam in American universities, Khaleel Mohammad believes "even when studied under different rubrics, whether as faith, civilization, history, or in the contemporary world, the focus mostly remains on Islam as a force that opposes western domination rather than as a religion that is followed by more than a billion people who come from different cultures, languages and interpretations." As for the emphasis on the subfields of Islamic studies (Qur'anic studies, Islamic law, Islamic philosophy, Sufism, Islamic history, Islamic arts and architecture, Islam and politics, Islam and women, etc), Khaleel Mohammad identified Islam and politics and Islam and women as the two areas that seem to have received an inordinate amount of attention because the general pejorative view, at least regarding women, is one that fits well with what a nation that views itself at war with Islam seems to want. The politics is studied as part of the contemporary need and while it may not have any underlying agenda, the professors seem to be generally working out of the "us" and "them" mindset. Khaleel Mohammad said he makes this observation after having been invited to speak at several classes and observing the language used during the discussion.

Nasr of George Washington University agrees that the field of Islamic studies has expanded greatly in the past decade, but he adds that the mainstream study of Islam is still based on a "truncated view of Islam." According to Nasr, the two trends occurring in the past few decades are the emergence of a generation of scholars of U.S. origin that are writing on Islam, and the immigration of foreign Islamic scholars to the U.S. "The problem that exists is that most of (U.S.) scholars don't know much about Islam," he said. Nasr added that many contemporary Muslim scholars are not like the Muslim scholars of the old school, saying some were simply looking to sell their name. Nasr also cited language deficiencies as being a major factor in the inability of these scholars to adequately address the issues related to the classical Islamic humanities.

The pioneers in the field of Islamic studies in the U.S. have been mostly Christian Lebanese, Orientalists, or American men of religion, according to Khaleel Mohammad. He mentioned Philip Hitti as one of the pioneers of the study of Islam and Islamic history in the U.S., and "Joseph Schacht the orientalist is still famous although many of his theories have been debunked. Duncan B. MacDonald and Samuel Zwemer, founders of the Hartford Seminary that today publishes the *Muslim World* started their early approach to Islam on a highly negative note, and any reading of the early issues of this journal will show their initial agenda. Only from the 1970s did the journal start changing," Mohammad observed.

Elaborating on the role of Christian seminaries in the development of the discipline and how that role has evolved over the last century and half, Mohammad said that in the initial phase:

> Almost all studies on Islam were done from a Christian perspective, since the only religion that yet challenged Christianity was, and remains, Islam. The Hartford Seminary is a prime example. Documentation in this regard is available in Carl Ernst's *Following Muhammad*. The initial translation of Muslim literature into English and European languages was done not out of genuine scholarship, but to present a negative view of Islam in the minds of the readers. Only since the 1970s has there been any change, and while the universities have somewhat managed to maintain a generally academic approach, after 9/11, the proliferation of courses that focus on jihad, Islam and politics and extremist movements within Islam, along with the popular literature threaten to cause a great retrogression.

As noted earlier by Nasr, the entry of Muslim scholar in the Islamic studies programs in American academy is an important new development regarding these questions: What has been the role of Muslim scholars in redefining the discipline of Islamic studies in American universities? In what ways these scholars have influenced the field? What has been the contribution of the emerging indigenous American

Muslim scholarship to the study of Islam in American campuses? Mohammad said:

> The scholarship of Fazlur Rahman of University of Chicago was, to my mind, a watershed period for redefining Islamic Studies. Since then, Ismail al-Faruqi, Mahmoud Ayoub, Maysam al-Faruqi, the Kassam sisters, etc have contributed great academic and intellectual imprints on the subject. People are now capable of viewing Islam through the lenses of genuine examination and awareness of the vast variegated interpretations of Islam, rather than through the monolithic medievalism presented by Schacht et al.

Khaleel Mohammad believes that the "emerging indigenous American Muslim scholarship is yet to be of a great impact, although scholars like Sherman Jackson have distinguished themselves in Islamic law." The indigenous Muslim population is still too marginally represented in the field, said Mohammad. The problem of funding has always been a critical factor in developing graduate programs in universities. What about funding of Islamic Studies programs? Mohammad noted:

> There are some private chairs at universities, as in Toledo, Stanford, Youngstown, for example. For the most part, funding seems to come from the U.S. government or the universities themselves, or in some cases, from the Arab governments...Now, after 9/11, most universities are leery of taking funding from abroad, as was found in the case of Harvard in particular. Most Muslim communities are struggling to establish themselves since the relaxation of immigration laws in 1965. We have thus a yet young community that in just a few cases may be willing to support Islamic Studies programs. In Toledo, as I mentioned, there was a chair established at the local university. In San Diego, the local community funds a Center for Islamic and Arabic Studies, but such funding is not up to the required level to have a chair or an elaborate research program.

On the role of the mainstream professional academic associations and learned bodies (American Academy of Religion, Middle East Studies Association, The Middle East Institute, and social science associations), their annual conventions, and scholarly journals in the shaping of the Islamic studies in the U.S., Mohammad believes that "the mainstream academic associations have been a positive influence on Islamic studies." However, after 9/11, only the AAR and MESA seem to have largely maintained the course of scholarly approach. It is at these conferences that hires are usually made and where the scholarly bent of a professor may be determined by his/her presentation and this still remains the norm for letting one's scholarship be known.

On the question of the major contributions of American scholarship to the field of Islamic studies as compared to the contributions of European scholars on Islam, Mohammad contends:

> American scholarship has been largely for the North American press in matters of history and law. European studies were more, in the early part of the last century, extremely polarized, and while in the U.S., Joseph Schacht was a main figure, he had several like minded Orientalists in Europe. This trend still continues, although from Holland in particular a generally academic approach to Islam seems to be the norm. If Wansborough, Patricia Crone, and David Cook are any indication of the scholarship from England at a certain period, their revisionism has generally lost steam. In the US, despite the popular pejorative presentations, most scholars seem to have maintained a high level scholarship in law and philosophy, as well as in Qur'anic studies, history and mysticism. Names like Wael Hallaq, Carl Ernst, and Tamara Sonn come to mind.

As for the positive trends in the study of Islam in recent years in the U.S., Mohammad believes these

> ...trends can be traced to the development of more courses by professors who in many cases come from within the tradition, or have been taught outside of the normal polemical approach to Islam. Scholars such as Azizah al Hibri, Maysam al-Faruqi, Rifat Hassan show that within Islam there are several trends for the empowerment of women, and they therefore break the stereotypes. Wael Hallaq, himself a non-Muslim, has debunked Schacht and his ilk almost in total and these have in fact set a ball rolling to reexamine much of what had become accepted as the norm in Islamic studies. Over the next twenty years, I believe that, as Professor

Akbar Ahmed has described this as "the century of Islam," we should expect more positive developments.

In the context of current developments, the impact of the events of 9/11 has been of critical importance for the field. Mohammad believes this

> ...impact has been two-edged. For the popular literature, there has emerged a vast horde of hateful writers who purvey the nastiest Islamophobia. But on the other hand, on campuses, the general interest in Islam has also made universities pay a lot of attention to courses on Islam. While many courses harbor an underlying anti-Islamic message, others are generally neutral, with many professors taking the ethical stance of truly trying to educate. The general and pervasive discontent with the war [in Iraq] has had a positive impact as, initially, while people may have denigrated Muslims, now they are beginning to reexamine the campaign of disinformation and prevarication that caused their illusions before the war.
>
> Several courses on 'Abraham religion' have been designed. For example, I teach a course on violence in Abrahamic religions, as well as one on "violence and non-violence." The students can examine first hand that violence is not the monopoly of any one religion, and can in fact trace facts that they have not hitherto accessed about their own past. This generally creates more of a desire to examine the Abrahamic roots of Islam and to explore the vast cultural differences that exist within a particular religion. I agree with Professor Ahmed in that this is the century of Islam, meaning, that the study of Islam will be much more neutral, objective, extensive and pervasive.

APPENDIX A

Questions for Conversation, Discourse, and Dialogue on the State of Islamic Studies in American Universities

1. How would you compare the study of Islam with the study of other religions in American campuses from the perspective of comparative religious studies? Do the scholars of comparative religion apply the same intellectual standards and same theoretical and methodological tools in the study of Islam as they do in the study of Christianity and Judaism or Hinduism?

2. What, in your view, has been the main focus in the study of Islam in the U.S.: Islam as faith? Islam as world civilization? Islamic history? Islam in the contemporary world? or Islam as an issue of U.S. foreign policy?

3. Which subfields, from among the various subfields of Islamic studies (Qur'anic studies, Islamic law, Islamic philosophy, Sufism, Islamic history, Islamic arts and architecture, Islam and politics, Islam and women, etc.) have received greater attention in the U.S. and why?

4. Who have been the pioneers in the field of Islamic studies in the U.S. and what has been their unique contribution to the field?

5. What was the role of Christian seminaries in the development of the discipline? How has that role has been evolved over the last century and half?

6. What has been the role of Muslim scholars in redefining the discipline of Islamic studies in American universities? In what ways they have influenced the field? What has been the contribution of

the emerging indigenous American Muslim scholarship to the study of Islam in American campuses?

7. Who has been funding the Islamic studies programs over the years: federal government, private foundations, individual philanthropists, and overseas Muslim governments? What was the role of Muslim communities as well as Muslim governments and overseas Muslim philanthropists?

8. What was the role of the mainstream professional academic associations and learned bodies (American Academy of Religion, Middle East Studies Association, The Middle East Institute, and social science associations), their annual conventions, and scholarly journals in the shaping of the Islamic studies in the U.S.?

9. What, in your view, have been the major contributions of American scholarship to the field of Islamic studies as compared to the contributions of European scholars on Islam?

10. Can one describe the present phase of Islamic religious scholarship in the U.S. as "post-orientalist" phase? If so, what evidence supports this contention?

11. What positive trends, if any, one can identify in the study of Islam in American universities in recent years? What caused these trends? How significant are these trends?

12. What, in your view, has been the impact of 9/11 on the field of Islamic studies? Is this impact transitory, or it is likely to have long-term consequences for the field?

APPENDIX B

List of Scholars in Conversation, Discourse, and Dialogue on
the State of Islamic Studies in American Universities

Prof. Seyyed Hossein Nasr, George Washington University

Prof. John Voll, Georgetown University

Prof. Osman Bakr, Georgetown University

Prof. Yvonne Haddad, Georgetown University

Prof. Ahmad Dallal, Georgetown University

Prof. Sumaiya Hamdani, George Mason University

Prof. Charles Butterworth, University of Maryland

Prof. Luis Cantori, University of Maryland

Prof. Mahmoud M. Ayoub, Temple University

Prof. Khalid A. Y. Blankinship, Temple University

Dr. Zain Abdullah, Temple University

Dr. Shalahudin Kafrawi, Moravian College

Prof. Carl Ernst, University of North Carolina

Prof. Khaleel Mohammad, San Diego State University

Prof. Sulayman Nyang, Howard University

Dr. Mumtaz Ahmad, Hampton University

Dr. Zahid Bukhari, Georgetown University

NOTES

1   There are another 900 departments in seminaries, yeshivas, and Bible colleges that are ministerial training schools rather than academic programs.

CONCLUSIONS

TO say that Islam has become a major topic of discussion in the United States since September 11, 2001 is to state the obvious. Not only that Islam and Muslims have generated a great deal of interest among academic institutions, media outlets, policy makers, think tanks but also among various religious groups and the general public. Educational institutions across the country are struggling to cope with this increasing interest in Islam as a religion, world civilization, political power, and strategic concern for U.S. national security. Enrollment in introductory and advanced courses on Islam and those focused on contemporary Islamic developments has increased substantially at campuses around the country. Several educational institutions have created new positions for teaching Islam in their existing religious studies departments as well as in social science disciplines.

Academic circles in the U.S. have also been engaged in two debates in the post- 9/11 environment. One debate focuses on the question of liberal and moderate Islam versus the extremist interpretation of Islam, and who has the legitimate authority to represent and interpret Islam and to exercise ijtihad in Islam. The second debate concerns the nature and outcome of Middle East area studies centers. This second debate started, ironically, with two contradictory claims. First, Middle Eastern and Islamic scholars have claimed that U.S. study of Islam, the Islamic world, and especially the Middle East, has been tainted with anti–Muslim and anti–Arab biases. On the other hand, some think tanks and politically inspired writers claim that the academic establishment of Middle Eastern and Islamic studies in the U.S. has been pro–Islam and pro–Arab.

The study of Islam and Muslim societies in the form of area studies programs at American campuses initially arose primarily in response to the post–World War 11 environment, in which the U.S. emerged as a superpower with active involvement and political–military investment in the affairs of the Islamic world. The main objectives of these area studies centers have therefore been to train experts who could assume positions in government, universities, and in the corporate sectors; inform, educate, and influence the formulation of foreign policy; and produce a body of knowledge – albeit suitable to the U.S. strategic interests – that would filter down to public schools and public opinion.

Thus, unlike European universities where the emphasis has been on classical Islamic studies, American universities have remained largely focused on modern Islamic developments. The overwhelming and paradigmatic context of the Cold War defined the programmatic emphasis of scholarly activities in the American academy and procured funds for such activities. Within this context, there was, at least in the formative phase, not much interest in traditional scholarship on Islam, such as Arabic philology, textual studies of the Qur'an, hadith, fiqh, Islamic history and other classical Islamic sciences. Things began to change, however, when prominent European, Arab and Muslim scholars moved from their home bases to major centers of American learning such as Chicago, Harvard, Princeton, Columbia, Pennsylvania, and UCLA and laid the foundation of classical and medieval Islamic studies.

The field of Islamic studies in the United States has gone through several phases in its development: from early polemical works of Christian missionaries who wanted to study Islam in order to convert Muslims in Lebanon–Syria and the Holy Land to the post World War 11, cold war–tainted interest in the religious, cultural and political affairs of the Muslim World; from the emergence of a more nuanced, phenomenological approach to the study of Islam in the 1970s to a post-orientalist discourse of the 1980s; and now to the post-9/11 focus on Islam and the Muslim World as a source of threat for the U.S. national security.

A major failure of Islamic studies and Muslim world area studies programs in American universities has been their total disconnect both from public opinion and the direction and conduct of U.S. foreign policy toward Islamic societies. The intellectual products of the programs have not trickled down to public school systems, popular media, and the public. School textbooks, popular literature, and media portrayals of Islam, Muslims, and the Islamic world, remain full of old (and new) stereotypes, misinformation, outright distortions, and sometimes highly slanderous material.

It was in this context that our project sought to undertake a comprehensive examination of the state of Islamic studies in the U.S. The idea was to investigate the factors that have tended to influence the contents and directions of the field of Islamic studies: social biases and prejudices, the traditions of previous scholarship, a particular direction of contemporary national policy, and the impact of the events of, and associated with, 9/11. The current state of relations between the U.S. and the Muslim world, as well the recent debates about Islamic education and study programs in American campuses, have, in our view, necessitated a thorough and rigorous study of Islam in American universities. The project, therefore, sought to fill this important need and was intended to achieve the following objectives: (a). to understand the historical roots and legacy of the study of Islam and Islamic societies in American academic institutions: (b) to critically examine, analyze, and evaluate the current state of Islamic studies in American universities; (c) to collect comprehensive data on the programs of Islamic and Muslim world studies in American colleges and universities; (d) to prepare case studies of some of the major centers of Islamic studies in the country; (e) to critically examine the theoretical frameworks and methodological approaches employed in the study of Islam as a faith, culture, civilization, and history in American academia and (f) to stimulate a candid, healthy, and critical debate on the status of Islamic studies in the U.S.

As can be seen in the preceding chapters, using both qualitative and quantitative research, the project sought to develop an understanding of the origins, history, and growth of the discipline. Our methodological perspectives of our authors combined an interpretive orientation with the "standard" social scientific approach. That is, besides collecting data through standard social science techniques (review of literature, internet websites, content analysis of selected publications, and structured interviews through questionnaires), we devoted considerable effort to collecting individual narratives of scholars and students through special interviews and informal discussions. These personal narratives, and the interpretive orientation of our research methodology, we believe, was much more enlightening and rewarding in terms of guiding the research and enhancing our understanding of the perception of the actors.

We have also tried to achieve a subjectively understandable meaning of the scholars' attitudes and behavior regarding conventions of American academic life. To examine the value and contribution of the Islamic studies programs on American campuses, the project team actively engaged thoughtful scholars, students, and alumni of these programs in panel discussions, focus groups, and dialogue, where they shared their diverse individual and collective experiences. We organized two formal focus group discussion sessions: one at Georgetown University in Washington, D.C. and the other at Temple University in Philadelphia. Besides these two formal brainstorming sessions, we mailed the questionnaire to more than seventy professors of Islamic studies. Some scholars were also contacted individually to respond to these questions and share their thoughts, experiences, and observations on the state of Islamic studies in American academia. "Conversations, Discourse, Dialogue" contains the critical thinking and discussion of seventeen scholars on the state of Islamic studies in American universities in a very innovative, systematic, and organized manner. The chapter "Conversations" contains the scholars' insights on the pertinent issues of comparison of the study of Islam and its intellectual standards with the study of other religions; focus and subfields of the discipline; pioneers and their unique contributions to the field of Islamic studies; role of Christian seminaries, Muslim scholars, emerging indigenous American Muslim scholars, and mainstream professional and academic organizations and learned bodies in the development of the field. They also discuss contribution of American scholarship to the field as compared to the contribution of European scholarship. Another important topic that generated considerable interest during the conversation was the role of the funding of the programs of Islamic and Middle Eastern studies over the years. Along with the scholarly papers included in this volume, these conversations constitute an immensely valuable contribution to the current debate on the state of the Islamic studies in America. Based on personal statements and experience of several years of teaching Islamic studies, the participants in these conversations share insights that are rarely articulated in formal scholarly monographs.

The state of Islamic studies in American universities was also analyzed by conducting a survey of 105 introductory courses on Islam (ISLAM 101). The survey report presented in this volume ("Islam 101: A survey of 'Introduction to Islam' Courses in American Colleges and Universities") analyses the characteristics of the instructors, the course goals, required texts and authors, class size for each course, the methods of student evaluation, and the frequency of course offering over the period of semesters or years. This part of our research is probably the first ever comprehensive study of introductory courses on Islam in American academia and will be of immense value to researchers, scholars and educational planners in religious studies and the humanities.

It was encouraging to note that a general agreement seems to be emerging among teachers as to what should be included in an introductory course on Islam. Themes such as Islamic beliefs and practices, intellectual currents, Islamic history, Islamic sources, and Islam in the modern world were found as the most widely-used course goals in the introductory classes. The gender of the instructor, however, makes a difference of focus in the selection of course topics.

Unlike the general agreement regarding the content of an introductory course on Islam, there was little consensus on the selection of required textbooks for teaching Islam. More than 200 books were used as required texts to cover different parts of the course syllabi. The top four books noted in our analysis were: *An Introduction to Islam* by Fredrick Mathews Denny; *Islam: The Straight Path* by John L. Esposito; *Approaching the Qur'an: The Early Revelations* by Michael Sells; and *Koran*, translated by N.J. Dawood. Among the authors, Fredrick Mathews Denny, John L. Esposito, Michael Sells, and Fazlur Rahman were found as the top four scholars whose books were used as required texts by the instructors.

There is certainly a strong demand to learn about Islam through academic courses, as the average class size in our analysis was 40-42 students per course. Two-thirds of these courses were offered either every semester or once a year. All instructors teaching an introductory course on Islam have post-graduate degrees from reputable institutions, but many lack genuine expertise and background in Islamic studies as such. Only one out of eight instructors has primary expertise in Islamic studies. The trend to borrow instructors from other disciplines, such as religious studies, political science, history, Middle Eastern languages, and even engineering, is still prevalent in some schools. The male-female ratio among the instructors was 4:1 and less than one-fourth of the instructors were Muslims.

The study of specialized sub-disciplines within Islamic studies has made considerable strides in recent years, especially in the areas of Sufism (as Marcia Hermansen shows in her chapter), modern Islamic history, Islamic intellectual thought, and contemporary Islamic discourse. Saba Mahmood charts the history and methodology and theoretical underpinnings of Islam and gender studies in American universities and points to the limitations of using western feminism models in studying the issues related to Islam and women. Among the social science disciplines, anthropology seems to have led the way in developing a body of literature with more sensitive, nuanced, and discerning approaches to the study of Islamic societies. Saba Mahmood's chapter in this volume is most insightful in understanding the anthropological approaches to the study of Islam in general and Islam and gender in particular.

As can be seen in the preceding chapters, Islamic studies in the U.S. has undergone several stages, and its present state in U.S. academic institutions cannot be understood without taking into account the path taken by the discipline since its early beginnings. There is a general consensus among our contributors in this volume that the field of Islamic studies in the U.S., although not yet on par with the study of Christianity and Judaism, has reached a high level of intellectual sophistication in recent years as a result of interventions by a new generation of American scholars of Islam and the Muslim world. This is demonstrated by the body of literature produced in recent years and the consolidation of the various branches within the field.

Conclusions

The discipline of Islamic studies has an assured future in the U.S. due to the following: its own strength as an institutionalized tradition within the American academy; the global status of Islam; and the political, economic, and cultural interests between the U.S. and the Muslim world. The events of 9/11 further created a demand for the growth of Islamic studies in American universities, although not always for the right reasons. Both the consolidation of tradition and the political imperatives associated with Islam and the Muslim world will ensure continued and increased funding for Islamic studies programs by the U.S. government, private foundations, Arab governments, and individual Muslim philanthropists in the U.S.

The most concrete and visible manifestation of Islam in the U.S. is the American Muslim community. Unlike the European scholarship on Islam and Muslims in the West, American scholarly works on Islam and Muslims in America have been mostly of general nature and are not grounded in empirical studies of local Muslim communities and their religious and ethnic diversities. An exclusive emphasis on the promotion of Islamic studies as an academic discipline in total isolation from the concrete reality of the American Muslim community and the Islamic world at large may serve some pedagogic goals, but it will not be of much help to Muslims in their present political predicament. Hence, our programmatic emphasis in the future should be equally focused on strengthening the study of American Muslim community and creating a better understanding of its role in the larger American society; and creating a more discerning understanding of the realities of Islamic societies.